PRAGMATICS AND NON
COMMUNICATI

The way we say the words we say helps us convey our intended meanings. Indeed, the tone of voice we use, the facial expressions and bodily gestures we adopt while we are talking, often add entirely new layers of meaning to those words. How the natural non-verbal properties of utterances interact with linguistic ones is a question that is often largely ignored. This book redresses the balance, providing a unique examination of non-verbal behaviours from a pragmatic perspective. It charts a point of contact between pragmatics, linguistics, philosophy, cognitive science, ethology and psychology, and provides the analytical basis to answer some important questions: How are non-verbal behaviours interpreted? What do they convey? How can they be best accommodated within a theory of utterance interpretation?

TIM WHARTON is an Honorary Research Fellow at University College London. He is a member of the International Pragmatics Association and is a regular contributor and reviewer for a number of international journals in language, philosophy and cognition. His previous book publications include contributions to *The Pragmatics Encyclopedia* (2009), for which he was a consultant editor, and *Pragmatics and Theory of Mind* (2009). Prior to his academic career, he was a singer-songwriter and has written and recorded a number of songs which are still used as teaching resources for those learning English as a foreign language.

PRAGMATICS
AND NON-VERBAL
COMMUNICATION

TIM WHARTON

CAMBRIDGE
UNIVERSITY PRESS

CAMBRIDGE UNIVERSITY PRESS

Cambridge, New York, Melbourne, Madrid, Cape Town, Singapore, São Paulo, Delhi

Cambridge University Press
The Edinburgh Building, Cambridge CB2 8RU, UK

Published in the United States of America by Cambridge University Press, New York

www.cambridge.org
Information on this title: www.cambridge.org/9780521691444

First published 2009

Printed in the United Kingdom at the University Press, Cambridge

A catalogue record for this publication is available from the British Library

Library of Congress Cataloging-in-Publication Data
Wharton, Tim.
Pragmatics and non-verbal communication / Tim Wharton.
p.   cm.
ISBN 978-0-521-87097-9 (hardback) – ISBN 978-0-521-69144-4 (pbk.)
1. Nonverbal communication.   2. Body language.   I. Title.

P99.5.W53 2009
302.2′22–dc22

2009024541

ISBN 978-0-521-87097-9 hardback
ISBN 978-0-521-69144-4 paperback

*This book is dedicated to my two beautiful daughters,
Xani and Zoë, and to the memory of Mary Wharton.*

Contents

Acknowledgements

I have tried to write this book in a way that does not presuppose any specialised competence in pragmatics, linguistics or any other of the various disciplines discussed. Many of the chapters are based on material which has been published elsewhere, but which has been revised in such a way as to highlight various threads that have emerged and produce a homogeneous whole. I am grateful to the publishers of this original material – Blackwell (publishers of Wharton 2003b), Elsevier (Wilson and Wharton 2006) and Mouton de Gruyter (Wharton 2008) – for their permission to use it. Material revised from Wharton (2003a) published with kind permission of John Benjamins Publishing Company. I would also like to express my gratitude to the Linguistic Agency division at the Centre of the Study of Mind in Nature Project at the University of Oslo, whose financial support during the final stages of the completion of this book was a great help.

I owe a huge debt of gratitude to numerous friends and colleagues who have supported me during the time it has taken this book to evolve. The largest part of this goes to Deirdre Wilson, and I would like to take this opportunity to thank her not only for comments on draft versions of this book (and the PhD thesis from which it developed), but for all her help and support over the years: her generosity and kindness have proved as much of an inspiration to me in my personal life as her unerring ability to keep the bigger picture in mind while studying the fine detail has inspired me professionally.

Other colleagues I would like to thank for comments and criticisms on the various talks and papers out of which the following chapters have emerged include: Nicholas Allott, Diane Blakemore, Robyn Carston, Billy Clark, Herb Clark, Coralie Chevallier, Christopher Dukes, Thorsten Fretheim, Richard Horsey, Patricia Kolaiti, Hannes Rakoczy, Paula Rubio, Seth Sharpless, Stephen Skelly, Neil Smith, J. L. Speranza, Dan Sperber, Mark Textor, Micheal Tomasello and Rosa Vega-Moreno. This list is certainly not exhaustive and I apologise to anyone I have left out. I would also like to thank the anonymous reviewers who commented on earlier versions of this book when it was still in proposal stage, and Helen Barton and the editorial team at Cambridge University Press for all their patience and hard work. Needless to say, all errors that remain are my own.

Personal thanks also go to Katharine Bradley, Peter Eastham and Roma Loban, for their advice and wisdom, to Tamsin Wharton, for all her support over the years, to my beautiful daughters Xani and Zoë, and to my late mother Mary Wharton, and my father Roy. Finally, I thank Laura for being herself and allowing me to be myself.

CHAPTER I

Natural pragmatics

A wagging tongue . . . proves to be only one part of a complex human act whose meaning must also be sought in the movement of the eyebrows and hand.

(Erving Goffman 1964, pp. 133–4)

INTRODUCTION

Sentences are rarely uttered in a behavioural vacuum. We colour and flavour our speech with a variety of natural vocal, facial and bodily gestures, which indicate our internal state by conveying attitudes to the propositions we express or information about our emotions or feelings. Though we may be aware of them, such behaviours are often beyond our conscious control: they are involuntary or spontaneous. Almost always, however, understanding an utterance depends to some degree on their interpretation. Often, they show us more about a person's mental/physical state than the words they accompany; sometimes, they replace words rather than merely accompany them.

The approach favoured by many linguists is to abstract away from such behaviours. Generative linguists sift out extraneous, paralinguistic or non-linguistic phenomena, and focus on the rule-based grammar – the *code* that constitutes language. This strategy has reaped rich rewards. Over the past thirty years linguists have suggested intriguing answers to the classical questions of language study (Chomsky 1986), and are now in a position to ask questions it was once not even possible to formulate (Chomsky 2000). Linguists working within functionalist frameworks (see, for example, Bolinger 1983) have addressed non-verbal communicative behaviours, as have some conversational and discourse analysts (Goodwin 1981, Brown and Yule 1983, Schiffrin 1994) and those looking at human interaction and communication from a more sociological or anthropological perspective (Garfinkel 1967, Goffmann 1964, Gumperz 1964, 1982 Hymes 1972). However, they do not seek to offer a cognitive explanation of the phenomena they describe. As with the work of generative linguists, distinctions important from a pragmatic view are sometimes left unexplored, and the question of how the natural properties of utterances might interact with the linguistic ones is largely ignored.

There are two main reasons why the pragmatist should cast a broader net. Firstly, thanks largely to the influential work of Paul Grice (1957, 1967, 1968, 1969, 1975, 1982, 1989),[1] it is now increasingly recognised that verbal communication is more than a simple coding–decoding process. Any attempt to characterise linguistic communication should reflect the fact that it is an intelligent, inferential activity involving the expression and recognition of *intentions*.[2] Secondly, the aim of a pragmatic theory is to explain how *utterances* – with all their linguistic and non-linguistic properties – are understood.

Consider the following examples:

(1) Jack (yawning, and very pale, with dark patches under his eyes): I feel a little tired, but I'm OK, honestly . . .

(2) **Ouch**, that flaming hurts! **Ow!** Oh! Oh! Oh! Oh! (KCW 17 – BNC)[3]

(3) Lily (to Jack, with a stern facial expression, in an angry tone of voice, gesturing furiously): You're **late**!

(4) Jack (faking a smile, and lying): It's absolutely delicious, really . . .

(5) [During the italicised section of the utterance the speaker performs an iconic gesture in which he appears to pull something down from the upper front space above him down towards his shoulder]: He grabs a big oak tree and *he bends it way back*.[4]

In all these examples, the non-verbal phenomena indicated will affect the way the utterance is understood: in (1), physical manifestations of Jack's tiredness indicate to his audience that he is not anywhere near as well as he would like them to believe; in (2), the speaker's natural expressions of pain says as much as the words he utters; in (3) Lily's frown, her aggressive tone and her gestures will calibrate the degree of anger her audience takes her to be conveying; in (4), Jack fakes a natural behaviour – a smile – which indicates that he is being ironic, and means the opposite of what he has said; in (5), the speaker augments her spoken message with a natural iconic manual gesture which is integrated somehow into the interpretation of the utterance.

The task of describing and explaining precisely what is conveyed by these and all the non-verbal phenomena introduced above falls squarely within the domain of pragmatics. Despite this, natural pragmatics remains an under-explored discipline, and the central aim of this book is to redress the balance. The examples above suggest various generalisations. In the first place, it seems clear that non-verbal behaviours may contribute either to overt communication (speaker's meaning) or to more covert or accidental forms of information transmission (compare (3) above with (1)). This point is generally missed in the literature on non-verbal communication. In the second place, many such behaviours convey non-propositional information about mental states or attitudes (see example (2)), or alter the salience of linguistically possible interpretations, rather than expressing full propositions: as Jill House (1990) puts it – they form the 'packaging' rather than the 'content' of the message. Thirdly, such behaviours are integrated both with each other – facial expression, prosody and gesture are closely linked (see example (3)) – and with linguistic inputs during the comprehension process (see all examples).

The question of how the interpretation of such natural phenomena is to be accommodated within a cognitively oriented pragmatic theory provides what I hope will be a discernible thread throughout the book, and can be analysed into a number of more specific questions: (A) What is the relation between natural non-verbal behaviours and intentional communication? (B) How are non-verbal behaviours interpreted? (C) What do they convey? (D) What is the relation between natural non-verbal behaviours and those non-verbal behaviours that are not natural?

The answers we provide to these questions will depend to a considerable extent on how we characterise notions such as *natural*, *language*, *pragmatics* and *communication*. Before providing an overview of the structure of the book, I will start with a few remarks about each of these.

Regarding the term 'natural', it should be clear from my opening paragraph that what I have in mind is to contrast natural phenomena, on the one hand, with human language, on the other. In a more general sense, of course, the human linguistic code is itself entirely 'natural' (hence, 'human natural language'). This observation is central to the view of language adopted in this book: language is not 'learned', it 'grows' (Chomsky 1988, p. 134). Similarly, the most 'natural' response in a given communicative situation is more often than not a linguistic one; so just as language is natural in a certain sense, so is language use. Indeed, there is a sense in which – as Mary Catherine Bateson (1996, p. 10) puts it – 'everything is natural; if it weren't, it wouldn't be. That's *How Things Are*: natural.' Even if we adopt an anti-Chomskyan stance and characterise language as an entirely cultural phenomenon, it is still natural in this general sense. As anthropologist Dan Sperber once suggested to me (personal communication): 'everything that is – or at least everything that is in time and space – is natural, including all things cultural, artificial, etc.'

The notion of naturalness I have in mind is rather more specific. My concern is with phenomena that *mean* naturally, in the sense of Grice (1957): the antonym of the intended sense of 'natural', then, is not '*un*natural', but '*non*-natural'. For Grice, 'means naturally' is roughly synonymous with 'naturally indicates', so in the same way that black clouds might be said to mean that it will rain or spots mean someone has measles, Lily's smile might be said to mean she is happy, or Jack's frown to mean he is displeased. This kind of meaning can be clearly contrasted with the kind of meaning inherent in language (often described as arbitrary or conventional), which Grice called 'non-natural'; so the word 'pluie' means 'rain';

'Lily está feliz' means 'Lily is happy', or what that remark meant was 'Jack is displeased'. Here, linguistic meaning contrasts with natural meaning.

In this book, I will be focusing on a particular subset of phenomena that mean naturally. I will be mostly concerned with the kind of communicative behaviours or states alluded to in my opening paragraph: affective tone of voice, facial expressions, spontaneous expressions of emotion. In this subset I also include 'natural' gesticulation and manual gesture, with the (important) caveat that some gestures used in verbal communication are not natural in the sense I intend. The kind of gestures illustrated in Fig. 1.1 are cases in point.

All these gestures are highly conventionalised and culture-specific. The relationship between the gesture and what the gesture conveys is arbitrary, and the meaning conveyed 'non-natural' in Grice's sense, rather than 'natural'. However, to ignore this dimension of gestural behaviours would be to neglect a hugely important facet of the pragmatics of non-verbal communication. Similarly, the kind of 'gestures' put to use by signers as part of the various deaf sign-languages are not – in a crucial sense – 'gestures' at all: they are part of language, and would also fall on what Grice called the non-natural side of meaning.

It might be suggested that the above discussion could have been avoided by using the terms 'paralinguistic' or 'non-linguistic', rather than 'natural'. I'm not convinced. For one thing, there is disagreement over what these terms mean. Some people treat 'paralanguage' as including only those vocal aspects of language use that are not strictly speaking part of language: intonation, stress, affective tone of voice, rate of speech, hesitation (if that can be considered vocal) etc. On this construal, facial expression and gesture are non-linguistic. Others treat the paralinguistic as including most or all of those aspects of linguistic communication that are not part of language *per se*, but are nonetheless somehow involved with the message or meaning a communicator conveys. On the first construal, while the set of paralinguistic phenomena intersects with the set of natural phenomena I am concerned with, there exist both

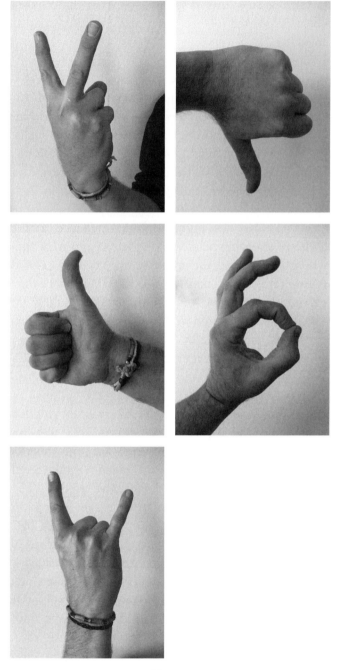

Fig. 1.1

paralinguistic phenomena that are not natural – deliberate frowns or fake smiles – and natural phenomena which might be co-opted for communicative use that I would not want to call paralinguistic on any conception – a bruise or a pale complexion, for example. In many ways, the second construal comes closer to what I have in mind; rising pitch is so often linked with rising eyebrows, for example, that it's perhaps not clear why we would want to say that while the former is part of a paralanguage, the latter is not. However, the notions of 'natural' and 'non-natural' meaning have been the focus of much debate within the Gricean pragmatic tradition, and since many of my arguments are directly concerned with this tradition, I will stick with them.

Many of those who use (and define) the terms 'paralinguistic' and 'non-linguistic' seem content not to define *language* (assuming, perhaps, that it is easily definable, or that since we all have an intuitive handle on what language is, a definition is not needed). In what follows, I adopt a broadly Chomskyan view of language as an autonomous, mentally represented grammar constrained by innately determined principles. I realise that this view of language is not to everyone's taste. Indeed, I face opposition from both sides, for Chomsky himself may well regard the kind of enterprise on which I am embarking as a fruitless one (2000, pp. 19–74). For those who work within other linguistic paradigms, I hope that this book will shed light on the interaction between the natural and non-natural aspects of linguistic communication irrespective of our theoretical differences. This interaction seems to have been little remarked on within any linguistic framework, and is in need of addressing from all kinds of perspectives. For the Chomskyan paradigm, I hope that if, as Chomsky once remarked, 'It is possible that natural language has only syntax and pragmatics' (2000, p. 132), some of the discussion in the chapters that follow might be of some value in clarifying the contribution of pragmatics.

The view of language I will adopt, then, is a cognitive, broadly Chomskyan one. Language is an Internal, Individual, Intensional object – Chomsky's *I*-language. Humans have a dedicated mental 'organ' or 'faculty of language' (2000, p. 168) – potentially a module (or set of modules). In a typically developing individual, this will mature, given exposure to the appropriate environment, from an initial genetically determined state to a 'steady state' that can be said to represent knowledge of language. To be in this state is to know a certain set of rules or principles: language is a principle-governed system. It is also a creative, combinatorial system with a finite number of elements (morphemes), which can be combined to create novel utterances of arbitrary length. The set of rules or principles a speaker of a language knows constitutes a mental grammar, a code pairing phonological and semantic representations of sentences. The view of language as an autonomous, innately constrained system fits well with the modular approach to mental architecture I take throughout the book, but my focus throughout will be on pragmatics and its interaction with language, rather than the nature of the linguistic system itself (for discussion of some of the general objections to the Chomskyan approach to language, see Chomsky 2000; for an overview of how a cognitive theory of pragmatics might fit in with broadly Chomskyan distinctions, see Carston 2002, pp. 1–14.).

Turning to *pragmatics*, my aim is to adopt a pragmatic theory that will provide an account of verbal communication – i.e. language use – that complements a broadly Chomskyan internalist or cognitive approach to language. For this reason, among others, I will adopt the framework of *Relevance Theory* (Sperber and Wilson 1986/1995), which was inspired by Chomskyan (and Fodorian) insights into language and mind, and is in the same spirit as their work. Of course, not all pragmatists sympathise with relevance theory, just as not all linguists sympathise with Chomsky, but I hope the questions raised in this book will be of interest to those who work within other pragmatic frameworks.

Relevance theory combines Gricean intention-based pragmatics with aspects of modern research in cognitive science to provide a cognitive-inferential pragmatic framework. It takes as its domain a theoretically defined subset of cases that might in folk terminology be referred to as instances of communication. 'Communication' is a very broad term. As Thomas Sebeok remarks:

all organic alliances presuppose a measure of communication: Protozoa interchange signals; an aggregate of cells becomes an organism by virtue of the fact that the component cells can influence one another. (1972, p. 39)

A pragmatic theory defined as a theory of communication in this very broad sense would indeed have to be what Chomsky (2000, p. 70) has termed a 'theory of everything'; it would be required to encompass every possible facet of human interaction that might conceivably be said to be (in Sebeok's terms) 'communicative'; from the socio-cultural right down to the sub-personal: from fashion to pheromones.

Relevance theory has a more narrowly delimited domain. It is not a 'theory of everything'; it is not even a general theory of communication, but focuses on a sub-type of human communicative behaviour: *ostensive* behaviour – behaviour by which a communi-cator provides evidence of an intention to communicate something. As noted above, language itself is seen as governed by a code which relates phonetic representations to semantic representations (or 'logical forms'). However, utterance interpretation is a two-phase process. The linguistically encoded logical form which is the output of the mental grammar is simply a starting point for rich inferential processes guided by the expectation that speakers will conform to certain standards of communication. In (highly) intuitive terms, an audience faced with a piece of ostensive behaviour is entitled to assume that the communicator has a good reason for producing this particular stimulus as evidence not only of their intention to com-municate, but of *what* they want to communicate. One of the objectives of this book will be to explain the interaction of 'natural' communicative phenomena and ostensive behaviour.

As well as meshing with the Chomskyan approach to language and cognition generally, relevance theory offers a framework within which the 'vaguer' aspects of human communication might be analysed. As Sperber and Wilson comment:

We see it as a major challenge for any account of human communication to give a precise description and explanation of its vaguer effects. Distin-guishing meaning from communication, accepting that something can be communicated without strictly speaking being *meant* by the communicator or the communicator's behaviour, is a first essential step. . . . Once this step is taken, we believe that the framework we propose . . . can rise to this challenge. (Sperber and Wilson 1986/1995, pp. 57–8)

As noted above, natural behaviours such as prosody typically convey emotional or attitudinal information, or create impressions or moods rather than express full propositions in their own right. As a result, they fall into the class of communicative phenomena with 'vaguer effects'. Throughout the book, I will provide examples of how the theory might deal with such cases, and go some way towards showing that Sperber and Wilson's framework can rise to the 'challenge' they describe.

Finally, pragmatics is by its nature a cross-disciplinary subject, with its roots in philosophy and linguistics, but reaching out into cognitive science, psychology, sociology and even the study of non-human animal communication. I have done my best to make the book self-contained and self-explanatory, and to present the arguments in a non-technical way. I therefore hope that it will be of interest to the reader who is neither a pragmatist nor a linguist.

OVERVIEW

In Chapter 2 I approach question (A) above (what is the relation between 'natural' and intentional communication?) by focusing on Grice's seminal paper 'Meaning' (1957). This is one of the most influential philosophical papers of the past fifty years, and has had a profound influence on linguists, pragmatists and cognitive scientists as well as philosophers. In this paper, Grice drew a distinction between natural and non-natural meaning, and attempted to characterise non-natural meaning (meaning$_{NN}$) in terms of the expression and recognition of intentions. For Grice 'what is meant$_{NN}$' is roughly coextensive with what is intentionally communicated, and his notion of non-natural meaning has had a major influence on the development of pragmatics. The notion of natural meaning has received much less attention: I use it as a starting point for investigating the role of natural phenomena in communication.

A controversial feature of Grice's account of intentional communication is the line he draws between *showing* and *meaning*$_{NN}$ (or showing and *telling*, or showing and *saying that*), where meaning$_{NN}$ typically involves a linguistic convention or code. This distinction has had important effects on the development of pragmatics. Following Grice, pragmatists have focused on the notion of meaning$_{NN}$ and abstracted away from cases of showing, which include the intentional display of 'natural' phenomena such as facial expression or tone of voice. I argue that while there is room for disagreement on whether cases of 'showing' always amount to cases of meaning$_{NN}$, there is little doubt that cases of 'showing' do qualify as cases of intentional communication of the kind a pragmatic theory should be able to handle: *meaning* and *communicating* do not always line up.

I end the chapter by considering some of the ways in which 'natural' phenomena may carry information for an observer. In some cases, they betray our thoughts and feelings to others in a way that does not amount to intentionally communicating them (see example (1) above). In others, they may be deliberately produced in a way that clearly amounts to intentional communication (see example (4)). In still further cases, they are involuntarily produced but may be deliberately (or overtly) shown (see example (3)). Intentional verbal communication, then, involves a mixture of natural and non-natural meaning, and an adequate pragmatic theory should take account of both.

Chapter 3 introduces the central tenets of relevance theory. In this chapter I pay particular attention to the relevance-theoretic notion of *ostensive–inferential* communication, which is explicitly designed to cover both showing and non-natural meaning. I argue that there is a continuum of cases between showing and meaning$_{NN}$, and that the existence of such a continuum has implications for the domain of pragmatic principles or maxims: it suggests that they are best seen as applying to the domain of overt intentional communication as a whole, rather than to the narrower domain of meaning$_{NN}$. In the rest of the book, I suggest ways of using this continuum as a conceptual tool for the analysis of both natural and linguistic behaviours.

An original feature of this chapter is its discussion of cases in which 'natural' and linguistic communication interact in the interpretation of utterances. I argue that natural communicative phenomena such as facial expression or tone of voice may play a vital role in understanding not only the propositional attitude that a speaker intends to communicate, but also the proposition she intends to express: compare example (3) above, in which Lily's tone of voice and facial expression calibrate the degree of anger her audience understands her to feel and to be expressing as part of her meaning, with (4) – in which Jack's 'smile' indicates that he is dissociating himself from the proposition he is expressing. As a result of the tendency of pragmatists to focus on meaning$_{NN}$, this type of interaction between natural and linguistic phenomena has generally been overlooked in pragmatics. I explore in some detail how it connects with the issue of semantic underdetermination, which is currently the subject of much debate among semanticists and pragmatists. Towards the end of the chapter, I introduce a distinction between translational and non-translational encoding (a development of Diane Blakemore's (1987, 2002) distinction between conceptual and procedural meaning) that will play a central role in my analysis of natural communicative phenomena.

Chapter 4 approaches questions (B) and (C) above (how do natural phenomena communicate, and what do they convey?) through the analysis of interjections: expressions such as *ouch, wow, yuk,* etc. which are generally seen as partly natural and partly linguistic. They are partly natural in the sense that many seem to have developed as stylised exaggerations of entirely natural responses, and partly linguistic in the sense that they differ from language to language. It has therefore been proposed that they are located on a continuum between display and language proper. I consider this continuum in some detail, and discuss its relationship to the showing–meaning$_{NN}$ continuum outlined in Chapter 3. I then examine the problems raised by previous attempts to characterise the meaning of interjections in purely conceptual terms, and argue that the aspects of interjections that differ from language to language are best analysed using the notion of non-translational – or procedural – encoding, introduced in Chapter 3. Towards the end of this chapter I suggest ways in which natural responses may, over time, become stylised and exaggerated so that they take on a coded element. This prefigures discussion of question (D) – what is the relation between natural non-verbal behaviours and those non-verbal behaviours that are not natural? – in Chapters 6 and 7.

In Chapter 5, I return to the kind of natural phenomena mentioned in my opening paragraph, and suggest that they fall into two distinct subsets – natural *signs* and natural *signals* – only one of which fits straightforwardly with Grice's distinction between natural and non-natural meaning. This distinction between natural signs and natural signals is based on the one made in Hauser's (1996) study of the evolution of communication. Natural signs (e.g. tree rings, footprints in the snow, the scent of ripe fruit) carry information which provides evidence for a certain conclusion (e.g. about the age of the tree, the presence of an animal, the ripeness of the fruit); indeed, Grice's notion of natural meaning was largely constructed by considering natural signs. However, Hauser's work enables us to distinguish natural signs from natural signals (e.g. the alarm calls of vervet monkeys, the waggle-dance of honey-bees), which have the *function* (Millikan 1984, Origgi and Sperber 2000, Sperber 2007) of conveying information: that is, they are inherently communicative and owe their continued existence to the fact that they convey information. I argue that the existence of natural signals presents problems for Grice's distinction between natural and non-natural meaning.

The sign–signal distinction seems to apply not only to animal but to human behaviour. Some natural human behaviours (e.g. shivers) are signs rather than signals: they carry information for observers, but do not have an indicating function. I suggest that they are interpreted purely inferentially, as providing evidence for a certain conclusion. Other human behaviours (e.g. smiles) are signals: they are inherently communicative, and do have an indicating function. I suggest that these have a coded element and are best analysed using the notion of a *natural code* (or natural signal, in the ethological sense). Using Grice's tests for distinguishing natural from non-natural meaning, I show that natural signals do not fall squarely on either side of his distinction. The existence of these inherently communicative natural behaviours thus suggests that Grice's original distinction between natural and non-natural meaning is not exhaustive.

I end the chapter by applying the distinction between translational and non-translational meaning drawn in Chapter 3 to the analysis of natural codes. As with interjections, I argue against attempts to analyse naturally coded behaviours such as facial expression in conceptual terms and propose a procedural account. The conceptual procedural distinction therefore applies to coded signals that are not strictly linguistic.

Chapter 6 begins with an examination of some of the implications of the analysis proposed in this book for the study of prosody. Firstly, prosodic inputs to the comprehension process are often seen as ranging along a continuum from the properly linguistic (e.g. lexical stress or lexical tone) to the 'natural' (e.g. an angry, friendly or agitated tone of voice) (Gussenhoven 2002, Pell 2002): this continuum has interesting parallels with Goffman's continuum presented in Chapter 4. In line with the distinctions made in the previous chapter, I argue that 'natural' prosodic inputs fall into two importantly different categories – signs and signals. Natural signals, like linguistic signals, are genuinely coded and inherently communicative; natural *signs*, by contrast, are interpreted by inference rather than decoding, and are not inherently communicative at all. Moreover, prosodic inputs of all three types may be exploited in overt communication, and when they are exploited in this way, they range along the showing–meaning$_{NN}$ continuum.

In this chapter I also address the question of what prosody encodes and argue that both natural and properly linguistic prosodic signals might encode procedural information of a type shared by borderline linguistic expressions such as interjections and properly linguistic expressions such as mood indicators. This makes it possible to see how there could be a continuum of cases between purely natural prosodic signals and non-natural ones, whether cultural or properly linguistic. Not all *non*-natural procedural codes are linguistic codes: they are better characterised as *cultural codes*. This notion can be used in the analysis of some aspects not only of prosody and interjections but also of other non-verbal behaviours, such as 'emblems' (Ekman and Friesen 1969): the culture-specific, coded gestures illustrated in Fig. 1.1 above.

The chapter closes with discussion of the work of Adam Kendon (1988, 2004) on gesture, which has inspired McNeill (1992) to suggest that gesture ranges along a continuum from 'gesticulation', those movements of the arms and hands that accompany speech, through what he calls 'pantomimes' and 'emblems', to sign-language proper: a continuum with clear parallels to both Goffman's continuum and the prosodic continuum discussed above. The chapter goes on to suggest that the distinction introduced in Chapter 3 between the deliberate production of behaviours and the deliberate showing of spontaneously occurring behaviours might shed light on how gestures and such behaviours are used and interpreted.

Chapter 7 looks in more detail at the psychological side of non-verbal communication. Since Grice's ground-breaking work, it is now widely accepted that mind-reading or 'theory of mind' (the ability to explain and predict the behaviour of others in terms of the mental states underlying that behaviour) plays a central role in human communication. Indeed, the model of communication out-lined in this book presupposes that humans are endowed with considerable mind-reading abilities. Various experimental para-digms have been devised to explore the communicative difficulties encountered by people with impaired mind-reading abilities (such as, for example, those with autism). The distinctions drawn in this book suggest a variety of further test cases which may contribute to our understanding of human mind-reading abilities. For example, natural signs and natural signals may present different problems for people with impaired mind-reading abilities, but this distinction is not normally considered in the mind-reading literature. Similarly, natural signs or signals that are overtly shown may cause different problems for those with impaired mind-reading abilities from those that are not overtly shown, but this distinction is also not normally considered in the literature on mind-reading. Finally, natural signs or signals that provide evidence of *physical* rather than *mental* states may be easier to interpret for those with mind-reading difficulties; again, this distinction is not normally considered in the literature on mind-reading.

The chapter concludes with a discussion of Lieberman's (2000) work on the sub-attentive processes involved in the production and interpretation of unintentional 'natural' prosodic signs and signals, and the production and interpretation of natural behaviours generally: what he calls the 'dance' of non-verbal communication. According to Lieberman, sub-attentive impressions created by behaviours of this type are dealt with in the basal ganglia. There is thus some evidence of a neurophysiological basis for the distinctions between accidental, covert and overt information transmission introduced earlier in the book.

In the final chapter, Chapter 8, I contrast the showing–meaning$_{NN}$ continuum outlined in Chapter 3 with the other continua discussed at various points in the book. I argue that, in fact, these are two very different kinds of continua: in the first place, the showing–meaning$_{NN}$ continuum includes only inputs exploited in overt communication; in the second, it includes not only natural and linguistic signals but also overtly used natural signs. I explore the relationship between the two kinds of continua, and suggest some possible applications: for instance, *synchronic* versions might be seen as 'snapshots' of the kind of communicative stimuli humans have at their disposal, and a *diachronic* perspective might shed light both on historical linguistics, and on the processes that underpin human communication from an evolutionary perspective. We end where we came in, with Paul Grice, and his 'mythical' account of the evolution of meaning$_{NN}$, which, I argue, may have implications for what we regard as the function of language itself, and for how it may have evolved.

NOTES

1. Page references to Grice's work are all from the published versions of these papers in Grice (1989).

2. When I speak of human communication as 'intentional' I use the word in what Hauser (1996, p. 23) calls the 'rich, philosophical sense'. Thus, human communication exploits the cognitive ability to attribute mental states – in particular intentions – to others. I point this out because later in the book I discuss various ethological concepts, and ethologists tradition-ally use 'intentional' in a different sense. '*Intention* movements' in non-human animals, for example, are movements that reliably predict a certain course of action: the term implies no pre-meditation on the part of the animal, and nothing 'intentional' in the 'rich, philosophical sense' on their part.

3. BNC = British National Corpus. I have used attested examples where possible (particularly in Chapter 4), but the reader will notice that I also use constructed examples in the book. This is for two reasons. Firstly, a written corpus does not record many of the kind of non-verbal behaviours in which I am interested: tone of voice, facial expression, etc. have to be inferred by the reader in both corpus and constructed examples. Secondly, most of my arguments are theoretical rather than descriptive, and made-up examples serve as well as attested ones to illustrate a theoretical point.

4. This example is from McNeill (1992, p. 25); the speaker is describing a scene from a story in a comic-book.

CHAPTER 2

Natural and non-natural meaning

Take Bach's *Well Temper'd Clavier*. To me it means molecular harmony. To my father, it means a broken sewing machine. To Bach, it meant money to pay the candlemaker.

(David Mitchell – *number9dream*)

GRICEAN MEANING$_{NN}$

Among the ghosts that haunt the corridors of departments that profess (and foster) an interest in pragmatics, there are a great many philosophers of language. Though with the passing of time the influence of some of these has faded, there can be little doubt that the spirit of Paul Grice continues to exert a powerful influence. Not only was his work among the most influential in laying the foundations for much of modern pragmatics, but his insights continue to provoke debate (and controversy). We may owe the term 'pragmatics' to Charles Morris (1938), but Grice certainly ranks highly among a select few to whom credit is due for shaping (and continuing to shape) the discipline as we know it today.

To pragmatists, indeed linguists generally, Grice is remembered best for his *Theory of Conversation*, outlined in the *William James Lectures* delivered at Harvard University in 1967. But whilst this is a book with its roots firmly in pragmatics, it is another area of Grice's work – his *Theory of Meaning*, first outlined in his paper 'Meaning' (1957) – that is the focus of this chapter.[1]

Although the two 'theories' are often regarded as distinct, they are not unrelated. Indeed, it could be argued that they are mutually illuminating to the extent that we fail to do justice to either if we consider them independently of one another.[2] Grice's theory of conversation and his theory of meaning were part of a much larger programme; a programme Grice never finished (nor indeed could ever have hoped to). On the back cover of Grice's 1989 anthology *Studies in the Way of Words*, Simon Blackburn describes Grice as 'a miniaturist who changed the way other people paint big canvases'. I respectfully disagree: while it's easy to form the impression that Grice was a miniaturist because of the capacity he had for taking infinite pains, I think this misses the point that the canvas he envisaged was – to borrow a phrase used by Daniel Dennett – 'Vanishingly Vast' (1995, p. 109).[3]

Grice's approach to meaning is neatly summed up by a quote from his 1989 *Retrospective Epilogue*: 'what words mean is a matter of what people mean by them' (1989, p. 340). Meaning was to be understood in terms of propositional-attitude psychology; ultimately, the meanings of words reduced[4] to the beliefs, desires and intentions of communicators who uttered them. As well as shaping modern pragmatics, then, another part of Grice's legacy is one particular view of 'semantics', which has been pursued most notably in the work of Stephen Schiffer (1972)[5] and Russell Dale (1996). This view is summed up by Jerry Fodor as follows:

English inherits its semantics from the contents of the beliefs, desires, intentions, and so forth that it's used to express, as per Grice and his followers . . . English *has no semantics*. Learning English isn't a theory about what its sentences mean, it's learning how to associate its sentences with the corresponding thoughts. (Jerry Fodor 1998, p. 9)

Grice's paper 'Meaning' was at least partly conceived as a response to Stevenson (1944), whose own account, Grice argued, failed to capture the crucial difference between expression meaning and speaker meaning. Having failed to recognise this distinction, Stevenson's framework would never be able to capture what for Grice was the very essence of meaning: that the linguistic meaning of expressions should ultimately be characterised in terms of speaker meaning – that words do indeed mean what people mean by them.

Grice was not the first to argue for this kind of view. Although we have no evidence that he read her work, Grice was returning to issues that had first been raised over fifty years earlier by a certain Lady Victoria Welby:

though we do now and then recoil from a glaring misuse of a term in the 'rising generation' and lament such a lapse from *our* good ways, we never see that the fatal seed has been sown, that fatal tradition of a far more extensive misuse has been handed on, by us; that in scores and hundreds of instances we have carefully habituated the child, trained it, to say one thing when it means another.[6] (1911, pp. 62–3)

Grice begins his paper 'Meaning' with an attempt to pin down the specific type of meaning he was to be concerned with: *non-natural*$_{(NN)}$ meaning. In order to do this, Grice distinguished it from a notion he called *natural*$_{(N)}$ meaning.[7] The natural/non-natural distinction was intended to capture what he later described as:

a reasonably clear intuitive distinction between cases where the word 'mean' has what we might think of as a natural sense, a sense in which what something means is closely related to the idea of what it is a natural sign for (as in 'Black clouds mean rain'), and those where it has what I call a non-natural sense, as in such contexts as 'His remark meant so-and-so'. (1989, p. 291)

Grice was not the first to consider this distinction. Effectively, he was carrying on a tradition that dates back through the work of Hobbes to at least as early as William of Ockham,[8] and arguably back as far as Plato's *physis–thesis* opposition, first characterised in the *Cratylus*.[9] In this dialogue, Socrates and Hermogenes discuss the origins of language, and debate whether word meanings are the result of some 'natural affinity' shared between form and meaning, or whether they are simply conventionally agreed upon. This too is a subject to which I will return in later chapters.

Although Grice's 1957 paper was primarily concerned with meaning$_{NN}$ it will suit my aims to dwell for a while on the notion of meaning$_N$, which lies at the very heart of the notion of 'natural pragmatics' discussed in this book. I will therefore start by looking at some of the tests Grice used to distinguish between natural and non-natural meaning.

Grice began by providing examples of the two types of meaning. Consider (6) and (7) below, the first a case of meaning$_N$, and the second a case of meaning$_{NN}$:

(6) Those spots mean measles.
(7) That remark means he has measles.

He then proposed a variety of ways in which the two types of meaning might be distinguished. The first was based on the idea that cases of meaning$_N$ are *factive*, in the sense that *x means$_N$ p* or *x meant$_N$ p* entail *p*. By contrast, cases of meaning$_{NN}$ are non-factive. An utterance such as 'his remark means *it is raining*' does not entail that it is raining at all. Grice's intuitions are, as always, dependable. Consider (8):

(8) That hissing sound means$_N$ there is a snake under the table.

If *U*'s utterance of (8) is true, then it will indeed always follow that there is a snake under the table. (If there isn't a snake under the table, then an audience might quite legitimately respond 'Well, it looks like that hissing sound *didn't mean* there was a snake under the table.') Compare this with a scenario in which *U* asks *A* what *B* meant by the remark 'Il y a un serpent sous la table', to which *A* replies 'That remark means there is a snake under the table.' Here, *A*'s utterance can be true whether or not there actually is a snake under the table, and the remark will still *mean* (or have meant) the same thing (and *B* will still mean or have meant the same thing by her utterance of it) regardless of the facts of the matter.

The difference between factive and non-factive uses of 'mean' underlay a further series of tests in which Grice contrasted the results of paraphrasing utterances containing uses of the word 'mean' (in both senses). While (9) is a plausible paraphrase of utterance (6), (10) is not a plausible paraphrase of utterance (7). It may be true, but it does not convey the same sense of 'means' as that in the original utterance. (It may, in fact, paraphrase a parallel case of *natural* meaning.)

(9) The fact that he has those spots means he has measles.
(10) ??The fact that he made that remark means he has measles.

This test confirms that (6) is a case of meaning$_N$ and (7) is not.

A further test, this time for recognising meaning$_{NN}$, involved paraphrases directly quoting the meaning in question. Example (11) below is not a satisfactory paraphrase of (6), but (12) is a satisfactory paraphrase of (7).

> (11) ??Those spots mean 'he has measles'.
> (12) That remark means 'he has measles'.

This confirms that (7) is a case of meaning$_{NN}$, and (6) is not.

In another test, Grice argued that while no conclusion about *what is (was) meant by (something)* can be drawn from an utterance that describes a case of meaning$_N$, such a conclusion can legitimately be drawn from an utterance that describes a case of meaning$_{NN}$ (see (13–14)):

> (13) ??What was meant by those spots was that he has measles.
> (14) What was meant by that remark was that he has measles.

This test supports the view that (6) is a case of meaning$_N$, while (7) is a case of meaning$_{NN}$. Grice's primary concern, of course, was meaning$_{NN}$, and in particular, how it might be characterised in terms of intentions and the recognition of intentions. I will argue later in the book that these tests do not apply so smoothly to certain cases of what is intuitively a type of natural meaning, and I will suggest an explanation for this.

Returning to the 1957 paper, Grice moved through a series of carefully constructed examples in order to identify precisely what type of intentions are required in cases of meaning$_{NN}$:

A first shot would be to suggest that 'x meant$_{NN}$ something' would be true if x was intended by its utterer to induce a belief in some 'audience' and that to say what the belief was would be to say what x meant$_{NN}$. This will not do. I might drop B's handkerchief near the scene of a murder in order to induce the detective to believe that B is the murderer; but we should not want to say that the handkerchief (or my leaving it there) meant$_{NN}$ anything or that I had meant$_{NN}$ by leaving it that B was the murderer. (1989, p. 217)

The problem here is that the fact that the 'communicator' (or handkerchief-dropper) has these intentions is entirely incidental to the 'audience's' (or detective's) response. The two are not linked in any way; nor can they be, since the 'audience' is entirely unaware of the 'communicator's' intentions. Grice then turns to a series of further examples, where – in contrast to the handkerchief-dropper example – the 'communicator' openly (hereafter *overtly*) provides evidence of their intention to induce a belief:

Clearly we must at least add that, for x to have meant$_{NN}$ anything, not merely must it have been 'uttered' with the intention of inducing a certain belief but also the utterer must have intended the 'audience' to recognize the intention behind the utterance. . . .

[(A)][10] Herod presents Salome with the head of St. John the Baptist on a charger.

[(B)] Feeling faint, a child lets its mother see how pale it is (hoping that she may draw her own conclusions and help).

[(C)] I leave the china my daughter has broken lying around for my wife to see. (1989, p. 218)

For Grice, however, this was not enough. There is still a sense in which the presence of the communicator's intentions in the above examples is (at least partly) incidental to the occurrence of the intended response. In (A), for example, Salome can infer that St John the Baptist is dead solely on the strength of the evidence presented, and independently of any intentions Herod has in presenting her with his head (similar remarks carry over to (B) and (C)). Grice wanted to distinguish between merely (albeit overtly) showing someone a particular object or a certain type of behaviour – from which in his view it did not follow that the object or behaviour meant$_{NN}$ anything (or that anything was meant$_{NN}$ by the 'show*er*'), and something's being meant$_{NN}$ by the object or behaviour in question (or by the person responsible for using it in a certain meaningful$_{NN}$ manner):

What we want to find is the difference between 'deliberately and openly letting someone know' and 'telling', and between 'getting someone to think' and 'telling'.

In Grice's view, the distinction might be drawn in the following way:

Compare the following two cases:

(1) I show Mr. *X* a photograph of Mr. *Y* displaying undue familiarity to Mrs. *X*.
(2) I draw a picture of Mr. *Y* behaving in this manner and show it to Mr. *X*.

I find that I want to deny that in (1) the photograph (or my showing it to Mr. *X*) meant$_{NN}$ anything at all, while I want to assert that in (2) the picture (or my drawing and showing it) meant$_{NN}$ something (that Mr. *Y* had been unduly familiar), or at least that I had meant$_{NN}$ by it that Mr. *Y* had been unduly familiar. What is the difference between the two cases? Surely that in case (1) Mr. *X*'s recognition of my intention to make him believe that there is something between Mr. *Y* and Mrs. *X* is (more or less) irrelevant to the production of this effect by the photograph. Mr. *X* would be led by the photograph at least to suspect Mrs. *X* even if, instead of showing it to him, I had left it in his room by accident; and I (the photograph shower) would not be unaware of this. But it will make a difference to the effect of my picture on Mr. *X* whether or not he takes me to be intending to inform him (make him believe something) about Mrs. *X*, and not to be just doodling or trying to produce a work of art. (1989, p. 218)

In any act which provides evidence of an intention to 'induce a belief' or to 'inform', notice that there are two layers of information to be retrieved by the audience. The first, basic layer is the information being pointed out – in Grice's example, the fact that Mr *Y* is being unduly familiar with Mrs *X* – and the second, the information that this first layer is being pointed out intentionally. In examples (A), (B) and (C) from the quote above, the communicator (Herod, the child, Grice) provides overt evidence of their intention to inform (the second layer), but in these cases the basic layer of information is derivable without reference to this intention. According to Grice, for a case to count as one of meaning$_{NN}$ this basic layer should *not* be entirely derivable without reference to the second layer (and, furthermore, this should be intended by the communicator). Grice concludes his formulation of meaning$_{NN}$ as follows:

'*A* meant something by *x*' is roughly equivalent to '*A* uttered *x* with the intention of inducing a belief by means of the recognition of this intention'.

This he later modified to the following more detailed definition (see Grice 1989, p. 92):

'U meant something by uttering x' is true iff, for some audience A, U uttered x intending:

(1) A to produce a particular response r
(2) A to think (recognize) that U intends (1)
(3) A to fulfil (1) on the basis of his fulfilment of (2).

In Lectures V, VI and VII of the *William James Lectures* (published as Grice (1968) and (1969)) Grice considered criticisms of the first of the above three clauses, which led him to make further modifications. This involved changing clause (1) in the above definition to read '"U meant something by uttering x" is true iff, for some audience A, U uttered x intending: *(1) A to think that U thinks that p*.' This made it possible to distinguish between what Grice called *exhibitive* and *protreptic* utterances. In an exhibitive utterance, U's intention is not to induce a belief in A, but rather to get A to think that U holds a particular belief: thus, the utterance exhibits U's belief. In a protreptic utterance, U exhibits a belief with the *further* intention of inducing the same belief in A (on the strength of A's recognising that U holds it too).

Stephen Neale remarks of this modification:

One worry about the suggested revision is that it does not comport well with the commonly held view that the primary purpose of communication is the transfer of information about the world: on the revised account, the primary purpose seems to be the transfer of information about one's mental states.[11] (1992, p. 549)

Although these changes do not affect the arguments to come in the next section, I will return to them in the final section of Chapter 8, when I consider the evolution of communication and language.

SHOWING AND MEANING$_{NN}$

Grice's account of meaning$_{NN}$ inspired (and continues to inspire) a great deal of discussion. On the one hand, philosophers such as Strawson (1964), Searle (1965, 1969, 1979) and Schiffer (1972) constructed a range of increasingly complex counter examples, many designed to show the need for ever higher levels of intentionality (which rapidly induce a kind of psychic vertigo). These, and some of the possible responses to them, are neatly summarised in Avramides 1989.

However, I would like to explore another way in which the above formulation might be challenged. Instead of focusing on the need for extra layers of intention over and above those proposed by Grice, it looks in particular at clause (3) of the above reformulation ('*A* to produce a particular response *r* on the basis of his recognition that *U* intends him to produce this particular response'), and at the central role Grice saw for the recovery of the second layer of information – the intention to inform – in deriving the first.

Schiffer addresses this point in his 1972 book *Meaning*:

[O]ne thing that might be said is that in presenting Salome with the head of St. John the Baptist, Herod might mean that St. John the Baptist was dead. This does not strike me as a wildly implausible thing to say. Consider an analogous case.

> (3a) *A*: 'Let's play squash.'
>   *S*:   Holds up bandaged leg.

Here, I think, one would say, intuitively, that by holding up his leg *S* meant that he could not play, or that he could play because his leg was injured; yet it would seem that the only difference between (3) [(A) – the Herod, Salome and St John the Baptist example – TW] and (3a) which is possibly relevant is that the 'inference' *A* has to make in the 'bandaged leg' example is slightly less direct than in the case of St. John the Baptist's head, although in both cases one could make the relevant inference without any assistance on the part of *S*.

Grice has objected to me that while we may say that (in (3a)) *S* meant he could not play squash by holding up his bandaged leg, he could not mean thereby that his leg is bandaged. But, in the first place, even this is not an objection to the point I am trying to make, which is that there is no relevant difference between (3) and (3a), so that if we may say that *S* meant that he could not play squash, then – by parity of reason – we may say that Herod meant that St. John the Baptist was dead (it was not suggested that Herod meant that there was a severed head on his charger). In the second place, I think that it is false that *S* could not mean that his leg was bandaged by holding up his bandaged leg. Consider

(3b) *A*: 'I've heard that your leg is bandaged. Is it true?'
     S: Holds up bandaged leg.

Here, I think, one would say that *S* meant that his leg was bandaged. (1972, p. 56)

Schiffer's argument, then, is that cases such as (1) from above (Grice's photograph example) – and, indeed, cases such as (A), (B) and (C) from the quote before that – should be regarded as instances of meaning$_{NN}$.

François Recanati also addresses this point, in his 1987 book *Meaning and Force*:

> Take Grice's example of Herod bringing to Salome the severed head of John the Baptist. By this 'utterance', the 'speaker' S (Herod) openly intends to provide A (Salome) with reason to believe that the following conditions obtain: John is dead, and S wants A to share this knowledge. Why should this not be considered a case of communication? Grice's reason for excluding this case is that for (an important part of) the speaker's intention to be fulfilled, it is not necessary that the intention be recognised: The severed head of John the Baptist, *by itself*, is evidence that he is dead, and to conclude that it is so, A does not have to recognise S's intention. Grice is right to point out that there are two sorts of cases: cases in which only the speaker's intention is intended to provide evidence (this is what Grice calls 'non-natural meaning', and it is indeed central in linguistic communication) and cases in which the 'utterance' is intended to provide evidence over and above the evidence provided by the speaker's intention. But there is no reason, it seems to me, to restrict the label 'Gricean communication' to the first category of cases, however important they are. (1987, p. 189)

My argument will run along similar lines, although as I mentioned in my introduction, my main concern (like Recanati's) is with intentional communication, not meaning$_{NN}$. While Schiffer and Recanati focus on the St John the Baptist example (A), I will focus on example (B), which will lead on to a discussion of natural behaviours and their role in overt intentional communication.

For a communicative act to be intentional in the required sense, I will argue, what is important is that evidence is provided of an intention to inform; it is much less important whether an audience might have been able to draw their own conclusions in the absence of

such an intention. As I will show, the very fact that a communicator
has provided evidence of an intention to inform may lead the
audience to make 'less direct' inferences about the communicator's
meaning.

Consider (15a–e) below, adapted from Grice's example (B) above.
In all these cases something has happened that produces a response
in an audience:

> (15a) Mary is asleep. Her mother notices that she is pale and concludes
>   she is unwell.
> (15b) Feeling unwell, Mary lies in bed with her eyes closed. She
>   intends her mother to see how pale she is but really doesn't care
>   if this intention is noticed or not.
> (15c) As (15b), except that here Mary's mother instinctively guesses
>   at Mary's intention to let her mother see how pale she is.
> (15d) Feeling unwell, Mary deliberately and openly lets her mother
>   see how pale she is, so she will notice and help.[12]
> (15e) Mary says to her mother 'I don't feel well.'

As I have pointed out, Grice noticed that before we can be said to
be dealing with a case of meaning$_{NN}$ certain intentions must be
present. Firstly, the response itself must be intended – this rules out
(15a) as a case of meaning$_{NN}$; secondly, the audience must recognise
the intention to produce that response – this rules out (15b); thirdly,
the communicator must intend the audience to recognise the intention to produce that response – this rules out (15c). The final all-
important condition, the one that rules out (15d), and makes (15e)
a case of meaning$_{NN}$, is that only in this example does Mary intend
the audience's recognition of her intention to produce the desired
response to play a crucial role in producing the response itself.
In (15d) Mary's mother can see for herself that Mary is unwell.

No one would propose that the scenario described in (15a) is a
case of intentional communication in any sense. Mary is asleep; she
does not intend to communicate anything. This might be better
described as a case of accidental information transmission: Mary's
pale complexion shows her mother that she is unwell. In fact, even
to describe this as a case of communication at all is to use the word
extremely broadly. Intuitively, there is no reason to say that an

individual walking down the street communicates every piece of information a passer-by might infer from his physical appearance, his demeanour, his clothes etc.

It is less obvious in (15b) and (15c) that we are not dealing with intentional communication in some sense. After all, Mary does intend to inform her mother of something. However, she is not being open about her informative intention, and while she might indeed be described as communicating intentionally, she is certainly not doing so overtly. (We might compare this with the 'handkerchief-dropper' example.)

But what of the cases in (15d) and (15e)? While it is certainly true that Mary's mother can see Mary's pale complexion and draw her own conclusions irrespective of Mary's intentions, I think (echoing Schiffer and Recanati) that there are good reasons to suggest that (15d) is an instance of overt intentional communication (though – as Recanati suggests – this concept needs to be distinguished from meaning$_{NN}$).

Firstly, Mary is being 'deliberate and open' about her intentions. Even if she only intended to inform her mother that she was feeling unwell (rather than also getting her to help), she is certainly conveying her informative intention overtly, rather than keeping it hidden, as in (15b) and (15c). There is a clear sense in which it is Mary herself who is showing her mother she is unwell, rather than just her pale complexion that is doing it (as in (15a)). Secondly, and more importantly, in these examples Mary intends not only to inform her mother that she is unwell, but also to indicate that she wants her mother to help. If Mary's mother does in fact infer that she wants help, I think we would be loath to say that she is drawing this conclusion entirely on her own responsibility, and not at least partly as a result of recognising Mary's informative intention. In general, someone who is 'deliberately and openly' letting someone know something encourages their audience to think that they have done so for a reason, and to continue looking until they have found it: thus, the best way of having an informative intention fulfilled is often to get the audience to recognise it. This reflects the point made by Schiffer in the quote above: the inference from 'Mary has a pale complexion' to 'Mary wants help' is less direct than the inference from 'Mary has a pale complexion' to 'Mary is unwell.' The motivation for making this less direct inference is the very fact that Mary – by acting deliberately and openly – has encouraged her mother to think that there is something extra to infer.

DELIBERATELY SHOWN NATURAL BEHAVIOURS

In Chapter 1 I mentioned three questions, the first of which was about the relationship between naturally occurring behaviours – natural signs in Grice's sense – and intentional communication. In the last section, I suggested one way of exploring the role that natural behaviours play in intentional communication.

In this section, I will be primarily considering cases where an individual behaves in a certain way – cries, shivers, smiles – as opposed to being in a certain state – pale, or covered in spots. I will discuss three examples: the first of these I regard as fairly unproblematic cases of overt intentional communication; the second I regard as potentially problematic, but plausible nonetheless; the third is an example from a group of natural behaviours on which I intend to concentrate in Chapter 5.

Consider crying. Crying is a natural sign that someone is distressed or unhappy. It is not hard to imagine a case (parallel to example (15a)) in which we see someone crying (perhaps in the street, or in a restaurant), and recognise that this person is in distress or unhappy, although the information has been transmitted (at least to us) entirely accidentally. Furthermore, I think we can also imagine (or recall) cases where, despite their best efforts to conceal them, tears[13] betray the true feelings of someone we are talking with. Perhaps they cover their face with their hands, or turn away, or hold something up in front of their face. Or perhaps they sit there crying, trying desperately, but failing, to hold back the tears. Here again, we were not intended to realise that this person is distressed or unhappy.

However, I think it is equally true to say that we can all imagine or recall cases (parallel to (15d)) where there has there been no attempt by the person we are talking with to hold back the tears: cases in which a person is, in a sense, crying openly. Someone behaving in this way might intend to inform us of their distress, and by openly displaying their natural behaviour, they might make it easier for us to recognise their informative intention.[14] The fact that they have openly displayed their tears creates in us the expectation that there is something extra to infer: for example, the reason why they are crying.

It is important to stress at this point that I am talking of behaviours that are deliberately *shown*, and not those that are deliberately *produced*: what I am concerned with are involuntary, spontaneous behaviours that are voluntarily shown, rather than voluntary behaviours themselves. In the above discussion I have been very careful to refer to crying 'openly' as opposed to crying 'deliberately and openly' for this very reason. The phrase 'crying deliberately and openly' brings voluntary behaviours to mind in a way that is potentially confusing. I am not concerned here with faked natural behaviours[15] or the tears of actors.[16]

Grice recognised that spontaneously produced facial expressions (for example) mean naturally, but he was perfectly happy to regard the voluntary production of otherwise natural behaviours as meaning *non*-naturally:

For consider now, say, frowning. If I frown spontaneously, in the ordinary course of events, someone looking at me may well treat the frown as a natural sign of displeasure. But if I frown deliberately (to convey) my displeasure, an onlooker may be expected, provided he recognizes my intention, *still* to conclude that I am displeased. Ought we then not to say, since it could not be expected to make any difference to the onlooker's reaction whether he regards my frown as spontaneous or as intended to be informative, that my frown (deliberate) does *not* mean$_{NN}$ anything? I think this difficulty can be met; for though in general a deliberate frown may have the same effect (with respect to inducing belief in my displeasure) as a spontaneous frown, it can be expected to have the same effect only *provided* the audience takes it as intended to convey displeasure. That is, if we take away the recognition of the intention, leaving the other circumstances (including the recognition of the frown as deliberate), the belief-producing tendency of the frown must be regarded as being impaired or destroyed. (1989, p. 219)

Grice is surely right on this. The deliberate production of an otherwise natural behaviour (in order to provide evidence of an intention to induce a response or belief) is a clear example of overt intentional communication (and for Grice, meaning$_{NN}$). But it is natural, involuntary, spontaneous behaviours and their possible role in overt intentional communication that I am considering here. My claim is that just because a behaviour may not have been deliberately produced, it does not follow that it cannot be deliberately (or intentionally) shown.[17]

The second example I would like to discuss involves a shiver. Jack and Lily are sitting outside a London café on a typical bright spring day in London. It's freezing cold, Lily is miserable, and she wants to go inside. She feels herself beginning to shiver, looks at Jack, and draws his attention to her involuntary shiver. As with deliberately shown crying, this creates an expectation in the audience, for in providing evidence of her informative intention, Lily makes it possible for Jack to infer not only that she is cold, but also that she is *cold enough to want to go inside*. Again, the inference from Lily's natural (but deliberately shown) shiver, which indicates 'I am cold', to 'I want to go inside' is, to adopt Schiffer's terminology once more, 'less direct'. I find this example plausible as a case of overt intentional communication too, but it is potentially problematic. For shivers are extremely transient things. There is therefore a great deal of potential for a shiver to be exaggerated, developed and stylised to a point where we might want to characterise it as being deliberately produced as well as deliberately shown. In which case, as we have seen, there is no doubt that the shiverer can be said to be communicating intentionally. (In Chapter 4 I propose that interjections such as *ouch* and *wow* might have originated and developed as stylised exaggerations of 'natural' vocal gestures.)

The third example involves a smile, which together with facial expressions in general will be the focus of the Chapter 5. If we accept that crying and shivering can be shown to an audience deliberately and openly, it is only a short step to accepting that the same is true of involuntary, spontaneous smiles (and other natural facial expressions). Jack gives Lily a bunch of flowers, and Lily responds by letting Jack see her spontaneous reaction – a smile. Of course, smiles are also susceptible to being exaggerated, developed or faked, but in the case of smiling, audiences are capable of detecting the differences between spontaneous and deliberate smiles. Evidence from clinical neurology suggests that different neural pathways are involved in the production of spontaneous and deliberate facial expressions (Rinn 1984), and physiological evidence supports the claim first made by Duchenne (1862/1990), and later Darwin (1872/1998) that different muscles are used in spontaneous and deliberate smiles. Ekman (1992) is not convinced that faked facial expressions are always detectable by an audience, but in the case of the smile they surely are. Firstly, fake smiles always mean *non*-naturally (see Grice's earlier remarks about a behaviour's 'belief-producing tendency'), and an audience must infer the intentions behind them – ask yourself when the last time was that you asked yourself 'what *did* he mean by that entirely natural smile?' (probably never), in contrast to the last time you asked yourself 'what did he mean by that phoney smile?' (probably not long ago). Secondly, fake smiles stick out like sore thumbs – take a look at the photos of yourself at that awful wedding you went to a few years back.

I conclude, then, that behaviours that might, from a Gricean viewpoint, be regarded as simply cases of natural meaning, can also be deliberately shown, and hence used in overt intentional communication.[18] This is not to suggest that they do not sometimes convey information in other ways (i.e. accidentally). However, it does enable us to make a clear distinction between those cases alluded to in Chapter 1, where natural behaviours betray our mental/emotional state, and those in which these behaviours are recruited for use in overt intentional communication. These observations might be represented as in Fig. 2.1.

I will later argue that some natural behaviours (which Grice only regarded as carrying meaning$_N$) have an indicating (more precisely, *signalling*) function. This raises a question about how these behaviours fit into Grice's natural/non-natural distinction, and in answering this question, Fig. 2.1 will require some fine-tuning.

Fig. 2.1

In the next chapter I introduce the pragmatic framework adopted in this book: relevance theory. I begin by arguing that there is a continuum of cases between showing, as construed above, and meaning$_{NN}$. At the showing end of the continuum lie clear cases of spontaneous, natural display (such as those mentioned above); at the other extreme lie clear cases of 'saying', where the evidence provided by a speaker takes the form of a linguistic utterance. In between lie a range of cases in which natural, conventional and coded behaviour mix to various degrees (e.g. pointing, stylised expressions of emotion, interjections). I will argue that this continuum is a useful tool for the analysis of non-verbal communication and its role in utterance interpretation. I will also consider some further theoretical issues that will be central to the framework proposed in this book.

NOTES

1. The paper was actually written some time before its publication. In his CUNY PhD thesis, Russell Dale (1996) remarks:

   Stephen Schiffer, Richard Grandy, and Richard Warner have all told me in personal correspondence that Grice originally wrote the paper for a seminar that he and Strawson were to give in 1948, but was reluctant to publish it. Strawson had the article typed out and submitted it for publication without Grice's knowledge. Strawson only told Grice after the article was accepted for publication. Stephen Schiffer has told me that Grice himself told him this story and Richard Warner has written to me that he also heard this story from Grice. (1996: Chapter 1, fn. 31)

   That Grice's paper – or ideas that were central to the paper – was circulating at Oxford well before its publication is confirmed in a review of Holloway (1951) written by H. Hart in 1952: in that piece, he remarks that 'in order that I should understand . . .[a]. . . statement in the specific sense of "understand" appropriate to statements, it is sufficient (and necessary) that I recognise from the utterance what the speaker *intended* me to believe or do' (p. 61). He then adds in a footnote (fn. 2) that it was a certain 'Mr. P. Grice' who first made this clear to him. Chapter 2 of Dale (1996) provides an excellent overview of the study of meaning in the twentieth century, from the work of Lady Victoria Welby (1893/1896/1911), to Ogden and Richards (1923) and Gardiner (1951), to Grice himself.

2. I follow Stephen Neale here: 'It is at least arguable that the Theory of Conversation is a component of the Theory of Meaning. And even if this interpretation is resisted, it is undeniable that the theories are mutually informative and supportive, and that they are of more philosophical, linguistic, and historical interest if the temptation is resisted to discuss them in isolation from one another' (1992, p. 512).

3. I think this is one of the reasons why we should not be in the least surprised that Grice's work is open to so many conflicting interpretations: we simply fill in the gaps that he was forced to leave – given the breadth of his task – in a variety of different ways.

4. Whether or not the term 'reduced' is appropriate to refer to the relationship between word meaning and propositional attitudes has been the subject of much debate. Schiffer takes it that Grice was indeed embarking on a reductionist programme; Avramides, on the other hand, argues it may be better to see Grice's analysis as a *reciprocal* rather than a *reductive* one. Dale (1996) insists that Grice, although he did not necessarily support 'reductionism' *per se* (see 1989, p. 351), was nonetheless engaged in reductive analysis, and uses observations based on the fact that 'Meaning' was written nearly ten years before its publication (see note 1) as evidence to counter Avramides' claims, some of which rest on some comments made by Grice in the 1957 paper. Date of publication (as I have found to my cost) is often an unreliable source of data.

5. Schiffer's 1972 book *Meaning* originated as a doctoral thesis with Grice, and outlined an approach he later came to call *Intention Based Semantics*.

6. I'm not convinced that we *train* our children to say one thing and mean another (well, I'm convinced that we don't), but I hope the quote illustrates Welby's perspective on meaning and how it might have influenced Grice.

7. Grice also suggested that meaning$_{NN}$ might ultimately be analysed in terms of meaning$_N$ – a point to which I will return in later chapters.

8. See *Summa Totius Logicae*, in which Ockham distinguishes examples of *naturaliter significare* from those of *significare per voluntariam institutionem*. He uses the following as examples of natural meaning: 'a stone means that wine is sold in the tavern', 'a smile means inner joy'. I may be

wrong, but is not the first an example of *non*-natural meaning? My thanks go to J. L. Speranza (personal communication) for bringing Ockham's examples to my attention.

9. See Hamilton and Cairns (1989).

10. I've changed Grice's original (1), (2) and (3) here to (A), (B) and (C) respectively, to avoid confusion – the numerals (1) and (2) feature in the next quote.

11. Here, Neale is echoing a point originally made in McDowell (1980).

12. The original wording in Grice's example is 'Feeling faint, a child lets its mother see how pale it is (hoping that she may draw her own conclusions and help).' I mention this because I would rather let the reader know 'deliberately and openly' that my 'adaptation' is precisely that. There are three key changes from the original, none of which, to my mind, affects the arguments to come, but which simplify the point I am trying to make. The first change is the introduction of the phrase 'deliberately and openly'. Since he is contrasting this example with a previous one in which an 'utterer' is not overt about their intention to inform (the 'handkerchief-dropper' example), it seems clear that what Grice had in mind in his original example was a case in which the child (in my adaptation, Mary) intends to have her intention recognised. In fact, the phrase 'deliberately and openly' comes from Grice's own characterisation of the 'feeling faint' example (and others) in the next paragraph (1989, p. 218 – and see below). The second change is the omission of the phrase 'draw her own conclusions'. I don't think that if the child is acting 'deliberately and openly' in showing her mother that she is pale, then the mother *is* 'drawing her own conclusions' any more (*cf.* cases of *accidental information transmission* mentioned below). The third change is the omission of the word 'hoping'. I made this change to avoid having to get into any discussion about whether 'hoping' necessarily involves 'intending'.

13. I will leave aside the issue of whether the 'tears' I describe as being hidden, held back, or openly shown are themselves a natural sign of distress, and how exactly they are linked with crying. After all, we can shed tears without 'crying' (to expel a foreign body) and cry without shedding 'tears' (the crying of infants is a case in point – for a few weeks/months a crying baby sheds no tears). Once young children have learned that tearful crying is a successful strategy for gaining the attention of their parent or carer, tears seem to take on a (slightly sinister) manipulative function. So often, if a child hurts herself, she will only start tearful crying when her parent or carer arrives at the scene.

14. I say '*might* intend' because I would not like to deny that there are probably cases in which crying openly does not amount to an intentionally (deliberately) shown act – expression of grief at a funeral, for example.

15. Another point worth considering is that there are actually two ways in which a facial expression (for example) might not be wholly spontaneous: it may be deliberately *produced* or it may be deliberately *concealed*. This point, and other problems that arise with a simple spontaneous/voluntary – deliberate/involuntary dichotomy, are discussed in Ekman 1997. Notice, too, that what may be perceived as deliberate showing might actually be the result of a communicator *suppressing the concealment* of a certain behaviour.

16. Though this last is an interesting one: many actors, asked to play a scene in which they are expected to cry, rerun emotional crises in their mind in order to recreate *real* tears.

17. Incidentally, it is not true that, as one interpretation of the above quote from Grice would suggest, a deliberate frown necessarily communicates displeasure: is there not such a thing as an ironic frown? Also, a parallel argument to the one Grice gives in the above quote could not strictly speaking be applied to spontaneous and deliberate *smiles*. As I discuss briefly below, spontaneous and deliberate smiles involve different muscles (and different neurology), and are thus quite easily perceived as 'real' or 'faked'. It would be interesting to investigate whether the same kind of differences exist between real and fake frowns. (I don't know of any study on this.)

18. A similar point – though from a more philosophical perspective – is made by Mitch Green in his 2007 book, 'Self-expression'; many of the ideas discussed in this chapter complement Green's views, and conversely.

CHAPTER 3

Pragmatics and the domain of pragmatic principles

There is a point where too much information and too much information processing can hurt. Cognition is the art of focusing on the relevant and deliberately ignoring the rest.

(Gigerenzer and Todd 1999, p. 21)

RELEVANCE THEORY AND THE SHOWING—MEANING$_{NN}$ CONTINUUM

In his William James Lectures on 'Logic and Conversation', delivered at Harvard in 1967, Grice proposed that human verbal communication is a cooperative activity driven by the mutual expectation that, in general, participants will obey a Cooperative Principle and Conversational Maxims of Quantity, Quality, Relation and Manner. In outlining his theory of conversation, one of Grice's main aims was to cast light on some of what he regarded as 'illegitimate applications' (1989, p. 3) of certain philosophical 'manoeuvres' by members of the ordinary language philosophy movement. This movement had influenced him greatly at Oxford in the nineteen-forties and fifties; in opposing the central tenets of the 'idealised' language philosophy of Frege, Russell and Carnap, it was instrumental in the birth and development of modern pragmatics.[1]

Jerry Fodor's chief objection to modern pragmatic programmes (an objection shared by Chomsky) is that the processes involved in utterance interpretation are 'global' rather than 'local': any type of information, drawn from any domain, may make a difference to the outcome of the interpretation process, and in Fodor's view such processes are not amenable to scientific study (Fodor 1983).

In many ways as Robyn Carston points out: 'the relevance-theoretic framework . . . can be seen as a response to the challenge presented by these sceptics' (2002, p. 2). Relevance theory sees cognition and communication as relying heavily on 'fast and frugal heuristics' (Gigerenzer, Todd and the ABC Research Group 1999), which make it possible to pick out potentially relevant inputs to cognitive processes (e.g. sights, sounds, utterances, memories, conclusions of inferences) and process them in a way that enhances their relevance. The claim that humans are equipped with such heuristics does not entail that they have an 'unbounded' form of all-seeing, all-knowing rationality. Rather, evolution has left us with economical rules-of-thumb that enable us to make the most of our finite cognitive capacity.

Relevance theory (Sperber and Wilson 1986/1995, Blakemore 2002, Carston 2002a, Wilson and Sperber 2002) is built around two principles. The Cognitive Principle of Relevance makes a fundamental assumption about human cognition: the human cognitive system is geared to look out for relevant information, which will interact with existing mentally represented assumptions and bring about positive cognitive effects (e.g. true implications, warranted strengthenings or contradictions of existing assumptions). Relevance itself is a property of inputs to cognitive processes, and is defined in terms of positive cognitive effects gained and processing effort expended: other things being equal, the more positive cognitive effects gained, and the less processing effort expended in gaining those effects, the greater the relevance of the input to the individual who processes it.

The human disposition to search for relevance is seen as an evolved consequence of the tendency toward greater efficiency in cognition (Sperber and Wilson 2002).[2] In Dan Sperber's words (which are echoed in the epigraph to this chapter):

Cognitive efficiency involves making the right choices in selecting which available new information to attend to and which available past information to process it with. The right choices in this respect consist in bringing together inputs and memory information, the joint processing of which will provide as much cognitive effect as possible for as little effort as possible. (1996, p. 114)

The disposition to search for relevance is, furthermore, routinely exploited in human communication. Since speakers know that listeners will pay attention only to stimuli that are relevant enough, in order to attract and hold an audience's attention, they should make their communicative stimuli appear at least relevant enough to be worth processing. More precisely, the Communicative Principle of Relevance claims that by overtly displaying an intention to inform – producing an utterance or other ostensive stimulus – a communicator creates a presumption that the stimulus is at least relevant enough to be worth processing, and moreover, the most relevant one compatible with her own abilities and preferences. Recall from the last chapter that the motivation for making the kind of 'less direct' inferences discussed there is the very fact that a communicator has created in her audience an expectation that there is something worth their while to infer. Relevance theory is an attempt to flesh out the notion of what makes communicated information worthwhile.

As pointed out in Chapter 2, in contrast with Grice's (1957) aim of characterising meaning$_{NN}$, relevance theory aims to provide a characterisation of overt intentional communication generally. Utterances are not the only kind of ostensive stimuli, and a communicator might provide evidence of her intention to inform by means of a look, a gesture, or – as we saw in Chapter 2 – even a natural sign. Ostensive stimuli often involve a mixture of what Grice would have called natural and non-natural meaning, and this is one reason why relevance theory does not attempt to draw a line (as Grice wanted to) between "'deliberately and openly letting someone know" and "telling"' (1989, p. 218).

Recall my claim in the last chapter that in any act carried out with the intention of revealing an informative intention, there are two layers of information to be retrieved. The first, basic layer is the information being pointed out, and the second is the information that the first layer is being pointed out intentionally. What makes a certain ostensive act a case of either 'showing' or 'meaning$_{NN}$' is the precise nature of the evidence provided for the first layer of information. In cases of showing, the evidence provided is relatively direct – Schiffer's bandaged leg, for example. In cases of meaning$_{NN}$, the evidence provided is relatively indirect – a linguistic utterance, for example. Sperber and Wilson (1986/1995, p. 53) discuss the relationship between the two notions:

> Is there a dividing line between instances of ostension which one would be more inclined to describe as 'showing something', and clear cases of communication where the communicator unquestionably 'means something'? . . . What we have tried to show . . . is that there are not two distinct and well-defined classes, but a continuum of cases of ostension ranging from 'showing', where strong direct evidence for the basic layer of information is provided, to 'saying that',[3] where all the evidence is indirect . . .

As I have suggested, this has implications for what should be seen as the domain of pragmatic principles or maxims: it provides evidence that they are best seen as applying to the domain of overt intentional communication as a whole, rather than merely to the domain of meaning$_{NN}$. Relevance theory recognises both showing and meaning$_{NN}$ as instances of overt intentional or – as they term it – ostensive–inferential communication. Most cases of showing – in which the evidence provided is fairly direct – still require an extra layer of inference in order to recognise the communicator's full informative intention[4] (recall that in example (15d) from Chapter 2 (p. 28) Mary's mother still has to make the less direct inference that Mary wants help), and the extent to which an audience is required to make this extra inference is a matter of degree. Consider Scenario One below in the light of Grice's photograph example (see p. 24 above):

Scenario One:

I am a private detective, hired by Mr X to follow Mrs X (he suspects that she is having a relationship with Mr Y). I have taken a photograph of Mrs X and Mr Y together; the quality is poor (I used a telephoto lens, and there is a little camera-shake), and a blurred image of the couple can only just be seen in the distance (though on close inspection it is unmistakably them).

There is a subtle, but to my mind clear, difference between this photograph example and Grice's original one. As far as I can see, it is this. If I leave my photograph in Mr X's room by accident, it is no longer so obvious that Mr X's accidentally coming across the photo will induce the same effect on him as my showing it to him. It is only by close inspection that he could even see this was a photo of Mrs X and Mr Y. Crucially, then, it may only be in virtue of my showing it to him that Mr X would take the time and effort to look at the photograph closely enough to make out exactly who it shows. In other words, whether or not the photograph has the effect I desire may well depend on Mr X's successful recognition of my intention to produce some effect on him by means of the recognition of that intention.[5]

A possible response might be that the degree to which Mr X is required to attribute intentions to me in this scenario is minimal. Still, the requirement is there, and it seems clear that the recognition of my intention to inform Mr X does indeed play some role, however minimal, in accounting for the effect of my photograph on him.

Or consider Scenario Two:

Scenario Two:

I am a private detective, and also a keen amateur photographer. I have taken another (better) photo of Mrs X and Mr Y, and I have developed it myself. As a photographer, I am proud of the colour, the contrast and the general quality of the print. I show a friend of mine the photograph of Mr Y displaying undue familiarity to Mrs X.

How does my friend respond? In the context provided so far, there is a tendency to assume that my friend would probably say something like 'My goodness, Mr Y is certainly having an affair with Mrs X', or even 'I hope you're going to show this to Mr X.' However, suppose I tell you that my friend is a professional photographer. Suddenly, a variety of other responses may be appropriate: 'The colour is great' or 'I love the quality of the light' or 'Aren't those new polarisers terrific?' And what does my colleague's response depend on? What he takes my intention to be in showing him the photograph.

In fact, I think the point can be made even more clearly. You are walking down the street and a complete stranger comes up to you and thrusts a photograph in front of your face. Having recovered from the initial shock, most people would probably react in the same way: with utter confusion. Of course, like me, you might say 'Lovely!' or 'How interesting!' but that would only be because you thought that by responding in such a way you might get rid of this mad photograph-shower. Actually, I bet most people wouldn't know what to think: the problem being that although it would be perfectly clear that you were being shown a photograph, it would be far from clear exactly what it was you were being shown a photograph of (or what you were being shown the photograph for).

Indeed, even in Grice's original photograph example is there not a sense in which Mr X must attribute an informative intention to the photograph-shower? It will, after all, make a difference to Mr X's response whether he takes the shower to be intending to inform him about Mrs X and Mr Y, rather than just showing him the quality of the colour, or the light, or the new polariser he has invested in. As Deirdre Wilson pointed out to me in conversation, even if you and I are in the same room as two other people – say Mrs X and Mr Y – engaged in (as she put it) 'unfaithful activities', some degree of intention-attribution will still be required if I attempt to point out something about them to you: other things being equal, I might just as well be pointing out something Mr Y is (or isn't) wearing, as drawing attention to the (potential) inappropriateness of their behaviour. Thus, not only must what is meant$_{NN}$ be regarded as only a subset of what is intentionally communicated, but there is a continuum of cases between showing and meaning$_{NN,}$ rather than the dichotomy Grice envisaged in his 1957 paper.

It might be objected that in broadening the domain of pragmatic principles in this way, we run the risk of allowing in all manner of cases in which what is communicated is so weak or so vague that it cannot be adequately characterised. The correct response, I suggest, is that overt communication often is weak and vague, and that a theory of human communication should at least try and accommodate these vaguer aspects. We saw in Chapter 2 that there are clear cases of overt intentional communication that do not qualify as cases of meaning$_{NN}$ according to Grice's definitions; we now see that even if we wanted to maintain a distinction between overt intentional communication and meaning$_{NN}$, there is no convenient cut-off point between the two. If we attempt to limit our attention to what are uncontroversially cases of meaning$_{NN}$, then we are forced to ignore a whole range of communicative exchanges that deserve explanation.

To help account for the vaguer aspects of communication, including the communication of impressions, emotions, attitudes, feelings and sensations, Sperber and Wilson argue that the informative intention is better characterised as an intention to modify not the hearer's thoughts directly, but his *cognitive environment.* An individual's cognitive environment includes not only all the facts or assumptions that he is currently aware of, but also all the facts or assumptions he is capable of becoming aware of given his cognitive abilities and his physical environment – in relevance-theoretic terms, the set of facts or assumptions that are *manifest* to him (i.e. that he is capable of perceiving or inferring). The notion of manifestness plays a central role in the relevance-theoretic characterisation of an informative intention, which is defined not in Gricean terms, as an intention 'to produce a particular response r', but rather as an intention 'to make manifest or more manifest to the audience a set of assumptions I' (p. 58).[6]

An assumption may be manifest to different degrees. The more salient a manifest assumption is, and hence the more likely to be mentally represented, the more strongly manifest it is. Vague communication typically involves an intention to bring about a marginal increase in the manifestness of a very wide range of assumptions that are weakly manifest in the cognitive environments of both communicator and audience, resulting in an increased degree of similarity or mutuality. Indeed, the mutual cognitive environment of two people engaged in communication is constantly calibrated, refined and readjusted by what Matthew Lieberman (2000) calls 'the dance of non-verbal communication'.

Consider the following example. Jack and Lily have arrived by ferry at a small Greek island. They disembark. Having scanned the quayside, he smiles at her and sighs as his whole body visibly relaxes, the tensions of the journey (indeed, the past few months) leaving him. Then he looks back ostensively to the quayside again, urging her to look too. She gazes along the quayside. What is Jack drawing her attention to? Is it the taverna at the water's edge, the octopus drying in the breeze, the ragged cats sniffing the nets, the bougainvillea in the kastro beyond the main square, the brilliant light? Is it one, many or all of these things? Is it none of these things themselves but rather the effect they are clearly having on Jack?

But Lily does not turn to Jack and say 'What do you mean?' She acknowledges him and smiles back, because she understands. The sights, sounds and smells perceivable in her physical environment interact with her inferential abilities and her memories to alter her cognitive environment in a way he could have foreseen, making it possible for her to have further thoughts, memories and feelings similar to his own. This is all that Jack intended: to share an impression with Lily. He did not mean anything in the strong Gricean sense. His intention cannot be pinned down to one specific proposition or small set of propositions. It was simply to make more manifest to Lily whatever assumptions became manifest to him as he scanned the quayside.

On other occasions, when the intention might be to communicate something equally intangible, and equally hard to spell out in words – emotions, feelings or an impression – it might also be preferable to use a behaviour that falls somewhere between showing and meaning or saying. Communication of this type may be described as *weak* communication, and the resulting implicatures as weak implicatures. A conclusion is weakly implicated if its recovery helps with the construction of a satisfactory overall interpretation, but is not essential because the ostensive stimulus provides evidence for a wide array of roughly similar conclusions, any of which would do. Thus, Jack's gaze and sigh above convey a wide array of *weak implicatures*: he shares an impression with Lily rather than conveying a definite message.

Consider now what might be communicated by Lily's ostensive sigh in (16) or (17):

> (16) Jack: How are you enjoying your linguistics course?
>   Lily: [Looks at Jack and sighs]
> (17) Lily comes home after a day at work, slams the door, catches Jack's eye and sighs.

In (16), Lily's sigh provides strong evidence for a definite conclusion (she is not enjoying her linguistics course) and weaker support for a range of further conclusions (her linguistics course is difficult, she is worried or anxious about it, is in need of help or sympathy, etc.). In (17), her sigh does not provide evidence for a single, definite conclusion, but creates a diffuse impression, by marginally altering the strength or salience of a wide array of conclusions. As these examples show, ostensive use of a non-verbal behaviour may convey a more or less definite meaning when addressed to a hearer with more or less definite expectations of relevance.

A conclusion may be described as strongly implicated (or as a strong implicature) to the extent that it (or some closely similar proposition) must be derived in the course of constructing a satisfactory interpretation (i.e. one that satisfies the expectation of relevance raised by the utterance). As noted above, it is weakly implicated (or is a weak implicature) to the extent that there is a wide range of roughly similar conclusions, any of which would do (Sperber and Wilson, 1986/95: Chapter 1, Sections 10–12, Chapter 4, Section 6; Wilson and Sperber, 2004). Thus, Lily's sigh in (16) quite strongly implicates that she is not enjoying her linguistics course, while her sigh in (17) conveys a wide array of weak implicatures but no strong implicatures: that is, it creates an impression rather than conveying a definite message. Typically, a spoken utterance involves a mixture of strong and weak communication. Relevance theory provides a framework in which this fact can be accommodated and explained.

Given the vagueness of what may be communicated by the cases of 'showing' described above, it seems clear that the communicator's informative intention does not always reduce to an intention to communicate just a single proposition and propositional attitude (or even a small set). In the next chapter I will argue that interjections such as *aha*, *wow* and *ouch* are often used to communicate in similarly vague ways, marginally increasing the manifestness of a very wide range of assumptions.

The showing–meaning$_{NN}$ continuum, then, has a variety of applications. At various points along it, we can see the varying degrees to which hearers are required to consider communicators' intentions in order to get from the evidence they provide to the first, basic layer of information they are communicating. It therefore provides a 'snapshot' of the types of evidence used in ostensive acts and the role inference plays in them. At one extreme of the continuum lie clear cases of spontaneous, natural display; at the other extreme lie clear cases of linguistic coding, where all the evidence provided for the first, basic layer of information is indirect. In between lies a range of cases in which more or less direct 'natural' evidence and more or less indirect coded evidence mix to various degrees: for example, in pointing and stylised expressions of emotion. Equally importantly, the continuum provides a theoretical tool which allows us to conceptualise more clearly the observation made above that ostensive stimuli are often highly complex composites of different, inter-related behaviours which fall at various points along the continuum between 'showing' and 'meaning$_{NN}$'.[7] In the next section I discuss further consequences of the shift to a relevance theory framework.

SEMANTIC UNDETERMINACY AND LEXICAL PRAGMATICS

One of many parallels between relevance theory and Grice's pragmatic framework is that relevance theory distinguishes between the explicit and the implicit content of an utterance. The explicit–implicit distinction drawn in relevance theory bears some similarity to Grice's famous distinction between saying and implicating, the distinction which – together with his Cooperative Principle and Maxims – provided the first systematic way of drawing a line between the content of whatever direct speech act was performed and any wider meaning the speaker intended to convey.

Consider what might be communicated by cases of metaphor or irony such as those in (18) and (19), or by Jack's indirect answer in (20):

> (18) The face of Greece is a palimpsest bearing twelve successive inscriptions.[8]
> [meaning that Greece is rich in history and culture]
> (19) There's nothing remotely interesting in Greece.
> [meaning that Greece is rich in history and culture]
> (20) Lily: I want a holiday somewhere rich in history and culture.
> Jack: Have you ever visited Greece?
> [meaning that Greece is rich in history and culture]

In Grice's framework, a hearer bridges the gap between what the speaker has said in these utterances and what they have implicated (represented in the square brackets) by assuming that the speaker is conforming to the Cooperative Principle and maxims of conversation (or at least the Cooperative Principle).

Although Grice avoided using the term 'truth conditions', it is generally agreed that his notion of *what is said* was intended to coincide with *the proposition expressed by the speaker*, or the *truth-conditional content* of an utterance.[9] On one reading at least he appears to have had a fairly minimalist view of what saying (and hence what is said) actually was. As Herb Clark puts it:

> But what is saying? According to Grice – though he was vague on this point – it is the literal meaning of the sentence uttered with its ambiguities resolved and its referents specified. (Clark 1996, p. 143)

This interpretation of Grice can be traced back to an often-quoted section of Lecture II of the William James Lectures (originally published in Cole and Morgan (1975) as 'Logic and conversation', later published as Chapter 2 of Grice (1989):

> In the sense in which I am using the word 'say', I intend what someone has said to be closely related to the conventional meaning of the words (the sentence) which he has uttered. Suppose someone to have uttered the sentence *He is in the grip of a vice*. Given a knowledge of the English language, but no knowledge of the circumstances of the utterance, one would know something about what the speaker had said, on the assumption that he

was speaking standard English, and speaking literally. One would know that he had said, about some particular male person or animal x, that at the time of the utterance (whatever that was) either (i) x was unable to rid himself of a certain bad kind of character-trait or (ii) that some part of x's person was caught in a certain kind of tool or instrument. (Approximate account, of course). But for a full identification of what the speaker had said, one would need to know (a) the identity of x, (b) the time of utterance, and (c) the meaning, on the particular occasion of utterance, of the phrase 'in the grip of a vice' (a decision between (i) and (ii)). (II p. 5; cf. 1989, p. 25)

Many people working on Grice's saying–implicating distinction have noticed that what is said, on this construal, does not always coincide with what is intuitively the truth-conditional content of an utterance. As Kent Bach (1994, p. 124) puts it: 'in Gricean terms, the distinction between what is said and what is implicated is not exhaustive'. This discrepancy has prompted a tremendous amount of work using Grice's distinction as a point of departure for constructing a broader notion of explicit content that would coincide more closely with the truth-conditional content of an utterance (Wilson and Sperber 1981, Levinson 1989, 2000, Sperber and Wilson 1986/1995, Bach 1994, Recanati 1993, 2004 Clark 1996, Carston 2002a).

There are a variety of ways in which what is said, construed in the fairly minimal sense of 'conventional' (i.e. linguistically encoded) meaning plus reference assignment and disambiguation, falls short not only of the speaker's intended meaning, but also of providing a truth-evaluable proposition at all. Consider (21), (22) and (23):

(21) Everyone is ready.
(22) Jack drinks too much.
(23) Have you seen Xani's picture?

In (21), there seems little doubt that some process of contextual enrichment distinct from reference assignment and disambiguation is needed to establish what proposition the speaker intended to express. Firstly, 'everyone' here would normally be understood as referring to everyone from a particular domain of individuals, and some inference would be needed to establish which domain the speaker had in mind. Secondly, some inference would also be needed to understand what the speaker thinks that everyone is 'ready' for (e.g. to begin the exam, to listen to the talk, to get on the plane, and so on). Similarly, what proposition the speaker is taken to express by uttering (22) will depend on inferences about what the speaker Jack drinks too much to do (e.g. to operate heavy machinery, to be entrusted with driving everyone home from the office party, and so on). In (23), the linguistically encoded meaning of 'Xani's picture' leaves open the precise nature of the relationship between Xani and the picture (e.g. whether it is one she painted, one she likes, one she owns, and so on), and this has to be inferred in establishing what proposition she intended to express.

Various proposals have been made as to how far Grice's notion of *what is said* can be stretched to accommodate these additional inferential processes – and many more that have come to light in the last thirty years. These proposals impact in various ways on how we might conceive of the relation between semantics, pragmatics, and the notion of what is said. Kent Bach argues that the inferential aspects of truth-conditional content are best analysed as a separate level of meaning between what is said and what is implicated. He calls this the level of impl*i*cature, and his construal of what is said is necessarily a very minimal, semantic one (see Bach 1994, 1999, 2001 for further discussion). Francois Recanati, by contrast, replaces Grice's notion of *what is said* with a much richer one, and envisages a wide variety of pragmatic processes as contributing to this enriched notion of 'what is said' (see Recanati 2004).[10] Those working within relevance theory reject the notion of what is said entirely, partly because of the now widespread confusion about how to define it, and introduce a new technical notion of explicature, parallel to Grice's notion of 'implicature', which is intended to coincide with what the speaker has explicitly communicated (in the case of a declarative, the intended truth-conditional content of the utterance).

In relevance theory, explicatures are recovered via a mixture of linguistic decoding and inference, and explicitness is treated as a matter of degree: the greater the proportion of linguistic encoding to inference, the more explicit the communicated content. To illustrate, compare three ways that Lily might reply to Jack's question 'Do you like the gift?':

> (24) (smiling happily) I think it's wonderful. I like it very much and I feel absolutely delighted.
> (25) (smiling happily) I do.
> (26) (smiling happily) I've *always* wanted an electric toothbrush.

What (24) linguistically encodes is an incomplete logical form that Jack will decode and inferentially enrich into a fully propositional form which he will take to constitute the basic explicature of the utterance. What (25) encodes is very fragmentary indeed, and Jack has to do considerably more inferential work to identify the intended explicit content (or explicature) of the utterance. What (26) encodes is an incomplete logical form that Jack must not only develop into an explicature, but complement with an implicature in order to derive an answer to his question.

A central claim of relevance-theoretic pragmatics is that explicatures and implicatures are developed in parallel, with the explicit content being adjusted or 'fine-tuned' in various ways in order to yield the implicatures required to satisfy the audience's expectations of relevance. In addition to the types of pragmatic inference illustrated in (21), (22) and (23) above, the encoded content of individual lexical items occurring in an utterance may have to be narrowed or loosened (assigned a narrower or broader denotation) in context in order to yield the expected level of implicatures. In the framework of relevance theory, there is a straightforward 'fast and frugal heuristic' which hearers can use to determine the appropriate degree of narrowing or loosening, and more generally, to identify the speaker's 'meaning'. I will illustrate how this heuristic works with an example.

Consider Jack's utterance of (27) below, as he talks to a friend on the telephone about how Lily will react when she opens her gift:

> (27) She's opening the parcel.

Given the assumptions of relevance theory, the hearer is entitled to presume that Jack's utterance will be at least relevant enough to be worth processing and, moreover, the most relevant one compatible with Jack's abilities and preferences. He is therefore justified in following a path of least mental effort in looking for the intended implications (or other positive cognitive effects), which should make the utterance relevant in the expected way. This may involve assigning reference to any referential expressions, disambiguating any ambiguous expressions, narrowing or loosening lexical meaning, and supplying particular contextual assumptions in order to derive the expected level of implications. Once his expectations of relevance are satisfied, it is reasonable for him to conclude that the 'meaning' he has inferred was the one the communicator intended.[11] The following comprehension heuristic – taken from Wilson and Sperber (2002, p. 13) – is therefore rationally motivated:

Relevance-theoretic comprehension heuristic

(a) Follow a path of least effort in computing cognitive effects: Test interpretive hypotheses (disambiguations, reference resolutions, implicatures, etc.) in order of accessibility.
(b) Stop when your expectations of relevance are satisfied.

In constructing the explicature of (27), the hearer must assign reference to the pronoun 'she'. According to the comprehension heuristic, he should follow a path of least effort and consider the most accessible candidate first. Given that they have just been talking about Lily, he will therefore form the hypothesis that Jack is referring to Lily. Moreover, given that the concept encoded by the verb 'opening' denotes a quite general action that may be performed in various ways, each of which would carry different implications, he is also likely to narrow it somewhat and take Jack to mean that Lily is opening the parcel in a certain way (e.g. untying the ribbon or undoing the sellotape, perhaps in a way characteristic of her). Contrast this with the sense of 'opening' conveyed in (28) and (29) below, which would have quite different implications:

(28) The dog is opening the parcel.
(29) The blue tit is opening the milk-bottle.

In (28) the sense of 'open' conveyed would more likely involve the tearing of paper (and gnashing of teeth); in (29) the sense conveyed is different again, involving as it does pecking through the foil top on a bottle of milk. Given the relevance-theoretic comprehension heuristic, the hearer of (27) can take it that if Jack had intended to convey that Lily was 'opening' the parcel in a non-standard manner (one less easy to imagine and hence more costly in terms of effort), he would not have chosen to convey this with the utterance he used.

What this suggests is that there is an interaction between decoding and inference not only at the level of what is explicitly communicated by a whole sentence, but at word level too: a particular word may be used to express not exactly the concept it encodes, but another related concept, which is easily constructed by drawing on encyclopaedic information, and is required to make the utterance relevant in the expected way (see Sperber and Wilson 1998, Wilson 2003 for discussion of verbs such as 'open'; see also Carston 2002a, Wilson and Sperber 2002, Wilson and Carston 2007). In such cases, the hearer constructs an ad hoc (i.e. occasion-specific) concept in order to satisfy the particular expectations of relevance raised by the utterance.

Consider the word 'bear', which encodes a concept that applies to all and only bears. In order to satisfy expectations of relevance, this concept might be narrowed in (30) to denote a subset of bears (e.g. polar bears), or broadened in (31) to include objects which are not strictly bears at all (e.g. large hairy dogs):

(30) The bear walked out across the frozen sea.
(31) I loved Emma, my Old English Sheepdog: she was a bear.

This kind of adjustment of conceptual content is a feature of relevance-theoretic pragmatics, and is seen as contributing to the explicit truth-conditional content of utterances, so that in appropriate circumstances the speaker of (30) (or (31)) would be understood as expressing a proposition containing a narrower (or broader) concept than the linguistically encoded one. A point that has been little remarked on is that – as we saw in example (3) from Chapter 1 – the interpretation of natural communicative phenomena ('paralinguistic' features) may affect the outcome of the lexical adjustment process, and thus contribute to explicit truth-conditional content too. Consider examples (32), (33) and (34) below:

> (32) Jack: Shall we sit out here?
>   Lily (shivering ostensively):   I'm cold.
> (33) Lily (furiously):   I'm disappointed!
> (34) Lily (smiling broadly):   I feel happy.

In (32), Lily and Jack meet outside a café. Lily's ostensive shiver accompanying her utterance of 'I'm cold' should be salient enough to be picked out by the relevance-theoretic comprehension heuristic and used in interpreting the degree term 'cold'. How much she is shivering will be treated as an indication of how cold she feels, and, in effect, will calibrate the degree of coldness Jack understands her to feel and to be expressing as part of her meaning. The fact that Lily has shivered ostensively – shown, as well as told him she is cold – motivates Jack's search for the 'extra' meaning Lily intends to convey in return for the extra processing effort required. In this case, Jack would be entitled to understand Lily as implicating that she is definitely cold enough to want to go inside. In a parallel example, Lily's ostensive shiver accompanying her utterance of 'It's lovely out here on the terrace, isn't it?' might provide Jack with a clue that she is being ironic, that actually she hates it on the terrace and would prefer to go inside. In both cases, openly shown natural behaviours affect the outcome of the interpretive process, guiding the hearer to a certain range or type of conclusions.

It is worth underlining here that these natural behaviours not only help Jack establish the implicit content of Lily's utterance, but also contribute to the explicit truth-conditional content he takes Lily to be expressing (or the explicature of her utterance). The truth conditions of her utterance of 'I'm cold' – and the truth-conditions of (33) and (34), which also contain degree terms – will vary according to the type or degree of coldness (or disappointment or happiness) she intends to communicate, which are indicated in her openly shown natural behaviour.

What is linguistically encoded by the word 'disappointed', for example, is a quite general concept which covers the full range of degrees and types of disappointment. What Lily intends to express in (33), however, is likely to be a narrower concept that is indicated by her tone of voice, facial expression, etc. Helped by these clues, Jack will understand her as expressing a narrowed concept – DISAPPOINTED* – that he sees as commensurate with the degree and type of disappointment Lily intends to convey. Similarly, what is encoded by the word 'happy' is also a quite general concept;[12] but Lily's utterance in (34) will be understood as conveying a narrower, occasion-specific sense, which is calibrated in this example by features of her smile. The overall interpretation process is relevance-driven, and the intentionally shown natural behaviours provide additional clues to the speaker's meaning, which is not encoded but inferred.

It's not just in the interpretation of degree terms that natural pragmatic factors play a role. Consider the following example, uttered whilst looking at a Pitbull Terrier (or holding up a picture of a Pitbull Terrier):

(35) The neighbours have a new dog.

Here, gaze direction or pointing would suggest a narrowing of the concept DOG to a particular type of dog (DOG*), and encyclopaedic information about this type of dog would give easy access to a certain range of implications. If (35) is uttered in a warning tone of voice, or with a terrified facial expression, this would also suggest a certain direction for narrowing, to dangerous or frightening dogs: thus, open expressions of emotion may affect not only the implicatures derived, but also the outcome of the lexical adjustment process.

According to relevance theory, an utterance may be used to convey not only a basic-level explicature which determines its truth-conditional content, but also a range of so-called 'higher-level explicatures'. These are constructed by embedding the basic explicature under a speech-act or propositional-attitude description, which may be explicitly indicated or pragmatically inferred. To illustrate, consider utterances (36) and (38) below, which would encourage a hearer to construct the higher-level explicatures in (37) and (39):

(36) Regrettably, your application has been unsuccessful.
(37) The speaker regards it as regrettable that my application has been unsuccessful.
(38) Frankly, you haven't got the job.
(39) The speaker is telling me frankly that I haven't got the job.

Notice, now, that this kind of attitudinal information can also be conveyed by entirely natural behaviours. So a speaker of (36) might convey her attitude without using the word 'regrettably', simply by speaking in a regretful tone of voice, and a speaker of (38) might indicate that she is speaking frankly simply by adopting a frank manner. Given the account of degrees of explicitness outlined earlier in this chapter, use of the words 'regrettably' and 'frankly' would make the higher-level explicatures more explicit, because of the extra element of linguistic encoding involved.

In everyday communication we simply take for granted the fact that a speaker naturally displays a certain degree of emotional intensity or attitude, and that (equally naturally) an audience can discriminate and interpret subtle variations in tone of voice or facial expression. Many human paralinguistic behaviours of this type appear to work on analogue lines, and can be directly contrasted with the digital code of language (I return to this analogy in Chapter 6). We read natural signs much as the engineer studies the needle on an analogue pressure gauge, where the needle's movement is analogous to the rising and falling of the pressure. In Lily's utterance, her frown and angry tone of voice are in a similarly proportional or analogous relationship to the amount of affect she intends to convey. Depending on the gravity of her frown and the tone of voice she uses, Jack might decide she is mildly annoyed, quite angry or absolutely furious. Jack's ability to interpret these degrees of her annoyance or anger or happiness depends not on his knowledge of any digital code, but on his ability to discriminate tiny variations in her facial expression and tone of voice, much as the engineer reads the quivering needle.

Although we take the natural side of verbal communication for granted in our everyday conversational exchanges, in trying to construct a pragmatic theory, we should not. The contribution made by the more 'natural' aspects of complex ostensive stimuli to establishing a speaker's 'meaning' – including basic and higher-level explicatures – should be neither overlooked nor downplayed.

For individuals with autism or Asperger's syndrome, the 'natural' side of communication presents many problems, and this affects their regular interpretation of utterances. Consider the following, taken from the autobiography of Lianne Holiday Willey, who has Asperger's syndrome:

> If my husband were to tell me he was disappointed he had missed me at lunch, I would wonder if he meant to say he was sad – which is simply regretfully sorry; unhappy – which is somewhere between mad and sad; mad – which makes you want to argue with someone over what they had done; angry – which makes you want to ignore the person you are feeling this way towards; furious – which makes you want to spit; or none of the above. In order for me to really understand what people are saying I need much more than a few words mechanically placed together . . . Words by themselves are too vague. (Liane Holliday Willey 1993, p. 63)

In Chapter 7, I discuss these issues in more detail, and use distinctions I draw later in the book to suggest a variety of further test cases which may contribute to our understanding of human mind-reading abilities.

TRANSLATIONAL AND NON-TRANSLATIONAL ACTIVATION OF CONCEPTS

Typically, what a communicator C wants to communicate to her audience A is a (more or less complex) thought. I take it, following Fodor (1983) and others that thought takes place in some sort of modality-neutral conceptual representational system, or 'language of thought'. A conceptual representation may be seen as a structured set of concepts with semantic or logical properties which make it capable of representing possible or actual states of affairs, being true or false, implying or contradicting other conceptual representations, and acting as input to logical inference rules. On this computational–representational approach to the mind, inference is carried out by computational manipulation of conceptual representations under truth-conditional (or evidence-based) constraints.

If humans were telepathic and genuinely able to read each others' minds, C would simply transfer her thought into A's mind (or A would somehow retrieve it). However, humans are not telepathic, and in order to communicate her thought, C must produce some publicly observable behaviour which will lead A to entertain a thought with the same (or at least a similar) content to her own. The hedge here is important, for there are two ways of cashing out the phrase 'communicate a thought'. According to a code model of communication, C's thoughts are translated into a signal by use of a code, and translated back into identical thoughts by A. If human linguistic communication were coded, its goal would be to bring about reduplication of thoughts. As we shall see in later chapters, a purely code-based account may work well in the case of bee-dancing, but it does not adequately characterise human linguistic communication.

One effect of a shift to an inferential model is to open up the possibility that the goal of linguistic communication may be to bring about similarity, rather than identity, of thoughts.[13] Sperber and Wilson describe this situation as follows:

> The type of co-ordination aimed at in most verbal exchanges is best compared to the co-ordination between people taking a stroll together rather than to that between people marching in step . . . (Sperber and Wilson 1998, p. 199)

The code model of communication is designed to explain how communication can bring about duplication of thoughts of a type that one would expect if humans were indeed telepathic. Sperber (2001) calls it 'cognition by proxy', and argues that the fact that human linguistic communication is inferential has interesting implications for an account of how it evolved. I return to this issue in Chapter 8, and explore its implications for what we take to be the function of communication.

This is not to deny that there is, of course, a coded element to human linguistic communication. As discussed in Chapter 1, the grammar of a language just is a code which translates phonetic representations of sentences into logical forms or conceptual representations which capture their linguistic meaning. By the same token, some words do translate into concepts, the constituents of logical forms which provide 'blueprints' for the inferential construction of the fully propositional forms that the speaker is taken to have expressed. If I utter the words 'open' or 'bear' to a competent English speaker (i.e. someone who knows the code), the appropriate concepts will be activated in his mind; the same goes for a competent Portuguese speaker on hearing 'abrir' or 'urso'. We might describe this as the *translational* activation of concepts, and the kind of coding that gives rise to it as *translational* coding. As we saw in the last section, in an inferential model the encoded concepts may be narrowed or broadened in the course of inferential comprehension. But these lexical adjustment processes can only take place once the concept has been (translationally) activated.[14]

However, there is no particular reason to think that all linguistic meaning must be of just one type. For instance, it is widely accepted that 'discourse connectives' such as 'but', 'moreover', or 'after all' do not contribute to the truth-conditional content of utterances, and therefore cannot be treated as encoding concepts that contribute to the proposition the speaker is taken to have expressed or explicated (in Grice's terms, what is said). Consider (40) below, which suggests that the fact that Xanthe is very tall contrasts with the fact that she is eight:

(40) Xanthe is eight, but she's very tall.

According to Grice, 'but' and 'and' make the same contribution to truth conditions, and hence to what is said; however, 'but' also encodes an element of non-truth-conditional meaning (what Grice called a *conventional implicature*) which indicates that the speaker is also performing a higher-level speech act of contrasting the assertion that Xanthe is very tall with the assertion that she is eight.

This analysis is reminiscent of a distinction drawn by speech-act theorists between *describing* and *indicating* (Austin 1962, Searle 1969, 1979); indeed, Grice's analyses of discourse connectives fit comfortably into the broader speech-act framework. According to speech-act theorists, sentences not only express propositions (with a truth-conditional content) which are used to *describe* the world, but may also contain non-truth-conditional expressions which *indicate* what speech act ('illocutionary' act) the speaker is intending to perform, or what propositional attitude the speaker is intending to express. On this approach, the difference in meaning between (41), (42) and (43) below is captured by treating all three sentences as having the same propositional or descriptive content – Zoë goes to nursery at time t – but differing in their illocutionary force:[15] (41) has the force of a question, (42) of a request for action, and (43) of an assertion:

(41) Does Zoë go to school?
(42) Zoë, go to school!
(43) Zoë goes to school.

What does the distinction between describing and indicating amount to in cognitive terms? Following Diane Blakemore (1987, 2002), I start from the assumption that most regular linguistic expressions encode concepts that figure directly in the proposition expressed by an utterance, and therefore contribute to its truth-conditional content. In speech-act terms, these are descriptive expressions; in my terms, they activate concepts by *translational* coding. Other expressions, however, encode information that does not translate into conceptual constituents of the proposition the speaker is taken to have expressed, but rather results in the non-translational activation of concepts, via *non-translational* coding. In speech-act terms, these are indicating expressions; Blakemore calls them procedural expressions. Although (for reasons to be discussed later in the book) I have not directly adopted Blakemore's terminology, my notion of translational coding corresponds closely to her notion of conceptual coding, and my notion of non-translational coding corresponds closely to her notion of procedural coding.

The essence of this distinction between translational and non-translational coding can be demonstrated using an analogy. Consider the following. There are two ways a friend might help you get from A to B. He might choose to take you in his car and drop you there directly, or he might simply point you in roughly the right direction, trusting that you will find your own way. If the destination is the identification of a communicator's intended interpretation, this analogy brings out (albeit in highly intuitive terms) the difference between translational and non-translational coding.

However, it is important to recognise that the distinction being made here is one between two types of coding. A still further way of pointing someone in the direction of your intended interpretation is to provide evidence which involves no element of coding. Recall the examples from Chapter 2 where Lily deliberately and openly shows Jack her shiver, intending to communicate that she feels cold; or consider another where I point at a cloud, intending to communicate that it's going to rain. It could be argued that both of these cases result in the non-translational activation of concepts. In both cases, however, the audience works out the communicator's intended interpretation in the absence of any code. The kind of non-translational activation I am considering here is different in that it does contain a coded element that points the hearer in a direction they would not reliably take unless they knew the code.

To illustrate, consider (44):

(44) Jack: (referring to Lily) She's arrived.

The pronoun 'she' clearly encodes something, but what? David Kaplan (1977/1989) analyses pronouns in terms of a distinction between *character* and *content*. The content of a pronoun is its referent, which varies from occasion to occasion. The character of a pronoun is the linguistic meaning which determines a class of potential referents. In (44) the character of 'she' restricts the class of potential referents to females, and the content of 'she' on this particular occasion is Lily. Wilson and Sperber (1993) argue that, translated into more cognitive terms, Kaplan's analysis amounts to the claim that, rather than directly encoding a conceptual representation of the intended referent,[16] pronouns encode a procedural constraint which helps the hearer identify the intended referent by making a certain class of potential referents more salient. (The comparison with Kaplan is developed further in the next chapter, where I also consider Clark and Fox Tree's (2002) similar notion of a 'semantics of use'.) Continuing my earlier analogy, there are a variety of ways of 'pointing' someone in the appropriate direction. If your friend really wants you to get from A to B – and we invariably do want our interlocutors to arrive at the intended interpretation of our acts of ostensive communication – he might, in addition to pointing, tell you that B is a house with a red-tiled roof.

The comparison with pointing is apt, for this is one of the central ideas behind the speech-act distinction between describing and indicating. Within an overall inferential model of communication, the function of linguistic indicators is not to determine a unique interpretation, but rather to narrow the range of possible hypotheses from which the hearer must choose. In my terms, linguistic indicators are coded signals, but the code is non-translational: their function is to guide and constrain the inferential processes used to identify the intended interpretation.

As noted above, my distinction between translation and non-translational encoding corresponds closely to a distinction that has been explored in relevance-theoretic semantics between *conceptual* and *procedural* meaning. This distinction was first proposed by Diane Blakemore (1987) and developed in Blakemore (2002). The possibility of such a distinction is yet another consequence of adopting a fully inferential approach to ostensive communication.

In Blakemore's account, most regular content words (nouns, verbs, adjectives, adverbs) are seen as encoding concepts, constituents of conceptual representations. Typically, these contribute to the truth-conditional content of an utterance: they have logical properties, and act as input to inference rules. In Blakemore's terms, these words encode conceptual meaning; in my terms, they involve translational coding. Some linguistic expressions, by contrast, do not map directly onto concepts. Their function is rather to constrain the inferential processes used to construct or manipulate conceptual representations during the search for relevance. In effect, they guide the inferential comprehension process by narrowing the hearer's search space and indicating the general direction in which the intended meaning is to be sought. The encoded logical form of an utterance vastly underdetermines the intended overall interpretation (both explicit and implicit), and since processing effort is a factor in finding an interpretation that makes the utterance relevant in the expected way, linguistic indicators contribute to relevance by reducing the effort required to identify the intended explicatures and implicatures.

To illustrate, consider Blakemore's analysis of the discourse connectives 'so' and 'after all' in examples (45), (46) and (47):

(45) Jack visits the dentist every six months. His teeth are good.
(46) Jack visits the dentist every six months; so his teeth are good.
(47) Jack visits the dentist every six months; after all, his teeth are good.

On Blakemore's account, in (46) the word 'so' encodes a procedure which leads the hearer to interpret the first of the two propositions as a premise from which the second follows as a conclusion. In (47) the expression 'after all' encodes a procedure which leads the hearer to treat the second proposition as providing evidence for the first.[7] In both cases, the discourse connective is seen as encoding a procedural constraint on the derivation of intended implications (or implicatures).

This is not to suggest, however, that non-truth-conditional meaning is necessarily procedural. Consider example (48):

(48) Regrettably, your wisdom tooth will have to be extracted.

Although 'regrettably' in (48) is non-truth-conditional (in the sense that it is not normally seen as contributing to the truth-conditional content or basic explicature of (48)), there are good reasons to treat it as encoding a concept rather than a procedure (see Ifantidou-Trouki 1993, Ifantidou 2001). Firstly, it has conceptual counterparts which do contribute to the truth-conditions of utterances containing them, as in (49) and (50):

> (49) The incident at the dentist's was regrettable.
> (50) The dentist's actions were regrettably shortsighted.

The simplest semantic analysis would treat 'regrettable' in (49) and 'regrettably' in (50) as encoding the same concept, which would contribute to truth-conditional content in (49), but not in (50).

Secondly, illocutionary adverbials such as 'frankly', which are not standardly seen as contributing to the truth-conditional content of (38) above and (51) below, combine compositionally with other expressions to form complex adverbial phrases, as in (52):

> (51) Frankly, she's an absolute menace.
> (52) To put it frankly, and more frankly than I would dare if she had her drill in my mouth, she's an absolute menace.

Such compositionality is to be expected if these adverbials encode conceptual representations, but it is much harder to explain on a procedural account. This suggests an important modification to speech-act analyses of illocutionary force indicators, in that not all non-truth-conditional 'indicators' seem to work in the same way: some encode conceptual information while others encode procedural information. The conceptual–procedural distinction thus cross-cuts the describing–indicating distinction (Wilson and Sperber 1993, Blakemore 2002).

What exactly does procedural information look like? Drawing on the distinction made in cognitive science between the representational and computational aspects of cognition, we might characterise it as providing instructions to the hearer about the computational aspects of the comprehension process: this is how it is often described in discussions of discourse connectives such as 'although', 'however', 'so', 'after all', following Blakemore 1987. Thus, Blakemore (1992, pp. 150–1) writes: '"But", "after all", "moreover" and inferential "so" do not contribute to a propositional representation, but simply encode instructions for processing propositional representations.' However, when the full range of potentially procedural constructions is taken into account, it might be better to view procedural encoding in a broader sense, in terms not of instructions to the hearer but of the management of levels of activation (e.g. of conceptual representations, computations or expectations). On this approach, a pronoun might be seen as activating (or adding an extra layer of activation to) a certain class of candidate referents from which the hearer is expected to choose. Mood indicators might be seen as activating a certain range of propositional-attitude descriptions from which the hearer is expected to choose in constructing higher-level explicatures. So Jack's question to Lily in (53), may lead to her to form the higher-level explicature in (54):

(53) Have you been to the dentist?
(54) Jack is asking Lily whether she's been to the dentist.

This analysis could be generalised to discourse connectives too. Thus, 'so', 'but' or 'after all' could be seen as activating (or adding an extra layer of activation to) a certain type of inferential procedure, or a certain range of expectations about the type of cognitive effects to be derived. On this approach, what discourse connectives, mood indicators and pronouns have in common is that, rather than translating into the constituents of conceptual representations,[18] they involve non-translational activation of some sort. What is activated in different cases may be inferential rules or procedures, conceptual representations such as contextual assumptions or classes of candidate referent, or simply expectations of particular types of cognitive effects. In each case, the function of the procedural expression is to guide the comprehension process by reducing the search space the inferential processes are working in, thus indicating – in Sperber and Wilson's words – 'a rather abstract property of the speaker's informative intention: the direction in which the relevance of the utterance is to be sought' (1986/1995, p. 254).

In the next chapter I draw together some of the observations made in this chapter – in particular those concerning the showing–meaning$_{NN}$ continuum and the translational/non-translational (or conceptual/procedural) distinction – and use them to analyse a group of 'semi'-natural expressions that have received much attention in the literature: interjections.

NOTES

1. The term 'pragmatics' is not indexed in *Studies in the Way of Words*, nor is it mentioned much by Grice in the original lectures or subsequent published versions of those lectures (or other published work). However, Grice does use the word in Strands Seven and Eight of the Retrospective Epilogue of *Studies* when discussing his reactions to (what he calls) Strawson's 'Neo-Traditionalism' – that is, Strawson's reaction to Russell's 'Modernism': 'A few years after the appearance of *Introduction to Logical Theory* I was devoting much attention to what might loosely be called the distinction between logical and pragmatic inferences. . . . I canvassed the idea that the alleged divergences between Modernists' Logic and vulgar connectives might be represented as a matter not of logical but of pragmatic import' (1989, p. 375). Given that Russellian 'Modernism' was one of the targets of much of the work undertaken by the ordinary language philosophers, there's an interesting irony in the fact that Grice's 'pragmatics' was conceived largely in an effort to *defend* it.

2. The evolutionary function (in the sense of the fitness-enhancing effect) of human cognition is to provide individuals with information about themselves and their environment (and thus guide their behaviour). See Sperber 2001 for discussion.

3. Earlier versions of the continuum I am about to propose were dubbed the 'showing/*telling*' or the 'showing/*saying*' continuum. I now prefer 'showing/*meaning$_{NN}$*' continuum (though the reader will notice that I occasionally lapse into the earlier terminology). The reason for the change in terminology is that there are instances of meaning$_{NN}$ which are cases of neither saying nor telling. The reason for my occasional inconsistency is that it has only gradually become clear to me that whereas I originally thought there was a single continuum, there are actually *two*. (These two continua are conflated in, for example, Wharton 2000b, 2003a.) Indeed, I have since come to realise that this was one of the reasons I had problems conceptualising the continuum in my earlier work (a fact which was never clearer to me than when I tried to explain it to others). The issue is further complicated by the fact that *one* of these two continua – the kind of continuum proposed by people like Erving Goffman (1981) and Adam Kendon (1988) – might *indeed* be better called the 'showing–*saying*' (or 'saying *that*') continuum, since it is more a continuum between non-linguistic and linguistic coding, than between showing and meaning$_{NN}$. In Chapter 3 I explore the similarities between the two types of continua, and in Chapter 8 I stress the differences between them (whilst also noting that they interact in interesting ways).

4. Notice that an audience is only required to *recognise* a speaker's informative intention; he might not believe the speaker, in which case the informative intention will be recognised but not fulfilled. By contrast, the communicative intention may be *fulfilled* without being recognised, in that it can be evidenced without the audience consciously attending to it.

5. Sam Guttenplan has remarked to me that, in his experience, undergraduates are not usually convinced by Grice's photograph example, and suggests that this is because when Grice wrote the original article, photographs were more clearly strict causal products of reality. Nowadays, modern digital photography and computer image manipulation complicate the issue, and we more readily call the authenticity of the (purported) causal link into question.

6. The notion of manifestness is also central to the relevance-theoretic notion of a *communicative* intention, defined as an intention 'to make it mutually manifest to audience and communicator that the communicator has [an] informative intention' (p. 61). The notion of *mutual manifestness* is the relevance theory solution to the problems with Grice's original three-clause definition of meaning$_{NN}$ raised by (among others) Strawson (1964) and Schiffer (1972). It provides a more psychologically plausible alternative to the notions of common ground (Stalnaker 1978, Clark 1996) and joint knowledge. (See Avramides 1989, Chapter 2 for discussion of Strawson's and Schiffer's counterexamples and redefinitions; see Sperber and Wilson 1986/1995 Chapter 1 for further discussion.)

7. Although the focus in this book is on what I am calling natural 'behaviours', there are all manner of other ways in which natural signs are used in verbal communication. If I am sitting behind my desk when an undergraduate asks me if I will play in the annual Linguistics *vs.* Phonetics rugby match, I might reply 'I've broken my leg' whilst at the same time showing him my leg in plaster. If I am attending a particularly infuriating meeting and decide to register my disapproval, I might close my brief-case and walk out, while simultaneously commenting 'I'm closing my brief-case and walking out.'

8. From *Travels in Greece*, Nikos Kazantzakis (1965).

9. For readers unfamiliar with the notion of 'truth conditional content' I provide the following brief introduction. Consider a sentence such as 'Neil Smith spoke to Noam Chomsky from 3.00 to 3.15 on September 12th, 2001.' This sentence describes a particular state of affairs: it is about that state of affairs. It picks out two individuals in the world – Neil Smith and Noam Chomsky – and describes an action that took place – Neil Smith spoke to Chomsky – at a certain time on a certain day. One property that this sentence has – a property shared by all declarative

sentences – is that it can be true or false. Of course, whether or not the sentence is true depends on the facts in the world. But even though we may not know what the facts are so that we can judge this sentence to be true, we know what the facts ought to be in order to make it true. We know, for example, that a trans-Atlantic phone call at the appropriate time on the appropriate day would suffice. We also know that if Neil Smith were talking solely to me for the whole of this time, then it would be false.

Notice, however, that we can only say how the world needs to be for the sentence to be true if we know what the sentence means. Someone who did not know what it means – say, a mono-lingual Finnish speaker – could not say how the world needs to be for it to be true, nor make use of the facts in the world to evaluate its truth or falsity. To judge the truth or falsity of a sentence you need not only knowledge of the world, but you must also know what that sentence means.

As a consequence of this relationship between truth and meaning many people working in meaning are working with the assumption that the meaning of sentences (or – as we shall see – certainly aspects of it) can be explained in terms of truth. If you know what a sentence means, then you know what the world would have to be like for it to be true, and if you don't know what a sentence means, then you don't know what the world would have to be like for it to be true. This kind of evidence has led linguistics and philosophers to believe that linguistic meaning can be characterised in terms of the conditions in which a sentence would be true, or truth-conditions. Speakers know the meaning of a sentence *because* they know how the world would have to be for the sentence to be true.

10. Though crucially, Recanati does not regard these 'primary' pragmatic processes as inferential (see discussion in Chapter 7).

11. The processes of hypothesis formation and evaluation that an audience undertakes in identifying the speaker's meaning are non-demonstrative in character. So he may be *wrong*, but he can do no better.

12. Though see discussion in note 14.

13. Identity is, of course, a special case of similarity; so the inferential approach does not rule out the possible reduplication of thoughts, but does not make it a necessary condition on successful communication.

14. In her 2002 book, Robyn Carston wonders whether many *conceptual* encodings are 'not really full-fledged concepts, but rather concept schemas, or pointers to a conceptual space' (2002a, p. 360). In particular she considers the word 'happy' and asks: 'Could it be that the word "happy" does not encode a concept, but rather points to a conceptual region?'.

This is an interesting point, which might be seen as having significant implications for the distinction I am about to propose between translational and non-translational encoding. As Carston also points out, however, even if it turns out to be correct that some words encode 'pro-concepts', it will only be *some* words, and not all: 'There is a strong intuition that 'cat' encodes a concept CAT, which features in thought, and not just an abstract schema for constructing CAT* concepts or some pointer to knowledge about cats' (*ibid*. p. 362). In which case, the above distinction between translational and non-translational encoding is still motivated.

15. The distinction between propositional/descriptive content and illocutionary force is one version of John Austin's distinction between locutionary and illocutionary acts. See Recanati (1987, pp. 236–66) for detailed discussion of Austin's distinctions and the various interpretations of his work.

16. To propose that pronouns linguistically encoded conceptual representations of their referents would amount to suggesting that they are multiply ambiguous.

17. Sperber (2001) suggests that words indicating inferential relationships (e.g. 'since', 'but' and 'nevertheless') might have evolved as 'tools of persuasion' in the cognitive arms race sparked by communicators' need to show that their argument is cogent enough to convince even hearers who do not trust them much. This point may have implications for the evolution of procedural expressions. I return to evolutionary issues in Chapter 6.

18. In the case of the pronouns, the *output* of the procedure does provide a constituent of a conceptual representation. However, the constituent itself is not encoded by the pronoun.

CHAPTER 4

Interjections and language

I should explain to you, Socrates, that our friend Cratylus has been arguing about names. He says that they are natural and not conventional – not a portion of the human voice which men agree to use – but that there is a truth or correctness, which is the same for Hellenes as for barbarians.

Hermogenes in Plato's *Cratylus*

INTERJECTIONS

Interjections are often regarded as marginal to language. While we feel them to be partly natural, we also feel them to be partly coded (or conventionalised). Interjections seem to lie somewhere *between* showing and saying or meaning. This marginal linguistic status is reflected in various historical analyses. Latin grammarians described them as non-words, independent of syntax, signifying only feelings or states of mind. Nineteenth-century linguists regarded them as non-linguistic, or at best paralinguistic phenomena: 'between interjection and word there is a chasm wide enough to allow us to say that interjection is the negation of language' (Benfey 1869, p. 295); 'language begins where interjections end' (Muller 1862, p. 366). Sapir also described interjections as 'never more, at best, than a decorative edging to the ample, complex fabric [of language]' (1970, p. 7).

According to various definitions in the literature, 'interjections' represent a fairly heterogeneous class of items. Examples in English include *wow, yuk, aha, ouch, oops, ah, oh, er, huh, eh, tut-tut (tsk-tsk), brrr, shh, ahem, psst,* and even, according to some, *bother, damn, (bloody) hell, shit* (etc.), *goodbye, yes, no, thanks, well.* I will assume for the sake of argument that many of the above items *do* form a class, but will end up suggesting that interjections are very disparate and should not all be treated as contributing to communication in the same way.

Existing studies of the semantics and pragmatics of interjections raise three main questions:

(A) What do interjections communicate?
(B) How do interjections communicate?
(C) Are interjections part of language?

These questions have been approached from two largely opposite viewpoints. Ameka (1992), Besmeres and Wierzbicka (2003), Wierzbicka (1992), and Wilkins (1992) argue that interjections are 'semantically rich and have a definite conceptual structure which can be explicated' (Wilkins 1992, p. 120). They treat interjections as part of language, and propose complex semantic analyses; I refer to this as the *conceptualist* view. Others, notably Goffman (1981), contend that an interjection 'doesn't seem to be a statement in the linguistic sense'. Rather, it is 'a ritualised act, in something like the ethological sense of that term' (1981, p. 100). Interjections, according to this view, are not part of language, and are analysed in terms of the socio-communicative roles they play, rather than any linguistic content they may have.

In the light of the above questions, the aim of this chapter is to assess the relative strengths and weaknesses of these contrasting approaches and to suggest a new analysis of interjections which preserves the insights of both. This analysis will build on some of the discussion in the previous chapters. In particular, it will make use of a version of the showing–meaning$_{NN}$ continuum and also of the relevance-theoretic distinction between translational and non-translational (or conceptual and procedural) encoding. The conceptual–procedural distinction will be further discussed in Chapters 5 and 6, for the question remains whether, given the marginal linguistic status of interjections, an analysis with its roots in what is essentially a *linguistic* distinction is appropriate.

The view that interjections have, at best, marginal linguistic status can still be found in the contemporary literature: Quirk,

Greenbaum *et al* (1985, p. 853) describe interjections as 'purely emotive words which do not enter into syntactic relations'; Trask (1993, p. 144) describes an interjection as 'a lexical item or phrase which serves to express emotion and which typically fails to enter into any syntactic structures at all'; Crystal (1995, p. 207) concurs – 'an interjection is a word or sound thrown into a sentence to express some feeling of the mind'.

There are exceptions, though. As noted above, conceptualists see interjections as properly linguistic, with rich semantic structures. However, whilst the conceptualists are agreed that interjections are part of language, they do not agree on what exactly an interjection is. Introducing the conceptualist view, Ameka (1992) divides interjections into two main classes: *primary* and *secondary* interjections. A primary interjection is a word that cannot be used in any other sense than as an interjection, e.g. *oops*, *ouch*, *ow* and *oh* in (55) and (56):

(55) Keep still Bet. **Oops**, sorry! (KBE 84 – BNC)
(56) **Ouch**, that flaming hurts! **Ow**! Oh! Oh! Oh! Oh! (KCW 17 – BNC)

Primary interjections are non-productive in the sense that they do not inflect and are not movable between word-classes. Secondary interjections 'are those words which have an independent semantic value but which can be used . . . as utterances by themselves to express a mental attitude or state' (Ameka 1992, p. 111), e.g. *damn* and *shit* in (57) and (58):

(57) They've been working on Sarah's today. **Damn**! They're up to the roof aren't they? (KCT 190 – BNC)
(58) Oh **shit**, I mustn't swear tonight. No not allowed to swear tonight . . . (KBE 49 – BNC)

Both types of interjection are syntactically independent, in that they can constitute an utterance by themselves, and are only loosely integrated into the grammar of the clause containing them. In written texts, interjections are separated off from the main clause by means of a comma or exclamation mark. Furthermore, Ameka observes, they 'always constitute an intonation unit by themselves' (1992, p. 108).

Wierzbicka's definition of an interjection corresponds closely to Ameka's conception of a primary interjection. She suggests that it is preferable not to regard exclamations such as *damn* and *hell* as interjections, since their semantics is determined by the semantics of the nouns/verbs they are derived from: I shall follow her on this. While Ameka's definition is too broad for her, for Wilkins it is too narrow. He uses a variety of hedges in his formal definition of interjections (1992, p. 124), which 'catches elements that would be called "secondary interjections" . . . "interjectional phrases" and "complex interjections" by Ameka' (1992, p. 125). There is thus no general agreement on how interjections can be defined.

Since Goffman (1981) does not regard interjections as part of language, he does not define them in the same way. In fact, for the majority of expressions I shall look at in this book, he prefers the term *response cry*: 'We see such "expressions" as a natural overflowing, a flooding up of previously contained feeling, a bursting of normal restraints' (1981, p. 99). By 'response cry', Goffman is referring primarily to expressions such as *ouch, oops, yuk, wow, eh, ah, aha, oh*, etc., which he regards as non-words. Since 'nonwords as a class are not productive in the linguistic sense, their role as interjections being one of the few that have evolved for them . . . [they] can't quite be called part of language' (1981, p. 115). However, he does grant that since these cries are found cross-linguistically, and since certain forms stabilise within a given speech community, the term *semiword* might be appropriate. Swear words are of course highly productive. But while conceding that they are probably more a part of language than non-words such as *oops* and *ouch*, he does not see this as reason to exclude them from the class of response cries, which in his view fall on a continuum between displays and properly linguistic items.

One point of agreement between the conceptualists and Goffman is that *an interjection is capable of constituting an utterance by itself in a unique, non-elliptical manner.* Another point accepted by both camps is that interjections are tied to emotional or mental attitudes or states. From the examples on my introductory list, *wow* might be said to express excitement, delight, wonder, etc., *yuk* to express disgust or revulsion, *ouch* pain, *aha* surprise etc. Wierzbicka suggests that alongside these emotive and cognitive interjections, there are some volitive ones, used to express wants or desires: *psst*, *ahem*, *shh* and *eh*, for example, serve as requests for attention, quiet or confirmation. A second criterion, then, by which we might classify an expression as an interjection is that *an interjection expresses a mental or emotional attitude or state.*

These two criteria seem to me to provide an adequate working characterisation. In what follows, I will retain the conceptualists' primary/secondary distinction, and focus mainly on primary interjections, which have no counterparts in other syntactic categories. Focusing on primary interjections also allows me to largely abstract away from linguistic expressions such as *yes*, *no*, *thanks* and *goodbye*, which could be seen as fitting the above criteria, but are not central to the claims of this chapter. I will, however, consider the status of certain stylised imitations, such as 'ha ha', 'boo hoo', etc.

INTERJECTIONS AND CONCEPTS

The conceptualists might answer questions (A), (B) and (C) along the following lines: first, interjections communicate complex conceptual structures; second, communication is achieved principally by means of encoding conceptual structures; third, since interjections are viewed as having 'semantic' content, they are part of language.[1] Below in (59) is an example of the kind of analysis the conceptualists propose, Wierzbicka's conceptual structure for *wow* (1992, p. 164):

(59) *wow!*
    I now know something
    I wouldn't have thought I would know it
    I think: it is very good
    (I wouldn't have thought it could be like that)
    I feel something because of that

As can be seen from this example, conceptualist analyses of interjections are massively decompositional, and should be viewed in the wider context of Wierzbicka's programme to develop a

Natural Semantic Metalanguage. The Semantic Metalanguage is based on a set of around fifty primitives, designed to represent the innate building blocks of meaning: 'research of recent years has proved Wittgenstein wrong . . . words can be rigorously defined' (Wierzbicka 1994, p. 433). Wierzbicka extends this approach to interjections: 'we can capture the subtlest shades of meaning encoded in interjections relying exclusively on universal or near-universal concepts such as "good" and "bad", "do" and "happen", "want", "know", "say", or "think"' (Wierzbicka 1992, p. 163).

Although many subtle and intuitively appealing analyses have been proposed within this framework, there are several problems with the approach. Fodor (1981) argues that very few words are decomposable into satisfactory definitions: in this respect, the classic example 'bachelor' is exceptional. Fodor demonstrates that the task of analysing other relatively simple words into necessary and sufficient conditions presents serious problems.[2] Taking a standard decomposition of the word 'paint' as an example, he argues that *x paints y* is not satisfactorily defined as *x covers y with paint*.[3] To support his claim, he raises a series of objections, each of which he attempts to counter with a more complex definition. For instance, when an explosion at a paint factory covers a passer-by with paint, it is not the case that the factory (or the explosion) has painted the passer-by: perhaps, then, the definition should stipulate the involvement of an *agent*. However, in covering the surface of the ceiling of the Sistine Chapel with paint, Michelangelo, while certainly an agent, was not painting the ceiling, but rather painting *a picture on* the ceiling. With these counterexamples in mind, Fodor redefines *x paints y* as meaning *x is an agent and x covers the surface of y with paint, and x's primary intention in covering the surface of y with paint was that the surface of y should be covered with paint in consequence of x's having so acted upon it*. However, he finds a counterexample to even this most complex definition. For when Michelangelo dipped his brush in his paint pot, the above conditions were satisfied, but he was not painting his paintbrush: 'when it comes to definitions', Fodor concludes, 'the examples almost always don't work' (1981, p. 288).[4]

Along similar lines we can find counterexamples to the conceptualist structures proposed for interjections. Firstly, the definition in (59) includes the line *I think: it is very good*. But this overlooks the fact that *wow* can just as easily express negative feelings, such as disappointment, or outrage:

(60) *Wow*! That's really bad . . . (124 KD6 – BNC)

This point is also is raised by Wilkins (1992, p. 150). To account for it, and for the fact that neither Wierzbicka's nor Ameka's definition captures the immediacy of the reaction expressed by an utterance of *wow*, he proposes the more complex structure below (1992, p. 151):

(61) '*wow!*'
I_U have just now$_T$ become aware of this$_I$ something,
that I_U wouldn't have expected
[or 'that I_U wouldn't have thought I_U would become aware of']
This$_I$ something is much more $X_{[Pr\text{-}of\text{-}this\ I]}$ than I would have expected,
and this causes me$_U$ to feel surprised,
and to feel that I_U could not imagine this something being more $X_{[Pr\text{-}of\text{-}this\ I]}$
than it already is now$_T$.
I_U say '/wau!/' because I_U want to show how surprised
(and impressed)
I_U am feeling right now$_T$.

But as with Fodor's more complex definitions, there are still problems. For example, there are aspects of the meaning of *wow* that the structure in (61) does not adequately capture. Does '*this is much more X than I would have expected and . . . causes me to feel surprised*' 'rigorously' define the subtle shades of positive meaning that an utterance of *wow* might communicate? From surprise and being mildly impressed, through amazement and astonishment to jaw-dropping bewilderment? From satisfaction through enjoyment to absolute exhilaration? Also, is it true that *wow* communicates that the speaker feels they '*could not imagine this something being more X than it already is*'? Does a spectator at a firework display communicate that he feels that this is the most spectacular firework display he can imagine when he utters *wow*? Fodor's point that there are always counterexamples to be found, no matter how complex the definition, appears to hold for interjections too.

A second problem with the conceptualist approach is that an utterance of *wow* seems to communicate something altogether vaguer than the kind of structures they propose would predict. This is not to deny that interjections can communicate a great deal. However, the range of communicative effects an utterance of *wow* might give rise to, when combined with different intonations and facial expressions, seems to go well beyond anything capturable in a small set of conceptual structures such as those proposed above.

An analogy with some of the other natural behaviours humans use to communicate is instructive here. What a speaker might communicate by using an affective tone of voice seems too nebulous to be paraphrased by fixed structures such as (59) and (61). A facial expression or gesture might convey more than a string of words ever could, but it is not obvious that it is *encoding* anything like a determinate conceptual structure or logical form.

The context-dependence of interjections is a third problem for the conceptualist approach. Of course, (59) as it stands is not a fully propositional structure, because it contains uninterpreted indexicals (*I*, *it*, *now*) which have to be assigned reference in a particular context of utterance. Wilkins employs a variety of deictic subscripts (see (61)) to account for this context-dependency: 'each deictic element must be filled referentially before the interjection can be fully meaningful' (1992, p. 137). But the communicative content of interjections is so context-dependent that it seems implausible to suggest that the only contribution of pragmatic/contextual factors to their interpretation is the assignment of reference to indexicals. The conceptualist approach seriously underestimates the contribution of pragmatic/contextual or *inferential* factors to the interpretation of interjections. I will return to this point below.

The vagueness and context-dependence of interjections also relate to a fourth, more general problem with the conceptualist

account. As mentioned above, humans use a wide range of
behaviours to communicate. Consider, for example, how an individual might convey a feeling of pain. The means that might be
used range from allowing someone to see an entirely natural and
instinctive contorted facial expression, to producing a scream such
as 'aaaargh', a culture/language-specific *ouch*, or a fully linguistic
'it hurts like hell'. Few people would propose that grimaces or
screams encode conceptual structure, but communicate they do.
Interjections retain an element of naturalness and spontaneity that
suggests they fall somewhere *between* the natural and the linguistic.
With tone of voice, facial expressions and even gestures, they share
the property of being partly natural: the conceptualist approach
overlooks this.

A fifth problem is that intuitions do not support the claim that
interjections encode the kind of conceptual structure the conceptualists propose. Consider (62) below, Wilkins' conceptual structure
for *ow* (Wilkins 1992, p. 149):

> (62) '*ow!*'
> I suddenly feel a pain (in this part of my body) right now that I
> wouldn't have expected to feel.
> I say '[au]' because I want to show that I am feeling pain right
> now [and because I know that this is how speakers of English can
> show (other speakers of English) that they are in pain (in a
> situation like the situation here)]

While it is plausible that the italicised expressions in (63) and (64)
express the same (or similar) concepts, it is not obvious that the
same is true of those in (65) and (66), which do not *feel* synonymous in the same way:

> (63) Be careful with that *needle*!
> (64) Be careful with that *hypodermic*!
> (65) That flamin' hurts! *Ow*!
> (66) That flamin' hurts! *I suddenly feel a pain* etc.

It could, of course, be our unfamiliarity with the sheer complexity of the conceptual structure in (62) that is responsible for this
intuition. However, even if we strip the conceptual structure down

to its bare essentials, where *ow* encodes something like 'I feel pain', there are still problems. Example (67), for example, intuitively involves a conceptual repetition, while (68) does not:

(67) I feel pain, I feel pain.
(68) *Ow*, I feel pain.

And interjections are not systematically interchangeable with their conceptual counterparts; they do not, for example, occur in embedded positions, and there seem to be other reasons for this than purely syntactic ones:[5]

(69) If I feel pain, I'll tell you.
(70) If *ow*, I'll tell you.

In unpublished work, the philosopher David Kaplan (1997) has addressed (among other things) the linguistic difference between 'I feel pain' and *ouch*. Well known for his work on indexicals, Kaplan sees similarities between indexicals on the one hand, and expressives (interjections – *ouch*, *oops*) and epithets ('that bastard') on the other: all these expressions, he claims, are better analysed in terms of a *Semantics of Use* rather than (or as well as) a *Semantics of Meaning*. To account for the difference between 'I feel pain' and *ouch*, he introduces a distinction between *descriptive* and *expressive* content: while 'I feel pain' has descriptive (truth-conditional/propositional) content, *ouch* has expressive (non-truth-conditional/non-propositional) content. This distinction is similar to the distinction drawn by speech-act theorists between describing and indicating mentioned in Chapter 3; I return to this point below.

Kaplan's notion of descriptive content has clear parallels with the conceptualists' notion of conceptual/propositional content, and the application of his descriptive/expressive distinction suggests that one of the reasons *ow* and 'I feel pain' are not interchangeable in (67) and (68), or (69) and (70), is that while 'I feel pain' has descriptive meaning, *ow* has expressive meaning. In Kaplan's terms, the *modes* of expression are different.

A sixth problem relates to the fact that interjections do not contribute to the truth conditions of the utterances that contain them. In fact, the non-truth-conditional status of interjections may be one of the factors responsible for the intuitions in (67) and (68). Consider (71) and (72):

(71) I feel pain, the anaesthetic isn't working.
(72) *Ouch*, the anaesthetic isn't working.

Example (71) makes two assertions: it is true when and only when the speaker feels pain and the anaesthetic isn't working; by contrast, (72) only makes a single assertion, and is true if and only if the anaesthetic isn't working. The dentist could not respond to a patient's utterance of '*Ouch!*' in (56) with: 'You're *lying*, you can't feel any pain.' As noted above, conceptual representations have logical properties, and are capable of being true or false. As a result, a conceptual representation can contradict or imply other conceptual representations and act as input to logical inference rules. Since interjections do not seem to have these properties, it might be best to treat them as not encoding fully conceptual structures.[6]

To summarise, there are six problems with the conceptualist approach: firstly, there are problems with decompositionalist accounts of meaning generally; secondly, the communicative content of interjections is vaguer than the proposed conceptual structures would predict; thirdly, the highly context-dependent nature of interjections suggests a substantial pragmatic contribution to their comprehension; fourthly, the approach overlooks the fact that interjections share with certain paralinguistic behaviours the property of being partly natural; fifthly, the fact that they do not appear to be synonymous with their fully conceptual counterparts suggests they do not encode concepts; sixthly, the non-truth-conditional status of interjections suggests that a conceptual account is inappropriate, and that alternative semantic treatments should be explored.

INTERJECTIONS AND 'RESPONSE CRIES'

During the Wimbledon tennis championships in 1981, officials were confronted with an unusual problem. Some male players, notably Jimmy Connors, were regularly grunting loudly as they hit the ball. Their opponents . . . claimed the noises were distracting and were emitted deliberately to throw off their timing. When officials confronted Connors . . . he explained that he had no control over his grunting; it just happened when he hit the ball hard . . . Wimbledon officials then observed the different players, trying to discern which grunts were intentional and which were not. (Seyfarth and Cheney 1992, p. 78)

Goffman (1981) discusses interjections in terms of the socio-communicative roles they play rather than any linguistic content they may have. Of the questions that are the focus of this chapter, he is concerned with questions (A) and (C), and not question (B).

He considers three types of 'roguish utterances', which violate the conditions that normal 'talk' observes: *self-talk*, *imprecations* (swearing) and *response cries*. It is the latter two which are relevant here, and Goffman's distinction between response cries such as *oops*, *ouch*, *wow*, etc. and imprecations reflects the conceptualists' primary/secondary interjection distinction discussed in the last section.

Goffman would not endorse Jimmy Connors' claim that his grunts were unintentional. Indeed, his primary concern is the fact that such sounds are invariably intended for the benefit of others. The purpose of *strain grunts*, for example, is often to warn others to stand clear. He comments, 'these sounds are felt to be entirely unintentional, even though the glottis must be partially closed off to produce them and presumably could be fully opened or closed to avoid doing so' (1981, p. 105): Goffman fifteen, Connors love.

Goffman classifies response cries according to the functions they serve. Some exploit more or less instinctive, natural reactions for communicative purposes: with the *transition display*, for instance, a person might utter *brrr* when leaving a warm atmosphere for a cold one not only in order to restore some sort of physical equilibrium but also to 'fall into cadence with the others in the room' (1981, p. 101); with the *spill cry*, a person might utter *oops* on dropping something because it has the effect of 'downplaying import and hence implication as evidence of our incompetence' (1981, p. 102). According to Goffman, the main function of *ouch* (the *pain cry*) is to warn others that a threshold for pain is being reached, or about to be breached. Such response cries are not productive linguistically, and are therefore treated as peripheral to language proper.

Imprecations, by contrast, are highly productive linguistically. However, Goffman notes that an exclamation of *shit!* 'need no more elide a sentence than need a laugh, groan, sob, snicker or giggle – all vocalisations that frequently occur except in the utterances ordinarily presented for analysis by linguists'. Nor does it help 'to define *shit!* as a well-formed sentence with *NP!* as its structure'. He concludes that 'imprecations, then, might best be considered . . . as a type of response cry' (1981, p. 112).

One of the most important points that Goffman raises is that there may be a continuum between the properly linguistic and the non-linguistic, or between display (or showing) and saying. Since *ouch*, *oops*, etc. are not productive linguistically, according to Goffman they 'can't quite be called part of language' (1981, p. 115). Because of their productivity, imprecations are treated as part of language (73–75) (though recall that when used as interjections they are non-productive):

(73) That dentist is shit.
(74) The dentist got really shitty with me.
(75) He was the shittiest dentist I've ever had the misfortune to see.

The distinction, however, is not clear-cut: 'response cries such as *eek!* might be seen as peripheral to the linguist's domain . . . but imprecations . . . are more germane, passing beyond semiword segregates to the traditional material of linguistic analysis' (1981, p. 121).

An illustration of Goffman's proposal might be as follows: to show someone you are delighted with a gift you allow them to see your natural reaction, a smile; to tell them you are delighted you utter something like 'it's wonderful!'; to utter an interjection like *wow* is to communicate that you are delighted by adding a certain element of *coding* which takes it beyond mere display, but falls short of language proper.

There are clear parallels between Goffman's continuum and the continuum sketched in Chapter 3. Both deal with the whole range of communicative phenomena: from 'natural' display to the fully linguistic. Indeed, one of my aims here (and in my final chapter) is to examine ways in which the type of continuum proposed by Goffman and others might mesh with the continuum presented in Chapter 3. One obvious difference is that Goffman's continuum (unlike mine) appears to be based on the assumption that all communication involves at least some element of coding. It's unclear to me precisely what Goffman means by 'display', but since he nowhere discusses the role played in human communication by the expression and attribution of intentions, and since in other published works (see, for example, Goffman 1964) he talks of the 'rituals' and 'regulations' that 'govern' conversational exchanges, I take his continuum to be one between non-linguistic and linguistic coding.

Goffman, as we have seen, does regard it as important that some response cries are 'intentional', but he does not appear to be using the word in the 'rich, philosophical sense' mentioned in my introduction (see note 2, p. 17). I return to these issues in Chapter 8, and argue that while the continuum outlined in Chapter 3 can accommodate all the elements on a continuum of the kind envisaged by Goffman (and others), the reverse is not the case.[7]

Although he sees response cries as falling outside language proper, a strength of Goffman's account is that he is keen to illustrate their communicative adaptability. He points out that if you are being told by a friend about a particularly gruesome moment from their last trip to the dentist's, you might utter *ouch* sympathetically on their behalf.[8] Or you might use it as in (76):

(76) Dentist: That'll be £75 for the consultation and £30 for the cavity.
Patient: *Ouch!*

Here again Goffman is distancing himself from the view that primary interjections are a simple 'natural overflowing'. It is, after all, intuitively clear that while they are instinctive in some respects, *ouch* and most primary interjections are under our conscious control. If I bring a hammer down forcefully on my thumb, the four-letter word I utter is unlikely to begin with 'o' (though, as Goffman points out, it might if I were helping at the local playgroup).

A person screaming in agony does not scream *ouch!*. In this respect, we should be careful not to overestimate the expressive, instinctive nature of these primary interjections.

There are many interesting ideas in Goffman (1981). The question of what interjections communicate is, in almost all cases, beautifully explicated. In terms of the questions asked at the beginning of this chapter, the problem is that he says nothing about *how* interjections communicate. In this respect, whilst it affords some insights that are certainly worth preserving, his analysis does not provide a satisfactory theoretical alternative to the conceptualist approach. In the next section, I will look at some analyses of linguistic meaning which offer alternatives to the conceptualist account of interjections.

INTERJECTIONS AND MEANING: 'WHAT DO INTERJECTIONS COMMUNICATE?'

In Chapter 3 we saw that over the last 30 years, philosophers of language and linguists have explored the idea that not all linguistic meaning is descriptive, or conceptual. At various times a distinction has been made between truth-conditional and non-truth-conditional, or propositional and illocutionary content, and between describing and indicating, or saying and conventionally implicating. If interjections do not encode descriptive or conceptual meaning, it is worth exploring whether they can be analysed as non-truth-conditional indicators of some kind.

Recall from Chapter 3 that, in relevance-theoretic terms, when the proposition expressed by an utterance is part of what the speaker intends to communicate, it constitutes the basic-level explicature. This explicature (already the result of pragmatic inference required for disambiguation, reference resolution and various types of enrichment) may also be used to construct various higher-level explicatures by embedding it under a speech-act or propositional-attitude description. In this way, aspects of both speech-act theory and Gricean pragmatics are retained within the relevance theory framework.

To illustrate this approach once more, consider how Jack might interpret Lily's utterance in (77). Having recovered the proposition expressed, he might embed it under a speech-act description, as in (78), or a propositional-attitude description, as in (79). Assuming they are part of what the speaker intends to communicate, these would be higher-level explicatures of Lily's utterance in (77):

> (77) Lily (regretfully):   I've got a toothache.
> (78) Lily is saying that she's got toothache.
> (79) Lily regrets that she's got toothache.

This framework suggests a way of approaching question (A) – What do interjections communicate? Interjections might be analysed as indicators of higher-level explicatures containing the type of speech-act or propositional-attitude information the hearer is expected to infer. An obvious candidate for an interjection that might encode a similar sort of information to interrogative mood indicators – *cf.* example (53) from the previous chapter – is *eh*. Thus, in relevance-theoretic terms, a patient interpreting the dentist's utterance in (80) might form the higher-level explicature in (81), or perhaps (82):

> (80) Dentist: So you're having three teeth out, *eh?*
> (81) The dentist is asking whether I'm having three teeth out.
> (82) The dentist is requesting confirmation that I'm having three teeth out.

In many languages such particles appear to be fully grammaticalised. Japanese has an interrogative particle 'ka', added to the end of an interrogative utterance. Wilson and Sperber (1993) point out that certain dialects of French have an interrogative particle 'ti' which performs the function carried out by word-order in other dialects, and might be analysed along similar lines to 'eh'. Indeed, in English a similar questioning attitude toward the proposition is often conveyed by the word 'right?', or the tags 'aren't you?' or 'are you?'.

Wilson and Sperber (1993) also propose that the English interjection *huh* might be used to encourage the construction of higher-level explicatures involving a mocking, sceptical, critical, or more generally dissociative attitude toward an attributed utterance or thought. Consider (83), which might lead a hearer to derive the higher-level explicature in (84):

(83) Lily: Dentists are human, *huh*!
(84) It's ridiculous to think that dentists are human.

Cross-linguistic data suggest that many languages contain particles that might be analysed in a similar way. Japanese (Itani 1995) and Sissala (Blass 1990) have hearsay particles, [tte] and [re] respectively, which mark propositions as attributed to another speaker (or thinker). Sadock and Zwicky (1985, p. 161) note that Lahu has 'a very large number of particles that indicate attitudes, rational or emotional, toward a proposition'.

Since a feature of interjections in general is that they express attitudes, we might consider to what extent these attitudes are similar to those conveyed in example (83). Certainly, utterances of (85) and (87) might lead a hearer to form the higher-level explicatures in (86) and (88):

(85) *Aha*! You're here.
(86) The speaker is surprised that I am here.
(87) *Wow*! You're here.
(88) The speaker is delighted that I am here.

In speech-act terms both *aha* and *wow* in (85) and (87) can be analysed as contributing to expressive speech acts. In fact, all the examples I have considered so far seem to fit the speech-act framework, in that there appears to be an attitude, emotional or otherwise, being conveyed toward the proposition expressed – satisfying John Searle's (1979) definition of an *expressive* speech-act: 'the illocutionary point of this class is to express the psychological state specified in the sincerity condition about a state of affairs specified in the propositional content' (Searle 1979, p. 15).

However, not all uses of interjections fit this account. Consider (89) and (90):

(89) *Yuk*! This mouthwash is foul.
(90) *Wow*! This ice cream is delicious.

Here, the attitudes being conveyed are not attitudes to the proposition expressed by the immediately following utterances. The hearer of these utterances would not be expected to form the higher-level explicatures in either (91) or (92):

(91) The speaker is disgusted that the mouthwash is foul.[9]
(92) The speaker is delighted that the ice cream is delicious.

It seems that in these examples, attitudes are being expressed to objects rather than propositions: in the case of *yuk*, to the mouthwash (or the taste of it), and in the case of *wow* to the ice cream (or the sight or taste of it). As another example, consider (93):

(93) Child: (taking foul-tasting medicine) *Yuk!*

Here, the interjection stands alone as an utterance in its own right in the unique non-elliptical manner characteristic of interjections. Not only is the attitude not directed at any embedded propositional content, there *is* no propositional content to embed. For this reason, it is hard to analyse (93) as conveying a higher-level explicature or contributing to the performance of an expressive speech act, since there is no linguistically encoded logical form to embed under it.

This suggests that it may be worth considering whether what is communicated by the interjections in (89), (90) and (93) are properly described as emotional attitudes at all. In (93) in particular, what the interjection communicates seems to be something more like what is sometimes characterised as a 'feeling' or a 'sensation', as opposed to an emotion.

Rey (1980) describes full-fledged emotional states as involving an interaction between several elements: cognitive, qualitative and physiological. Thus, sadness is characterised as involving an interaction between a cognitive element – the knowledge that something has happened which you would prefer not to have happened, or the belief that something which you would prefer not to happen is going to; a qualitative element – that feeling of being 'down' (perhaps accompanied by behaviour consistent with feeling this way, such as drooping shoulders and a flat tone of voice); and a physiological element – chemical changes in the brain (in the case of sadness or depression, depletion of norepinephrine). Whilst emotional states crucially involve cognitive as well as qualitative and physiological elements, feelings or sensations need not. Seen in these terms, what is communicated by *yuk* in (93) is indeed a feeling or sensation rather than an emotion, and not an emotional attitude or propositional attitude proper. It seems, then, that the framework as presented so far is too restrictive: perhaps it is not possible to account for the meaning of interjections solely in terms of propositions and propositional attitudes, as existing speech-act and relevance-theoretic analyses seem to suggest.

As well as the example in (93), other interjections, such as *ouch* (see (56)), are difficult to account for in terms of propositional attitudes; these might also be said to communicate feelings or sensations rather than emotions: the speaker simply reveals something about her internal state. In Kaplan's terms this state is expressed rather than described. In cognitive terms, we might cash this out by proposing that there is something non-representational about what interjections encode. This proposal would be consistent with the arguments presented earlier in the chapter, and is one I explore below.

The question of what interjections communicate, then, requires various answers. In some cases they might be analysable as conveying speech-act or propositional-attitude information. In this regard, interjections such as *eh* and *huh* pattern with discourse particles such as those I mentioned earlier. The interjection *alas* might also express a propositional-attitude proper. Thus, instead of sighing regretfully and speaking in a regretful tone of voice, Lily might preface her utterance with *alas*, and in doing so express her attitude of regret more explicitly.

Other interjections (e.g. those in (85), (97)) also express propositional attitudes: emotional attitudes to propositions in the sense suggested by Searle. However, in some instances what an interjection expresses might be directed toward a percept or object which is the cause of a qualitative or physiological response, and not to a proposition (e.g. (89), (90)). In these cases, whether or not what is communicated is an *emotional* attitude depends on whether there is a cognitive element interacting with the qualitative and physiological ones. The cognitive element is not always present: indeed, it could be argued that interjections are primarily directed at the percepts and objects that are the causes of particular responses, and only by extension at propositions. Finally, some uses of interjections (see (56), (93)) clearly communicate feelings or sensations rather than propositional attitudes proper.

An adequate analysis of what interjections communicate should take account of all these observations. It should also address the fact that whatever interjections communicate – propositional attitudes, emotions, feelings or sensations – it does not seem to be achieved by encoding conceptual representations. I turn to this question in the next section.

INTERJECTIONS AND PROCEDURES: 'HOW DO INTERJECTIONS COMMUNICATE?'

In Chapter 3 I introduced a distinction between translational and non-translational encoding, based on the relevance-theoretic distinction between conceptual and procedural encoding. Having argued against conceptualist (or translational) accounts of interjections, I now want to explore the possibility of a non-translational/procedural approach. Many of the arguments I will use are based on those developed to test whether words encode conceptual or procedural information (for that reason I favour the term 'procedural' rather than 'non-translational' in much of what follows). In the next chapter, I will consider whether an analysis with its roots in *linguistic* distinctions is appropriate for items such as interjections, which have at best marginal linguistic status.

As we saw above, we already have good evidence against conceptual accounts generally. Furthermore, the tests for conceptual or procedural content described in Chapter 3 seem to support a procedural account. Interjections have *no* synonymous truth-conditional counterparts; they are linguistically *non*-productive and do not undergo compositional semantic rules. It seems plausible to suggest, then, that they encode procedural information which 'points' in the general direction in which relevance should be sought.

In an account along these lines the procedural information encoded in interjections might be seen as activating various attitudinal concepts or classes of concepts, but not in the standard translational way. For instance, *wow* would not encode a unique conceptual representation that a hearer translates as 'X is delighted'. Instead it might activate (or add an extra layer of activation to) a range of attitudinal descriptions associated with delight, surprise, excitement, etc. In the case of *yuk*, the attitude would be one of disgust or revulsion; in the case of *aha* it would be one of surprise, etc. In the case of *eh*, what would be activated is a range of interrogative propositional-attitude descriptions; in the case of *huh*, it would be a range of dissociative attitudes, and so on. Intonation and facial expression might provide further clues to the particular attitude involved and the intensity with which it is held.

What a hearer does with the attitudinal or speech-act information activated might vary in different situations. In utterances of (85) and (97), a hearer might use it to construct a higher-level explicature. In (89) and (90), by contrast, it might be understood as directed at an object or event; indeed, it may be that many interjections are primarily directed at suddenly perceived objects and events, and only by extension to propositions.

This kind of account would square nicely with the observation made in the last section that there is something non-representational about what interjections encode. It also means that we might see some interjections as working in a similar manner to more fully grammaticalised discourse particles – 'please', 'well', 'then', 'now' – with which they share a lack of syntactic integration.

It would also resolve five of the six problems with the conceptualist account outlined above: firstly, the approach is clearly non-decompositional; secondly, it could account for the vagueness of what is communicated, since a wide range of possible propositional-attitude descriptions may be equally activated, and there may be no need for the hearer to choose among them.

As to the third problem, the precise conceptual structure actually arrived at by the hearer will be different in different contexts, since the particular interpretation is the outcome of several overlapping inferential processes and is merely constrained by the semantics of the interjection. Even in the case of *eh*, one of the best candidates for being linked to a particular speech-act – i.e. a request for confirmation – it would be unsatisfactory to propose that this is what is encoded. Consider (94) below:

> (94) Dentist: I'm going to polish your teeth.
> Patient: *Eh?*

Here, the particle would not be understood as requesting confirmation in the same way as it does in (84). The patient may not have heard the dentist properly, and may simply be requesting her to repeat what she has said.

The fifth and sixth problems with the conceptualist account are also solved. The non-truth-conditional status of interjections, which is hard to explain on a fully conceptual account, is to be expected if they encode procedures, which often fall on the non-truth-conditional side. And under a procedural account, there is no expectation that *ouch* and 'I feel pain' will be synonymous, since one encodes concepts and the other does not.

While solving these problems, the procedural account preserves both the conceptualist intuition that there is a coded element to interjections, which is responsible for their language-specific nature, and Goffman's intuition that interjections are more than mere natural displays. It also allows us to incorporate aspects of the functional treatment that Goffman proposes, by suggesting a plausible way in which the communicative content he describes might actually be conveyed: via a combination of procedural encoding and inference.

However, one of the problems I raised for the conceptualist account still remains. I claimed that conceptualists overlook the fact that interjections seem to share with paralinguistic or non-linguistic behaviours the property of being partly natural (as well as partly coded). So far, apart from proposing that interjections might work by activating certain attitudinal descriptions, I have said nothing about this partly natural side of interjections, nor how it might be reconciled with the coded side. For while we intuitively regard words that encode procedural meaning (e.g. 'so', 'after all', 'however', 'moreover', 'I', 'he', etc.) as properly linguistic items, there remains a doubt as to the linguistic status of interjections.

Another issue that I have not yet addressed is the fact that interjections can constitute utterances in their own right in a unique non-elliptical manner; in such cases the higher-level explicature account proposed above would be problematic, since a higher-level explicature, by definition, takes an embedded proposition as its object.

In fact, the two issues are not unrelated, and a way of resolving both would be to see interjections themselves as working more in the manner of wholly natural phenomena, which on some occasions contribute to the construction of higher-level explicatures (when used by a hearer to flesh out a linguistically encoded logical form), but on other occasions contribute only to implicatures (when there is no accompanying utterance with which they could appropriately interact).

The issue of the linguistic status of interjections also remains open, and it has considerable bearing on the analysis being offered here. So far in the literature on the conceptual–procedural distinction, procedural meaning has only been attributed to linguistic expressions, and the question of whether a procedural account would be applicable to non-linguistic or semi-linguistic items has not been addressed. I turn to this question in Chapter 5. In the next section I look in more detail at the linguistic status of interjections.

INTERJECTIONS AND LANGUAGE: 'ARE INTERJECTIONS PART OF LANGUAGE?'

In Chomskyan terms, knowing a language is having a mentally represented grammar, or I-language. However, we may also want to think of 'language' in wider terms. The human production and understanding of natural language is mediated by the grammar in conjunction with other cognitive systems. The ability to produce and understand language in this wider sense includes the ability to carry out various pragmatic interpretation processes. It also includes the ability to attribute intentions and beliefs to others.

These observations are crucial in any attempt to answer question (C) above. For while interjections undoubtedly contribute to the interpretation of utterances, the same can be said for the whole range of natural phenomena discussed at various points in this book: although interjections may contribute to linguistic communication, it does not necessarily follow from this that they encode anything *linguistic*. For an interjection to be regarded as a part of language in the narrow sense discussed above, the mentally represented grammar must be involved: if interjections are part of language, they must encode linguistic information, i.e. what they encode must be stipulated in the grammar.

Ameka summarises the conceptualist viewpoint on question (C) as follows:

[D]ifferent interjections do have different degrees of integration within the linguistic systems of languages. . . . But the underlying commonality shared by all words which satisfy our characterisation of interjection is that they are linguistic signs. (Ameka 1992, p. 113)

It is clear from the first part of this quote that although they see interjections as part of language, even the conceptualists allow for some borderline cases. Ameka argues that there are three respects in which it might be argued that interjections are peripheral to language. These provide a convenient framework within which to approach question (C).

The first property of interjections that Ameka singles out is their 'paralinguistic' nature: 'there is no doubt that there is an intimate connection between interjections and gestures in general' (Ameka 1992, p. 112). Wierzbicka describes interjections as 'vocal gestures', which fits Goffman's intuitions that they are paralinguistic, and to a certain extent my own that they are partly natural as well as partly coded.

Wierzbicka does not, however, regard this as militating against a semantic analysis, and proposes to capture the difference between interjections and regular content words by omitting the 'I say' component from her proposed conceptual structures for interjections (simplified as in Wierzbicka 1992, pp. 162–3):

> (95) *Ow*
> I feel pain.
> (96) *I feel pain*
> I say: I feel pain
> I say this because I want to say how I feel.

This would remove interjections from the class of assertions, and leave them free to perform other speech acts – as expressives, for example. I find this an interesting proposal, and more in line with my own intuitions than other aspects of the conceptualist analysis. It seems to echo Kaplan's (and Searle's) descriptive/expressive distinction, in that (71) describes (conceptualises) a feeling, while (72) just expresses it.

Recall examples (84–88), repeated below as (97–100):

> (97) *Aha!* You're here.
> (98) The speaker is surprised that I am here.
> (99) *Wow!* You're here.
> (100) The speaker is delighted that I am here.

A hearer of these utterances might well be led to construct higher-level explicatures such as (98) and (100) above. Given Wierzbicka's intuitions, and the framework discussed earlier, the issue is whether he might also be expected to construct the higher-level explicatures in (101–102):

> (101) The speaker is saying that she is surprised that I am here.
> (102) The speaker is saying that she is delighted that I am here.

My intuition is that he would not, any more than he would construct (101) and (102) when a speaker says 'You're here!' and accompanies it with a surprised facial expression or a smile. This seems to support Wierzbicka's claim and might be taken as evidence that interjections are not part of language in the same way as regular content words. However, Wierzbicka is not dissuaded from her conclusion: 'interjections – *like any other linguistic elements* – have their meaning, and . . . this meaning can be identified and captured in rigorous semantic formulae' (1992, p. 188 – emphasis added).

Wilkins disagrees with Wierzbicka's claim that use of interjections does not amount to 'saying'. On the contrary, he suggests, native speakers are happy to accept that some interjections are 'said', and presents evidence from his own informal survey to support this. He found that native speakers regarded (103) and (104) as acceptable, but (105) and (106) as unacceptable. These latter expressions are, he argues, better reported using the verb 'go' (107–108):

    (103) 'Ouch!', she said.
    (104) 'Wow!', she said.
    (105) ??'Psst!', she said.
    (106) ??'Shh!', she said.
    (107) 'Psst', she went.
    (108) 'Shh!', she went.

He concludes that 'primary interjections are not merely vocal gestures' and 'interjections like *wow* and *ow* do have an 'I say' component in their decomposition, and may be regarded as illocutionary acts' (Wilkins 1992, pp. 147–8). He also claims his survey provides evidence that 'interjections that match the typical word phonology of English are regarded by native speakers as words' (Wilkins 1992, p. 148).

Here Wilkins touches on the second factor Ameka mentions: phonological atypicality. Wilkins' test in (103–106) suggests that there is a line beyond which items that are sometimes considered interjections (and are included in my original list) are not classified by native speakers as part of a language. Vowel-less vocalisations such as *psst* and *shh* are two examples. Other examples from my introductory list include *brrr*, *hmm*, [|] – the dental click usually orthographically realised as *tut-tut* (or *tsk-tsk*) – and *ahem*, often referred to as an interjection but in practical terms usually little more than an ostensive throat clear. *Oops* also fails to fit standard English phonotactics (in many dialects, English words do not begin with [ʊ]).[10] Similarly *ugh* differs from *yuk* in that the former ends in a velar fricative [x] that is not linguistically productive in many varieties of British English.

Essentially, Wilkins' argument is that since phonologically atypical interjections cannot be reported using the verb 'say', they are not part of the language. However, the situation is more complicated than he suggests, and the argument is not convincing. Not only can we use the reporting verb 'say' with many expressions which are clearly not words of the speaker's own grammar,[11] in metalinguistic uses such as direct quotation, but 'go' is a perfectly acceptable verb with which to report linguistic utterances (109–111):

> (109) And so the kid would say, 'Blah blah blah?' [tentative voice
>   with rising intonation] and his father would say 'Blah blah blah'
>   [in a strong blustery voice], and they would go on like that.[12]
> (110) She looked at me and said 'moi, je déteste les dentistes'.
> (111) So he comes into the pub and he goes 'where's that money you
>   owe me?'. 'What?', she goes, 'I don't owe you anything.'

Furthermore, combining the conceptual approach with Wilkins' claim that phonologically atypical interjections are not words would lead to considerable problems in accounting for the borderline expressions that Ameka alludes to. I don't think I am alone in having *yugh* [jəx] as well as *yuk* [jək] and *ugh* [əx] in my interjectional repertoire. Under Wilkins' account, *yuk* is part of language proper and communicates via its precise encoded conceptual structure: to suggest it does so solely by conceptual encoding, however, leaves no account of *yugh*, which must surely communicate in a similar manner.

The third and final issue in deciding whether or not interjections are part of language is their syntax-independence and non-productivity. Interjections are, as it is often put, 'thrown' (interjected) into utterances. They exist on the edges of utterances, always separated off from the main clause and rarely integrated into intonational units. They do not inflect or combine with other morphemes to change word-class, and often stand alone as utterances in their own right, seemingly without internal linguistic structure. If the crucial factor in deciding the linguistic status of interjections is whether or not the information they putatively encode is stipulated by the grammar, the fact that interjections operate independently of syntactic structure suggests they operate independently of the mental grammar.

In my introduction to this chapter, I stated that for the sake of argument I would assume that interjections represented a unified class. It should be clear by now, however, that this is not the case. As a further complication, consider (112–113):

> (112) At the Annual Dentist's Convention Mr. Pulley *wow*ed the audience with his encyclopaedic knowledge of gold teeth.
> (113) That is without doubt the *yuck*iest mouthwash I've ever tasted.

Wow and *yuk* are, of course, not secondary interjections: the linguistically productive expressions *to wow* and *yucky* (and *yummy*) are derived from the interjections rather than the other way round. This phenomenon complicates the picture even further, and the harder one looks, the more complicated it becomes.

Consider the utterances containing *eh* and *huh* in (80) and (83): although we cannot argue that these expressions are syntactically integrated, there is a sense in which they have to be 'thrown in' in a certain position in the overall utterance to perform the functions they do. With regard to phonology, recall Ameka's comment that interjections 'always constitute an intonation unit by themselves' (1992, p. 108). However, despite the comma in (114), *oh* could be the nucleus, or alternatively the pre-head of a larger intonational unit encompassing the whole phrase:[13]

> (114) Lily: That dentist's a complete sadist.
> Jack: *Oh*, I don't know. (As in 'she isn't really'.)

Interjections are such a disparate, non-unified group of expressions that a question based on the assumption that either all or none of them are part of language may be impossible to answer satisfactorily; any adequate account of interjections should reflect this heterogeneity. It should also reflect the evidence presented in this section, which suggests that many interjections are *not* part of language.

As mentioned above, the question remains whether, having argued against a conceptual and for a procedural approach to interjections, we can maintain the procedural approach in spite of this uncertain linguistic status. In the next section I focus on this *natural* side of interjections, and then suggest a way it might be reconciled with the *coded* side.

THE NATURALNESS OF INTERJECTIONS

Recall Goffman's suggestion that interjections occupy a position on a continuum between display and language proper; interjections do indeed seem to lie half way between the two extremes. There is a sense in which they are partly natural, as well as partly coded. Consider this from Sapir:

A Japanese picture of a hill both differs from and resembles a typical modern European painting of the same kind of hill. Both are suggested by and both 'imitate' the same natural feature. Neither the one nor the other is, in any intelligible sense, a direct outgrowth of the natural feature . . . The interjections of Japanese and English are, just so, suggested by a common natural prototype, the instinctive cries, and are thus unavoidably suggestive of each other. (1970, p. 6)

In *The Expression of the Emotions in Man and Animals* (1872)[14] Darwin considers whether 'the sounds which are produced under various states of mind determine the shape of the mouth, or whether its shape is not determined by independent causes, and the sound thus modified' (*ibid.* p. 96). In describing the natural human expression of surprise he notes: 'Certainly a deep sound of a prolonged *Oh!* may be heard from a whole crowd of people immediately after witnessing an astonishing spectacle' (*ibid.* p. 97). He goes on: 'If, together with surprise, pain be felt, there is a tendency to contract all the muscles of the body, including those of the face, and the lips will then be drawn back; and this will perhaps account for the sound becoming higher and assuming the character of *Ah!* or *Ach!*' (*ibid.* p. 97). Despite the fact that interjections that express pain are language specific – English *ouch*, French *aïe*, Spanish *ay*, Finnish *auts* – they do all begin with the same mid-front vowel that Darwin describes as being naturally expressive of pain. Darwin's observations of how humans naturally express surprise and astonishment (and wonder) suggest that certainly *oh* arises out of a natural behaviour. And he notes other natural expressions of surprise: 'the dropping of the jaw and open mouth of a man stupefied by amazement' (*ibid.* p. 284); the fact that 'when thus affected, our mouths are generally opened, yet the lips are often a little protruded' (*ibid.* p. 285). Given these observations, *aha* and *wow* might also be viewed as developments out of natural behaviours.

When discussing the natural expression of disgust, Darwin says: 'With respect to the face, moderate disgust is exhibited in various ways . . . by blowing out of the protruded lips; or by a sound as of clearing the throat. Such guttural sounds are written *ach* or *ugh* . . .' (*ibid.* p. 256). The interjection *yuk*, then, is closely related to the natural expression of disgust.

As Sapir points out in the epigraph to this section, this goes some way towards explaining why interjections, although not entirely involuntary reactions, *feel* so instinctive both to speaker and hearer. Standing alone in the kitchen, we do not utter 'I feel pain' if the kitchen knife slips, we utter *ouch*. In terms of interpretation, if you hear a spontaneous utterance of *ouch*, the evidence for that first layer of information, that the speaker is in pain, seems direct in a way that with 'I feel pain' it is not. In this respect, the continuum presented in Chapter 3 reflects the intuitions behind Goffman's own proposed continuum.

We have already seen that in relevance theory, there are degrees of explicitness not only at utterance level, but also at word level; a particular word may be used to express not exactly the concept it encodes, but another related concept which is more relevant in a given context. However, there is another way in which coding and inference may interact at the lexical level. Certain words, while they are clearly properly linguistic, appear to carry an extra element of 'showing', where the evidence provided for the first layer of information is more direct.

Onomatopoeic language is an obvious example (e.g. 'clink', 'clank', 'splash', 'sizzle'). In fact, iconic language generally is an example: stylised imitations of non-human sounds (e.g. *buzz*, *miaow*, *moo, oink*); also, stylised imitations of human sounds (e.g. *ha ha, tee hee, boo hoo, boo, hiccup*). In these last examples, there is an element of coding, which separates them from clear instances of showing such as laughing or crying, but also an element of showing, which separates them from clear instances of saying such as 'I am amused' or 'I am crying.' The link here between sound and meaning is not entirely non-natural or arbitrary. Indeed, we might argue that 'yuk', for example, originated as a stylised imitation of the natural expression of disgust discussed by Darwin above.

On this link between sound and meaning, Grice observed that:

Any link will do . . . and the looser the links creatures are in a position to use, the greater the freedom they will have as communicators, since they will be less and less restricted by the need to rely on prior natural connections. (1989, p. 296)

I return to this point in Chapter 8.

In stylised imitations of the type described above, and in onomatopoeic expressions generally, the link between sound and meaning is not *as* loose as in most other words, since some element of the natural connection remains. The fact that some stylised imitations have been grammaticalised to the point where they are linguistically productive suggests that the relation between coding and inference is even more complex. This point is illustrated in (115–117):

(115) The bacon was *sizzling* in the pan.
(116) The cows were *mooing*.
(117) He *hiccuped* loudly.

This is not to suggest that there are degrees of coding, or to attempt to blur the distinction between coded and non-coded meaning. The suggestion is that there might be different *types* of coding. In the above examples, there is an iconic element, and as a result the hearer is given more direct evidence of the first layer of meaning than in examples of pure coding.[15] Since many interjections seem to be exaggerations or developments of natural expressions of emotion, they might also be regarded as stylised imitations, and hence as iconic in some way; although for reasons discussed in the previous section, and in contrast with the examples in (115–117), they are not properly linguistic.

In fact, even some of those vocalisations which I have been treating as interjections, but which cannot be shown to be derived from natural expressions of emotion, are iconic to some extent. *Shh* does not convey emotion: but it could be argued that its voiceless quality, together with the fact that it can be uttered continuously, makes it a particularly suitable sound – though not *word* – for urging someone to be quiet. The showing–meaning continuum, then, can be seen to apply at a *lexical* level as well, but in a manner that is somehow orthogonal to the lexical pragmatic processes discussed in Chapter 3.

More evidence that these expressions are located along a continuum is that there really does appear to be a gradual increase in stylisation/codification among them. This is reflected in the parallel drawn by Goffman (1981) between interjections and *ritualised* behaviours, in the ethological sense of that term. Consider *shh*, *shush* and 'hush'; consider the progression noted earlier from *ugh* to *yugh* to *yuk* to 'yucky'. Similar progressions can be seen from [ostensive throat clear] to *ahem* to the highly stylised [ə'hə'həm], or from [dental click dental click] to *tsk tsk* to *tut tut* to 'he *tutted* loudly'. Right down at 'word' level there appears to be a continuum from more direct to less direct evidence: from *showing* to *meaning*.

In a more recent account, Clark and Fox Tree (2002) argue that the interjections *um* and *uh* are indeed part of language, and that they are used to signal that the speaker is initiating a pause. They contrast their view, much as I have done here, with Goffman's view that such sounds are mere 'fillers', sounds 'whereby the speaker, momentarily unable or unwilling to produce the required word or phrase, gives audible evidence that he is engaged in speech-productive labor' (Goffman 1981, p. 293). *Um* and *uh* have 'basic meanings', and are also used to implicate further meanings depending on context.

Clark and Fox Tree base their findings on an exhaustive and insightful study of a large number of corpora, and provide evidence that these two interjections signal different length pauses: *uh* for a short pause, *um* for a longer one. There is much to agree with, and in many ways their account complements, rather then contradicts, the procedural account suggested in this chapter. They advocate an approach that is similar to Kaplan's 'semantics of use' (see p. 79) and propose:

Uh: 'Used to announce the initiation, at *t*('uh') of what is expected to be a minor delay in speaking'
Um: 'Used to announce the initiation, at *t*('uh') of what is expected to be a major delay in speaking'

(Clark and Fox Tree 2002, p. 104)

Notice, however, that Clark and Fox Tree only deal with two interjections. What of the remaining ones? And notice also that even if Clark and Fox Tree are right to conclude that *uh* and *um* are words just like any other, then the claim cannot be carried over to phonologically and prosodically atypical interjections.

Moreover, the account does not mesh with the intuition that there is a natural side to interjections, even fillers such as *uh* and *um*. Clark and Fox Tree point to cross-linguistic variation among such fillers as evidence that they are conventionalised linguistic forms (2002, p. 92), but the degree of variation between, say, English *uh* and *um*, Spanish *eh* and *em*, French *eu* and *euh*, Hebrew *eh* and *e-h*, German *äh* and *ähm* is hardly conclusive, and suggests that the intuition that they may be stylised imitations of natural expressions is worth holding on to.

So to return to the three questions asked in my introduction to this chapter:
(A) What do interjections communicate?
I have argued that interjections communicate attitudinal information, relating to the emotional or mental state of the speaker. In some instances the attitude might be genuinely propositional: say, an attitude of questioning, or regret, or joy, or sadness, directed at an embedded propositional content. However, sometimes the mental state is directed not toward an embedded proposition, but toward a percept or object which is the cause of a feeling or sensation, and sometimes, what is expressed is merely a feeling

or sensation with no apparent cause. In all these cases, what is communicated may be extremely vague: in relevance-theoretic terms it involves only a marginal increase in the *manifestness* of a very wide range of assumptions. Such vagueness is captured by the procedural account: the greater the range of attitudinal concepts activated by the procedure, the greater the vagueness.

(B) How do interjections communicate?

Interjections are partly natural and partly coded. As Goffman suggests, they fall at various points along a continuum between display and language proper; Goffman's own continuum, as I mentioned, appears to be rooted entirely in the notion of coding, with all the items on it having some degree of codification, which increases towards the linguistic end of the spectrum. However, we can recast his intuitions in terms of the showing–meaning$_{NN}$ continuum introduced in the previous chapter. This captures the partly natural, partly coded nature of interjections, because whilst in one way interjections offer fairly direct evidence of the basic layer of information being communicated, in another their partly coded nature makes them *less* direct than completely spontaneous, natural sounds. The continuum also allows us to capture the heterogeneity and marginal linguistic status of the class in general. Seeing interjections in this way, we should not be surprised that the attitudes they communicate are not always propositional. Nor should we be surprised that what they convey is sometimes too nebulous to be paraphrased in determinate conceptual terms: they are *partly* natural responses.

In fact, there is good reason to suppose that some interjections are derived from natural expressions of emotion, and for this reason the continuum may have diachronic implications. The element of stylisation or coding in interjections takes them beyond pure showing; this stylisation is also present in some aspects of language proper, at the meaning end of the continuum. Other interjections are not 'natural' in this sense, but may also be iconic – e.g. *shh*: these also fall somewhere between showing and meaning. With all interjections, the evidence provided for the first layer of information is more direct than with saying, but less direct than with entirely natural behaviours.

I have argued that the coded element of interjections is procedural, and that what is activated by the use of an interjection might be used by the hearer in a variety of ways. When combined with a sentence, it may function in a similar way to other natural phenomena, by encouraging the construction of higher-level explicatures.

In an utterance which consists of *just* an interjection, and expresses no explicit proposition, it might be reasonable to suggest that a hearer can only use the procedural information in deriving implicatures: since the utterance has no encoded logical form, what is communicated falls entirely on the implicit side. In this respect, interjections would pattern with paralinguistic and non-verbal behaviours generally; for while these might help a hearer construct higher-level explicatures when interpreting a linguistic utterance, they cannot contribute to explicit communication when used alone as an ostensive stimulus. However, it might be felt that this account is slightly problematic. Since interjections do have a coded element, it may seem unsatisfactory to suggest that they only contribute to the implicit side of communication. I return to this issue in the next two chapters.

(C) Are interjections part of language?

Since there is a continuum involving different combinations of natural and coded information, we would expect to find expressions occasionally moving along it. In historical terms, when an interjection moves far enough along the continuum, it may become relatively productive ('to wow', 'yucky'), and some of its uses may be properly linguistic (verbs, adjectives etc.). When used as an interjection, though, it seems to retain its independence from the mental grammar.

The answer to this question, then, is no, interjections are not in general a part of language. But the continuum does offer a framework within which they might be seen as existing on the edge of language, integrated to a greater or lesser extent: to use Goffman's expression – *semiwords*. The conclusion that interjections are not part of language is supported by aphasiological evidence of a dissociation between interjections and language proper. Goodglass (1993) demonstrates that interjections such as *ouch* remain within the repertoire of certain grave aphasics. If an individual can retain interjections while losing language, it is hard to see how the former can be viewed as part of the latter.

A question still remains, however. I have argued that interjections, despite their non-linguistic status, might encode procedural information. How plausible is this claim? Having argued that interjections are not linguistic, what light can be shed on interjections by an analysis that has so far been used for purely linguistic items? For further evidence, I turn in the next chapter from the semi-natural to uncontroversially natural phenomena such as facial expressions and spontaneous expressions of emotion. I argue that a sub-set of these behaviours have an inherent signalling function: they are, in effect, *natural codes*.

This has two implications: firstly, it suggests that elements of Grice's natural/non-natural distinction, presented in Chapter 2, are problematic; secondly, it suggests that we need an account of precisely what kind of information these natural codes convey. If the type of coding they involve turns out to be non-translational too, it should provide an additional motivation for pursuing the procedural account of interjections offered above and may also take us a step further toward understanding the processes that underlie the interpretation of natural and non-natural ostensive stimuli.

NOTES

1. Of course, a great deal depends on how you interpret the word 'semantic' here. Wierzbicka (2000), for example, discusses the 'semantics' of human facial expression, and this suggests she has a somewhat broader conception of semantics than the one adopted in this book, where 'semantics' is taken to be the study of *linguistic* meaning. Despite these terminological differences, I think that on the strength of the quotes from Ameka and Wierzbicka (pp. 93–5), I am justified in taking it that according to the conceptualist view, interjections are part of language. See Chapter 5 for discussion of Wierzbicka's conceptualist analysis of facial expressions.

2. See Wierzbicka (1996, pp. 253–7) for her response to Fodor.

3. Fodor's discussion (pp. 287–90) is based on a definition originally presented in Miller (1978, p. 285) and widely used in the 'generative semantics' literature at the time.

4. Fodor maintains this view in Chapter 3 of his 1998 book: *Concepts: Where Cognitive Science Went Wrong*. 'There are practically no defensible examples of definitions; for all the examples we've got, practically all words (/concepts) are undefinable. And of course, if a word (/concept) doesn't have a definition, then its definition can't be its meaning' (1998, p. 45).

5. An anonymous referee of a published version of this chapter (see Wharton 2003a) points out that the non-embeddability of interjections (and 'expressive elements and constructions' generally) is also central to Banfield's (1982) account of represented speech and thought (essentially, *style indirect libre*). (Although it should be noted that Banfield is concerned with constraints on embedding in 'that' clauses (1982, p. 30–2).)

6. This is not to say that all conceptual meaning is truth-conditional meaning. (For further discussion see Wilson and Sperber 1993, Ifantidou 2001.)

7. I hope I am not attributing to Goffman views he never held; as I say above, the difference between the two types of continuum will (hopefully) become clearer in the final chapter. Until then, I would like the reader to bear in mind that since both types of continuum deal with the whole range of communicative phenomena – from display to the fully (linguistically) coded – the similarities between them are worth holding on to.

8. Both this use and Goffman's 'warning' example are 'pragmatically determined variants' according to Wilkins (1992, p. 150*n*.). He says nothing of the use in (18).

9. A dentist might chastise her sloppy assistant by saying 'I am disgusted that this mouthwash is foul', but would not communicate this by uttering (91).

10. I abstract away from a number of dialects in which the word 'up' begins with /U/.

11. There is evidence that Wilkins is confusing the direct quotation use of 'say', with 'say' as in 'state' or 'assert' (i.e. the more technical term I think Wierzbicka has in mind).

12. Clark and Gerrig (1990, p. 780).

13. The 'nucleus' is the final accented syllable in a word-group, which is strongly associated with the main focus of attention within that word-group. The term 'pre-head' is used to describe any unstressed, unaccented syllables which precede the first accented one.

14. All quotes are from the 1998 edition (edited by Paul Ekman – see references).

15. I am grateful to the anonymous referee who pointed out some interesting data relevant to this topic in a comment on a previously published version of this chapter (Wharton 2003a). Cuxac (1999) describes the way in which deaf children raised by non-signing parents spontaneously develop 'iconic' signs, which are then used to communicate by both the children and the parents.

CHAPTER 5

Natural codes

A six-word dictionary for grasshoppers (*Acrididae*):
Signal I: It is fine, life is good;
Signal II: I would like to make love;
Signal III: You are trespassing on my territory;
Signal IV: She's mine (of the female of course);
Signal V: Oh, how nice it would be to make love!
Signal VI: How nice to have made love!
(adapted from Moles 1963, pp. 125–6)

CODES, SIGNS AND SIGNALS

Codes, honeybee-dances and facial expressions

One of Grice's most lasting achievements was to provide an alternative to the code model view of communication. According to the code model, an utterance is a signal which encodes the thought or message a communicator wishes to communicate: in order to retrieve the speaker's 'meaning', all the hearer need do is decode the signal the speaker has provided into an identical thought or message. Construed in this way, linguistic communication works according to broadly the same principles as semaphore, or Morse code.

The assumption that human communication is a matter of coding and decoding was one of the key ideas underlying the semiotic programme (Peirce 1897, 1903, de Saussure 1916/1974, Vygotsky 1962). Indeed, this programme proposed that most aspects of human life – from language, customs and rites, to the media, the expressive arts and science – were best analysed as systems of 'signs'[1], or underlying codes and 'sub-codes' (Eco 1976), which underpin and facilitate every type of human social and cultural interaction.[2] As we have seen (and will continue to see), many approaches to 'meaning' and communication come heavily laden with semiotic baggage.

There are two rather different answers to the question of what constitutes a code. In the strict semiotic sense, a code is a system which pairs signals with messages, enabling two information-processing systems to communicate. 'Zoosemiotician' Thomas Sebeok, aspects of whose account of human communication I discuss below, summarises Shannon and Weaver's classic (1949) model as follows:

> One system, a source, influences another system, a destination, by dispatching alternative signals that are carried in the channel connecting them. The information source is conceived as producing one or more messages which must be transformed, or encoded, by a transmitter into signals which the channel has the capacity to carry; these signals must finally be transformed, or decoded, by a receiver back into messages which can be accepted by the destination. (1972, pp. 12–13)

There is also a broader notion of code, which is often used in the social sciences and is at least as common in ordinary linguistic usage. This treats a code as a collection of rules, regulations or 'conventions': self-perpetuating regularities in the sense of Lewis (1969). Thus, we might speak of a code of law or a code of politeness, the Christian code or a code of ethics.

While the two notions are clearly distinct, they do not have to be seen as mutually exclusive. Indeed, both have been recruited in explanations of human language. On the one hand, language might be seen as a system that pairs signals (sentences) with messages (meanings). On the other, many people (including Lewis, and Grice himself) have sought to analyse language as a set of signalling conventions. Grice, for example, saw aspects of his natural/non-natural distinction reflected in the distinction between natural and conventional 'signs'.

The sense in which I use the word 'code' in this chapter is the first one: the strict semiotic sense. Furthermore, I take language and the other phenomena I shall discuss to be codes only in this sense.

Given the Chomskyan perspective on language adopted in this book, it seems inappropriate to talk about language as a set of socially agreed-upon conventions while committed to the existence of an innate language faculty, or a Universal Grammar, which constrains the form of possible human languages in ways that most humans are unaware of. William Lycan sees major problems with Grice's and Lewis' attempts to characterise literal meaning in terms of a convention to use certain expressions with certain intentions:

most sentences of a language are never tokened at all; since hearers instantly understand novel sentences, this cannot be in virtue of pre-established conventions or expectations directed on those sentences individually. (1991, p. 84)

While many would disagree with any attempt to sever the link between human language and convention, few would advocate talk of conventions when discussing non-human animal communication systems. However, these are certainly codes in the strict semiotic sense. In that regard, the existence of what I will call *natural codes* should be uncontroversial.

Consider honeybees: the honeybee performs a complex dance in order to indicate to its conspecifics the location of a source of nectar (von Frisch 1967). The dance can 'transcend the here and now and . . . make reference to distant temporal and spatial variables in the environment rather than only to the immediate surroundings of the signaller' (Allen and Bekoff 1997, p. 108). The distance of the food source from the hive is indicated by the length of the dance; direction away from the hive is conveyed by the orientation of the 'waggle' component of the dance in relation to the position of the sun. Recent research (Dreller and Kirchner 1993, 1994) has suggested that there may well be an auditory, as well as visual, dimension to the bee's dance.

Would we want to characterise the 'meaning' of the bee dance as meaning$_N$ or meaning$_{NN}$? Recall the tests from Chapter 2: Firstly, is the meaning carried by these dances factive or non-factive? It seems fair to claim that it is factive: from the fact that the honeybee has performed the dance it follows that the nectar is there.[3] Secondly, is there any evidence that the interpretation of the dance relies on the deployment and attribution of intentions? As far as we know, there is none. This suggests that the dances of honeybees mean naturally.

With non-human primates the situation is more complex. Consider the vervet monkey. When it sees a predator – a leopard, an eagle or a snake – it emits a specific alarm call to alert the other monkeys in the group: a loud barking call for leopards; a short, double-syllable cough for eagles; and a 'chutter' sound for snakes. The fact that vervets do not automatically emit an alarm call on seeing a predator (Cheney and Seyfarth 1990) has been cited as evidence that their calls are intended for other vervets (see Dennett 1987). Notice, however, that the vervets' calls would still be factive as long as they were only emitted in the presence of a predator. What would provide stronger evidence that they were not factive would be cases in which vervets call in the absence of the appropriate predator: i.e. cases of deception. And even evidence of deception among vervets (and there is some – see Cheney and Seyfarth 1990) would still not show that intentions play a role in either their deployment or their comprehension. There are a variety of creatures that feign injury (plovers) or play dead (snakes) when confronted by a predator, and it remains unclear whether this amounts to deception of the 'intentional' variety (see Hauser 1996, pp. 586–94 for discussion). Moreover, even if we concede that deception does provide evidence of a form of intentionality, it certainly does not provide evidence of overt intentional communication: expressing and attributing intentions overtly is an entirely different and much more complex phenomenon – requiring much more sophisticated metarepresentational abilities – than covert intentional information transmission.

Still, there is a sense in which it is plainly unsatisfactory to see the meaning of the honeybees' dances as entirely parallel to paradigmatic examples of Gricean meaning$_N$ such as 'those black clouds mean rain'. There is nothing coincidental about the fact that a honeybee's dance 'means' something to another honeybee: the function of the honeybees' dance is precisely to convey information about the location of the nectar. By contrast, it is not the function of black clouds to convey the information that it is going to rain.

This observation is confirmed by applying some of Grice's tests for meaning$_{NN}$ to honeybee-dances. The results, which in the examples in Chapter 2 illustrate so neatly the 'reasonably clear intuitive distinction' Grice sought to demonstrate, are much less clear-cut in (118–119):

> (118) What is meant by the honeybee's dance is that there is nectar at location$_X$.
>
> (119) That honeybee dance means 'nectar-at-location$_X$'.

According to Grice, these paraphrases should be acceptable only if the type of meaning involved is non-natural. However, they seem quite acceptable in the case of honeybee dancing, although as we have seen, other tests suggest that this is a case of natural meaning. Why the tests become unreliable is unclear, but it seems to me that the most plausible explanation is that our intuitions concerning (118–119) simply reflect the fact that the dances of honeybees are inherently communicative: they are coded signals. Honeybees don't 'mean', as in 'intend', but something is surely meant (in one sense of the word) by their dances. In this sense, then, Grice's dichotomy is not exhaustive.

It might be objected at this point that Grice's 1957 paper was not at all concerned with non-human animal communication, and that the above observations are so utterly unrelated to the distinctions he was discussing as to be irrelevant. However, I do think that the complications raised by (118) and (119) have implications beyond the rather trivial observation that Grice's natural/non-natural dichotomy fails to accommodate the dances of honeybees. My reason is that the very same complications arise if we apply the tests to certain human behaviours. In particular, they arise with a subset of human behaviours that appear at first sight to be natural signs: facial expressions such as smiles, for example. It seems to follow that these behaviours have something in common with the honeybee dance, and moreover, something that is not easily accommodated by Grice's distinction between natural and non-natural meaning.

Consider again the three natural behaviours discussed in Chapter 2: (involuntary) smiles, crying and shivering. These are natural indications, respectively, that a person is happy (or at least not a threat), distressed and unhappy, or cold. Applying Grice's tests again, we see that the 'meaning' carried in all three cases is factive: a spontaneous smile naturally indicates that a person is happy at that moment; crying naturally indicates that a person is distressed or unhappy; a spontaneous shiver naturally indicates that a person is cold. This is borne out in (120–122) below:

> (120) The fact that he is smiling means he is happy.
> (121) The fact that he is crying means he is unhappy or distressed.
> (122) The fact that he is shivering means he is cold.

As we have already seen, the question of whether the attribution of intentions can be said to play a role in the interpretation of human natural behaviours is complicated by the fact that a species capable of monitoring its own (involuntary) production of such behaviours might also be capable of deliberately showing them in order to reveal an informative intention; furthermore, such behaviours might be exaggerated, developed or faked in communicative situations.

However, there is clearly a sense in which at least some of the messages carried by these natural behaviours are derivable without reference to the intentions of the person responsible for the behaviour: that is why we regard them as natural. It doesn't contradict my earlier position – that the deliberate showing of natural behaviours is an intentional act – to acknowledge the fact that natural behaviours convey information whether or not they are deliberately shown.

Despite the apparent 'naturalness' of all three behaviours, two in particular behave differently when Grice's tests are applied. The tests that yield interesting results when applied to honeybee-dances yield similar results when applied to smiling, but not when applied to shivering. That is, (123–124) are acceptable in a way that (125–126) certainly, are not.

> (123) His smile means 'I am happy'.
> (124) What was meant by that smile was that he is happy.
> (125) *His shiver means 'I am cold'.
> (126) *What was meant by that shiver was that he is cold.[4]

Remember again that I am talking about spontaneous smiles here. It could be argued that the intuitions that the tests rely on are confused by the fact that a fake smile can be used to mean non-naturally. I do not think this is the case. Consider a situation in which someone uses a fake, forced smile to mean$_{NN}$ something like 'I am not amused' (that slightly sardonic smile, which is often accompanied by a monotone ha-ha). In this case, (127–128) would be appropriate paraphrases:

> (127) Her (sardonic) smile means 'I am not amused'.
> (128) What was meant by her (sardonic) smile was that she was not amused.

And it seems clear that (127–128) are acceptable in a manner distinct from this, a manner more closely akin to the cases in (125–126).

Just as the dances of honeybees 'mean' in a slightly different way than black clouds, so a spontaneous smile 'means' in a different way than crying or shivering. In both cases, I will argue, the reason lies in the adaptive functions of the behaviours themselves.

Signs and signals

In deciding which instances of information transmission in the non-human animal world are to be regarded as properly communicative and which are not, Marc Hauser (1996, pp. 9–10) relies on an ethological distinction between *signals* and *signs*.[5] Signals are those behaviours that convey information and have been 'moulded by natural selection to do so' (Seeley 1989, p. 547). They have been 'designed to serve a particular [i.e. communicative] function' (Hauser 1996, p. 6). Philosopher of biology Robert Brandon (2005) explains this evolutionary sense of 'function' as follows:

And so if an *adaptation* is a product of the process of evolution by natural selection . . . then these things are adaptations. And so, I claim, they have functions. Their *functions* are their effects that make them adaptively superior to the trait variants with which they compete. (2005, see references)

The adaptive function of a behaviour is the effect which is historically responsible for the reproduction and propagation of that behaviour within a species (Millikan 1984, Origgi and Sperber 2000, Sperber 2007). Signals have a communicative function.[6]

Signs, on the other hand, do not have a communicative function, although they may be highly informative to an observer with enough background knowledge. Hauser provides two illustrations. First, he conjectures that forest monkeys, whose predators are chimpanzees, might use the presence of chimpanzee nests to avoid chimpanzees, and hence predation. However, the function of chimpanzee nests is not to inform forest monkeys of the presence of predators. In that case, chimpanzee nests are signs, but not signals, of the presence of predators. Second, predatory species such as lions and pythons might leave traces of their presence in the dusty soils they regularly travel. Certain prey species might learn that particular traces are associated with danger, whereas other traces are not. However, the traces cannot be said to have a signalling function, since they would continue to be produced whether or not they were observed. This sign–signal distinction is an ethological version of the distinction I alluded to in the introduction to this book, between indicators the function of which is to indicate, and those which have no such function.[7]

It is tempting to regard the ethological notion of a sign and Gricean natural meaning as entirely parallel: the nests indicate the presence of chimpanzees whether or not the forest monkeys take them that way; the tracks of lions and pythons indicate danger to certain prey species (if they are noticed). We can equally imagine these signs being interpreted by a human observer in the field, just as those black clouds are interpreted as meaning rain. However, as we have seen, it would be a mistake to draw such a parallel. The Gricean natural/non-natural distinction does not fully accommodate the distinction between signs and signals, because there are natural signals as well as natural signs.

However, the ethological signal–sign distinction does capture the difference between smiles and shivers noted above. Smiling, in fact, evolved as a signalling activity (van Hooff 1972, Fridlund 1994, Ekman 1999): its function is to indicate, or carry 'meaning'. The function of the shiver response, on the other hand, is to generate heat by rapid muscle movement. In ethological terms, smiles are signals, and shivers are signs:[8] natural behaviours, then, do not all work in the same way.

In the ethological literature, non-human animal communication systems are often referred to as codes (see Bradbury and Vehrencamp 1998, pp. 456–7 for one example). By the same token, the evolutionary link between signal and message in behaviours such as smiles suggests they too are best analysed as coded behaviours, governed by natural codes.[9] On this approach, one difference between the interpretation of smiles and shivers is while shivers (and other natural signs) would be interpreted in purely inferential terms, the interpretation of smiles and other spontaneous expressions of emotion would involve an element of the type of automatic decoding so typical of non-human animal communication.

In fact, although Shannon and Weaver's model was developed with engineering problems in mind, it seems a highly appropriate blueprint on which to model animal communication systems. The stimulus produced by the transmitting animal is the signal that encodes the message. The cognitive or affective state activated in the receiving animal is the decoded message. Of course, the encoding and decoding processes that govern the honeybees' dance – and non-human animal communication generally – are automatic. They occur without either the sending or receiving animal consciously recognising that the signal means anything, and are similar to perceptual processes in that respect.

In one sense, human natural codes are the same. We read facial expressions automatically, for example: they activate in us a particular mental or emotional state that correlates with the mental or emotional state – surprise, delight, anger, fear – of the communicator. In another sense, however, they are not. We not only read facial expressions automatically, but can reflect on their content, and, what is more, know that others can reflect on them too.[10] As a result, when natural coded behaviours are put to use in ostensive–inferential communication, the automatic decoding processes that govern their interpretation are supplemented by other equally specialised automatic – but this time inferential – processes that govern the interpretation of ostensive stimuli.

The work of Paul Ekman (1989, 1992, 1994, 1999) suggests that there is a whole range of spontaneous facial expressions that have evolved in humans to reflect a signaller's internal state, and might thus be analysed as natural codes; 'these expressions have been selected and refined over the course of evolution for their role in social communication' (Ekman 1999, p. 51). Ekman's claims that these expressions reflect the existence of underlying basic, universal human emotions, which are to some degree at least biologically inherited, have been criticised (see Fridlund 1994, Russell 1994). Fridlund, for example, denies that facial expressions are reliably correlated with underlying emotions, and stresses their social and manipulative communicative functions. Among the evidence he presents in support of this position are data from experiments on 'audience effects' in human smiling (Kraut and Johnson 1979). In these experiments, researchers monitored the smiles of people involved in various activities – ten-pin bowling, spectating at an ice-hockey match – and found that, in general, people smile more for the benefit of others than themselves. During a ten-pin bowling match, for example, 'subjects rarely smiled while facing the pins, but did so frequently when they pivoted to face their friends in the waiting pit' (Fridlund 1994, p. 153).[11] In a more recent set of observation-based experiments, Fernandez-Dols and Ruiz-Belda (1995) noticed that gold medallists in the swimming events at the Barcelona Olympics smiled a great deal when receiving their medals, and considerably less during the rest of the ceremony; this despite the fact that their 'happiness' at having won the medal was presumably stable throughout the whole period.

Hauser (1996, pp. 495–6) argues that the two approaches are not mutually exclusive: 'the debate actually confuses two levels of analysis. Whereas Ekman's work has generally focused on the mechanisms underlying facial expression (e.g. changes in physiology, brain state), Fridlund has considered the function of facial expression.' One thing is clear, however. Despite the disagreement over the putative role of actual emotions in the production of facial expressions, smiles and other spontaneous expressions of emotion differ crucially from facial reflexes such as eye-blinks or sneezes, or other non-communicative behaviours such as shivers: their function is to signal.

WHAT TYPE OF INFORMATION IS CONVEYED BY NATURAL CODES?

Sebeok's analogue codes and Peircean indices

Thomas Sebeok (1972) investigates the different types of coding humans might use in linguistic communication, and draws a distinction between digital and analogue coding. This distinction was intended to capture the differences between what he termed 'rational' and 'emotional' (1972, p. 10) human communicative content. Since human facial expression and other natural signals (e.g. tones of voice) appear to be primarily indicators of 'emotional' or 'affective' content, it is worth investigating how much Sebeok's distinction can tell us about human natural codes.

The analogue–digital distinction exists in a variety of guises.[12] Essentially, it is a distinction between codes or systems in which the repertoire of signals is either – in the case of analogue codes – graded, blended or continuous, or – in the case of digital codes – discrete or discontinuous. In a graded system the boundaries between the signals cannot be demarcated, whereas within a digital one they can.

As noted in Chapter 3, an analogue system works as follows. There is a variable of some physical quantity: the pressure of a certain gas in a certain system, for example. This variable is related to another variable, say the needle in a pressure gauge, in such a way that the variations in the former are in a proportional relationship to the variations in the latter. As the pressure in the system rises, so the needle on the pressure gauge rises; as the pressure falls, the needle falls. The movement of the needle is analogous to the rising and falling of the pressure, and the continuous fluctuation of pressure is reflected in the continuous movement of the needle.

In a digital system, the continuous flow of data – in our example the continuous fluctuation of pressure – is represented in terms of discontinuous or discrete units. To achieve this, the rise and fall of pressure has to be reanalysed into these units by some converter-mechanism: in short, the data are not measured, but counted. Rather than assessing the pressure by means of checking the quivering needle, the engineer consults a numerical (i.e. digital) read-out.

The principal advantage of digital over analogue systems is one of accuracy: digitally encoded information is 'all-or-none', while analogue information is 'more-or-less'. Before recent technological advances in the recording industry, studios employed analogue recording systems using magnetic tape. The sound-waves produced by voices or instruments were converted by microphones into analogous waves of electrical voltage, and stored on magnetic tape as further sets of analogous waveforms, this time magnetic.[13] In modern computerised recording, the sound-waves are still converted by a microphone into voltage, but the electrical waves are re-analysed by a converter into discrete, digital (in this case binary) units. Again, accuracy is the principal advantage: the sound is a cleaner, supposedly more faithful representation of the original. Furthermore, the digital representation allows much wider scope for modifying the original signal, i.e. altering the tuning or timing of individual notes (or part of individual notes).

However, just as words have their limitations, so do digital recordings. Modern – entirely digital – computerised recording studios employ state-of-the-art software to recreate the characteristic inaccuracies of analogue recording systems. Principally, this involves the reintroduction of extraneous 'noise' or 'hiss' to the sometimes antiseptically clean digital recording. They are thus (hopefully) imbued with some of the warmth and immediacy of older analogue recordings. This is one, but only one, of the reasons the old songs always sound best . . .

It is often taken to be one of the defining characteristics of human language that it is a digital, combinatorial system. The discrete units – words – can be combined into larger structures which have properties that are distinct from the properties of the elements, and are determined by the way in which the elements are combined according to recursive rules. This accounts for the fact that language is not only 'discrete' but also 'infinite',[14] and that the speakers of a language are capable of producing (and understanding) an unlimited number of distinct combinations, expressing an infinite range of meanings. In an analogue system there are no discrete elements to rearrange: the only way to distinguish a wide range of 'meanings' is to discriminate ever tinier and more subtle differences in the continuous signal.

As we have seen in examples used throughout this book, the potential of analogue and digital codes to complement each other is nowhere more clearly illustrated than by human linguistic communication. Consider as further examples (129–132)) below:

(129) Lily: Has John arrived?
(130) Jack: John has arrived.
(131) Lily: Has John arrived?
(132) Jack: (smiling happily, in a pleased tone of voice) John has arrived.

By fronting the auxiliary in (129), Lily forms an interrogative. One aspect of the difference in intended meaning between her utterance in (129) and Jack's in (130) is indicated by placing the discrete units of language in a different order. Now consider Jack's replies in (130) and (132). In terms of linguistically encoded content, these utterances are identical. However, there are differences in the way they would be understood. Crucially, this difference in meaning is not achieved by digital means – Jack's smile and affective tone of voice in (132) are in some sort of proportional or analogous relationship to the amount of affect he intends to convey: Lily reads his emotional state more in the manner of the engineer consulting the analogue pressure gauge than the digital read-out. Depending on the breadth of his smile and the tone he uses, she might decide he is mildly pleased, quite happy or absolutely thrilled. Furthermore, the extent to which Lily can interpret these degrees of happiness depends not on her knowledge of any digital code, but on her ability to discriminate subtle (sometimes tiny) variations in his tone of voice, much as the engineer studies the quivering needle; we have already seen how such behaviours help speakers and hearers calibrate the appropriate sense of a given concept and feed into the relevance-theoretic comprehension heuristic.

Of course, Jack might have tried to convey this information digitally, by saying 'I am mildly pleased that John has arrived' or 'I am quite happy that John has arrived' or 'I am absolutely thrilled that John has arrived.' Notice, however, that utterances such as these, produced in an entirely neutral tone of voice, would sound extremely strange, and it is unlikely Jack would be taken to have communicated his feelings very effectively.

The distinguishing features of human language listed by Hockett (1959) included not only discreteness but arbitrariness – de Saussure's (1916/1974) 'l'arbitraire du signe'. Arbitrariness was also a defining feature of Charles S. Peirce's notion of a symbol, which he distinguished from icons and indices. An iconic representation is one in which the relationship between the object and the representation is one of resemblance: a picture of a dog running is iconic of a state of affairs in which a dog is running. An icon 'has no dynamical connection with the object it represents; it simply happens that its qualities resemble those of the object' (quoted in Feibelman (1960, pp. 91–2)). An indexical representation is one in which the relationship is physically (or temporally) proportional or causal – the analogue pressure gauge described above is a good example: 'it is physically connected with its object . . . they make an organic pair' (ibid.). A symbolic representation is one in which the relationship between the signifier and the signified is arbitrary or conventional-ised[15] – the word 'dog' meaning dog, for instance. 'The symbol is connected with its object by virtue of the . . . symbol-using mind, without which no such connection would exist' (ibid.).

Sebeok attempts to draw parallels between Peirce's distinctions and the analogue–digital distinction. In his view, 'the most interesting thing about the property of arbitrariness is this: that it is a logical consequence of digital structuring in the code' (1972, p. 25); in effect, it doesn't matter what the discrete units into which the continuous data are reanalysed are, or what they are called: discreteness alone suffices to make the code arbitrary. Assuming that

Sebeok is right to treat 'digital' as lining up with 'arbitrary',[16] it is worth considering whether analogue encoding lines up with the Peircean notions of icons and indices, and to what extent this might help with the characterisation of natural codes.

It seems to me that analogue coding corresponds most closely to the notion of an index. In the first place, it seem intuitively clear that a picture of a dog running is not a coded representation of a dog, but simply a likeness; so Peirce's icons are not coded at all. Moreover, the causal and temporal links underlying Peircean indices parallel the kind of proportional relationship mentioned earlier as characteristic of analogue coding. These parallels are noted in a number of previous approaches. Jakobson and Halle (1956, p. 11) describe the expressive features of speech as 'physiognomic indices'. In an analysis with strong echoes of Peirce's discussion of indices, Bolinger (1983) describes intonation generally as exhibiting properties of 'dynamic indicators' (though the passage is entitled 'The inherent iconicism of intonation').[17]

The concepts of analogue codes and indices are certainly useful in approaching natural codes. The majority of human natural codes do indeed appear to work along analogue lines, and the concept of an analogue code at least takes us some way towards understanding how natural signals are interpreted. However, in order to say what kind of information human natural codes convey, we must go further and explain what analogicity and indexicality mean in cognitive terms. Moreover, there are several problems with the claim that natural codes in general operate solely on the basis of indices and analogue coding.

Firstly, semiotic accounts rely entirely on a code model of communication. However, a coding–decoding model is as inappropriate for analysing the intention-driven communicative interaction of humans as it is appropriate for analysing the dances of honeybees. Furthermore, semiotic approaches aim to provide a 'general' theory of communication in terms of coding and decoding, but as we have seen, there are two distinct types of communication: coded and inferential. Whilst it is true that in human communication these two types interact, neither should be regarded as more general than the other, since neither is essential for communication to take place: pure coding–decoding requires no inference, and inferential communication can take place in the absence of any code.

Secondly, the idea that natural codes must always be analogue is too restrictive. While the honeybee's dance functions on largely analogue lines, the codes used by vervet monkeys (Cheney and Seyfarth 1990) and certain birds (Okanoya 2002) – clearly natural codes in terms of the distinctions presented here – exploit discrete, digital signals. Thirdly, the idea that naturally coded signals are indices is not restrictive enough: although in a sense all 'natural' indicators are indices (the etymological similarity is not accidental), it is not the case that all indices are coded signals. Recall the example of the mechanical system. The amount a particular pipe bulges is also in an indexical relationship to the rising of the pressure; the engineer might indeed choose to assess the pressure system by checking the bulging seams. However, it is not the function of the bulging pipe to convey the information it does. It is a sign, not a signal.

The semiotic notions of analogue codes and indices are useful tools. They describe properties that human natural codes appear to have, properties which should be accommodated in a satisfactory analysis. However, something more is required in order to say what the information conveyed by a human natural code looks like in cognitive terms.

The conceptualist approach to facial expression

Wierzbicka (2000) also discusses the 'natural' properties of facial expression, and comes to similar conclusions to those I have drawn above regarding their inherent indexicality: 'those (if any) which are universally interpretable may have a "natural", i.e. iconic or indexical basis' (2000, p. 178); 'the basis for decoding lies either in similarity . . . or in co-occurrence' (2000, p. 156). Another point of agreement between us is that the 'naturalness' of certain human facial expressions does not preclude their being coded signals.[18]

However, there are several points on which we disagree. Wierzbicka begins, for example, by presenting arguments against what
she calls the 'Ekmanian paradigm', briefly discussed in the previous
section. She claims that the time is ripe for a new direction in the
study of human facial expression: 'A fresh breeze is blowing in
the field . . . and there is a widespread sense that the time has come
for a change of paradigm' (2000, p. 147). She lists ten basic assumptions fundamental to this new direction.[19] These assumptions lay the
foundations for what is essentially her main claim, that the coded
element of human facial expressions can be analysed in terms of the
same 'Natural Semantic Metalanguage' we saw in the previous
chapter being used to analyse interjections. Below is another example,
this time applied to the adjective 'courageous':

> (133) courageous
> X is courageous. —
> > X can do very good things when other people can't
> > because when other people think something like this:
> > > I don't want bad things to happen to me
> > X thinks something like this:
> > > it is good if I do this
> > > it is bad if I don't do it
> > > I want to do it because of this
> > this is good

Having extended the approach from adjectives to interjections,
Wierzbicka now applies it to facial expressions as in (134) below:

> (134) raising of the eyebrows
> > I know something now
> > I want to know more (about this)
> > I'm thinking now

In Chapter 4, I outlined what I regard as major problems with the
conceptualist approach to interjections; the same arguments carry
over to the proposed analysis of facial expressions. Of the numerous
issues that Wierzbicka's account raises, I would like to focus primarily on three main problems that I see with the approach. The
first is a general problem concerning the model of communication

it presupposes; the second is a more specific problem concerning the tools of the analysis itself; and the third concerns a specific area of confusion that seems to be present in the account.

The first, general problem recalls a point I have made at various places in this book against the semiotic program generally. The conceptualist approach to human communication appears to be based on just the kind of coding–decoding model which I am rejecting. Wierzbicka (1996, p. 8) talks of 'the meanings encoded by natural language', and largely ignores the kind of insights concerning the link between intention and meaning.

Consider the following comment on facial expressions: 'Human faces send messages, and these messages must be *decodable*' (2000, p. 178 – my emphasis). Whilst I agree that there may be a coded element to some facial expressions, I do not agree that for a facial expression to communicate something it necessarily has to encode anything at all. If I catch your eye during a boring presentation and look ostensively toward the door, I might communicate to you that I want to leave, but there is no reason to think that communication is achieved by my encoding anything. If I deliberately and openly let you see my spontaneous shiver, I am not encoding the conceptual structure 'I feel cold', any more than if I point to a cloud I am encoding the conceptual structure 'it's going to rain'. Information does not have to be encoded to be successfully communicated, and this is overlooked by NSM-based accounts. What is required are clear criteria by which we can decide whether a behaviour is coded or not (we have seen that evolutionary function is a key motivating factor behind Hauser's distinction between signs and signals), and if there is a coded element to a particular facial expression, we need to consider how this might be exploited in intentional-inferential communication.

The second, more specific, disagreement with Wierzbicka's account relates to the conceptual structures themselves, and how adequately they capture what is conveyed by natural codes. Facial expressions are marvellously versatile, and Wierzbicka is careful to include among her fundamental premises the assumption that 'semantic analyses (whether of verbal utterances or facial expressions) must distinguish between the context-independent invariant and its contextual interpretations' (2000, p. 151). There is a semantics/pragmatics distinction underlying conceptualist analyses, and she clearly explains that what is being characterised by these conceptual structures is what is encoded, rather than what is communicated.

Consider the eyebrow flash (or spontaneous raising of the eyebrows). This is one candidate for a universal facial expression[20] (though see Ekman 1999) that has been much discussed. In a seminal paper, Eibl-Eibesfeldt describes some of its various functions as follows:

We mentioned several situations in which eyebrow flashes of approximately the same stereotyped form occur: greeting, flirting, approving (yes), seeking (asking) confirmation, thanking and emphasising a statement (calling for attention) . . . Finally, we raise the eyebrows during disapproval, indignation, and when we look at a person in an admonishing way. (1972, p. 300)

Eibl-Eibesfeldt concludes that if there is a common denominator in all these functions it is that the eyebrow flash is a kind of 'attention' signal: 'the basic common denominator is a "yes" to social contact, and it is used either for requesting such a contact or for approving a request for such contact' (1972, p. 300). Wierzbicka comments that her structure is not inconsistent with interpretations relying on the technical expression 'attentional activity' (2000, p. 168).[21]

But it is hard to see how it is not. The gap between the conceptual structure in (134) and the uses described above is so vast that it seems implausible to suggest that they are all pragmatically derived variants of this context-independent structure. Furthermore, these rigid conceptual structures do not begin to capture the 'natural', i.e. 'iconic or indexical basis' Wierzbicka (I think quite rightly) attributes to facial expressions.[22] Conceptualist structures are entirely digital constructs and as we have seen, in the case of human natural codes, what is needed is some way of accounting for their analogicity.

Interestingly, although Wierzbicka remarks on the natural – or analogue/indexical – side of facial expressions, she chooses not to contrast it with the digital nature of language. On the contrary, one of her fundamental assumptions is that we should stress the similarities between the two: 'facial expressions can convey meaning comparable to verbal utterances' (2000, p. 151). This brings me to the third problem. In a sense, of course, it is true that the meanings conveyed by facial expressions are comparable to those conveyed by verbal utterances. You give me a gift, and I take it from you, smiling broadly. The meaning I convey to you might be paraphrased as 'Tim is delighted with the gift.' If I choose to convey this information to you by saying 'I am delighted with the gift', the meaning conveyed is certainly comparable. Notice, however, that it is only comparable if we take 'the meaning conveyed' by verbal utterances and facial expressions to be what they communicate, rather than what they encode. Given that there are two alternative models of communication, we cannot assume without argument that smiles and language work in exactly the same way (and if they do, then we may as well say that when I point at a cloud, I am encoding 'it's going to rain').

This element of confusion is unavoidable within the conceptualist framework. The root of the problem lies in the code model foundations upon which it is built. Inference is relegated to a minor role, an 'add-on' to a human communicative process that is seen as fundamentally a matter of coding and decoding. From this it follows that pretty much the only way to communicate a concept is to encode it, which in turn leads to a position on the relationship between language and thought that I also believe to be problematic.

One problem that Wierzbicka raises with work in the 'Ekmanian paradigm' is that Ekman's use of English words to label the emotions signalled by universal facial expressions results in an 'ethnocentric' view of their interpretation: since the English word 'anger' differs in meaning to the Italian word 'rabbia', the former cannot be said to name a 'universal category of human experience' (1994, p. 439). Actually, it is clear from Ekman's work that his claim that universal facial expressions reflect the existence of universal emotions does not in any way presuppose a one-to-one mapping between these emotions and the words used to label them in different languages: in fact, he is quite explicit on this point: 'we never claimed that facial expressions evolved to represent specific verbal labels. Nor did we say that the meaning of an expression is limited to or best captured by a single, specific word' (1994, p. 270).[23]

However, what Wierzbicka's criticisms also reveal is a Whorfian, relativistic view of the relationship between language and thought: 'speakers of other languages . . . think about human experience in terms of other non-matching conceptual categories . . . they do not read human faces as "angry" . . . but rather interpret them in terms of their own language-specific categories' (2000, p. 149). On this view, even if thought doesn't take place in words, it is still shaped by language; what runs through our mind when we think is the concepts that constitute the meanings of words. From this, it follows that most concepts are lexicalised. If they were not, the efficiency of thought processes, as well as communication, would be seriously compromised. Unlexicalised concepts would not even be entertainable, let alone communicable.

By contrast, the relevance-theoretic inferential view of communication suggests that much of our conceptual repertoire is not lexicalised. Individuals are capable of acquiring an enormous amount of information each day, and it seems implausible to claim that this information can only be stored in the mind if it can be encoded in a public language. Sperber and Wilson argue that, in fact, 'there are many times more concepts in our minds than words in our language' (1998, p. 196), and that in everyday thought we regularly entertain unlexicalised concepts. We also regularly communicate them; for as we have seen, a lexicalised concept is typically inferentially enriched during the comprehension process to yield the (slightly or substantially different) sense that the speaker is taken to have conveyed. This provides another argument against the position taken in NSM analyses, for it suggests not only that humans engage in non-verbal, non-coded communication, but also that words are routinely used to communicate ad hoc concepts which differ from the precise conceptual content they encode (see discussion of narrowing and loosening in Chapter 3).

I think these three arguments suggest that conceptualist accounts of facial expressions are at least implausible. According to these accounts, as in semiotic approaches generally, communication is seen largely as a coding–decoding affair; the proposed conceptual structures do not reflect the analogicity of human natural codes; and the relationship assumed to hold between language and thought leads to inevitable blurring of the distinction between what is encoded and what is communicated. So far, however, other than arguing that natural codes should be integrated within an inferential model, I have offered no alternative to the conceptually encoded structures that Wierzbicka proposes. Does such an alternative exist? We saw in the last chapter that it does: the information encoded in natural codes may not be conceptual at all.

CONCEPTS, PROCEDURES AND META-PROCEDURES

According to the account of interjections offered in Chapter 4, the information encoded by an interjection merely encourages the hearer to construct a higher-level explicature by embedding the proposition expressed under a speech-act or propositional-attitude description. In some cases, as we saw, there is no propositional embedding and the interjection is used to convey the speaker's reaction to a suddenly perceived object or event. The information encoded by the interjection is non-translational, where 'non-translational' meaning corresponds closely to the relevance-theoretic notion of procedural meaning.

Whether this non-translational account of interjections amounts to a properly procedural account remains to be seen. Firstly, the kind of information conveyed by non-translational encoding differs somewhat from the kind of information described as procedural in earlier accounts (Blakemore 1987, 2002). Indeed, although in Chapters 3 and 4 I presented my translational/non-translational distinction as a way of introducing the conceptual–procedural distinction, it was originally conceived of as a way of broadening the notion of procedural meaning (see Wharton 2001).

Recall from Chapter 4 that in much work on the conceptual–procedural distinction, procedural information is characterised in terms of instructions to the hearer. The notion of procedural information as a (potentially) vague indicator of an individual's mental state seems to contrast with this view. I believe that the broader view is worth exploring, however; indeed, a broader notion of procedural meaning seems to be required in any case to accommodate the full spectrum of linguistic devices currently seen as encoding procedural information (see discussion in Chapter 4).

Secondly, procedural analyses have only so far been proposed for properly linguistic items, whereas, as I remarked in Chapter 4, the linguistic status of interjections is marginal at best. If interjections are not part of language – and I believe that I have given good reasons why they are not – then some justification is needed for treating them as encoding the same type of procedural meaning as properly linguistic items. Notice, however, that much depends on whether we take the notions of procedural and non-translational encoding to be co-extensive, or whether we treat procedural encoding as a sub-type of non-translational encoding.

I will argue below that non-translational encoding does not apply exclusively to linguistic expressions. And in that case, interjections can be seen as encoding non-translational information whether or not they are part of language.

This point has clear implications for the analysis of natural codes. Natural signals such as facial expressions and affective tones of voice are certainly not part of a linguistic code. However, they are coded signals, and I want to argue that they too are best analysed along non-translational lines. Consider examples (135–136):

(135) Mary: (in a regretful tone of voice) I don't feel well.
(136) Jack: (smiling happily, in a pleased tone of voice) John has arrived.

On the analysis I envisage, hearers of these two utterances would be encouraged by the speaker's affective tone of voice or facial expression to form the higher-level explicatures in (137–138)) below:

(137) Mary regrets [that she doesn't feel well]
(138) Jack is happy [that John has arrived]

Notice that the higher-level conceptual representation in which the basic propositional content is embedded is activated non-translationally, on a similar pattern to the one I used to analyse interjections ((138), for example, is almost entirely parallel to example (88) from Chapter 4). My proposal, then, is that the coded element in all manner of natural behaviours – Mary's tone of voice in (135), Jack's smile in (136), vocal and facial gestures generally – are best analysed as encoding non-translational information.

There are a variety of arguments to support this claim. Like interjections (and many properly linguistic expressions that are seen as encoding procedural information), facial expressions do not contribute to the truth-conditional content of utterances. If Jack says to Lily 'I am happy', she might reply 'That's not true, you aren't happy.' If he simply looks at her and smiles, she would be unlikely to make the same accusation. Parallel arguments apply to crying and shivering (and to other non-verbal behaviours for that matter).[24]

Similarly, facial expressions do not combine to form larger 'phrases'. It is true, of course, that smiles, eyebrow flashes, frowns and gestures are 'discrete' signals which are clearly distinguishable from each other. However, they are not digital in the sense that they combine in different ways to form different meanings. This point is easily demonstrated by comparing the putative discreteness of the natural manual gestures that accompany speech, for example, with the genuinely compositional component 'gestures' of sign-language proper, which are true digital systems. This observation is found in the work of Adam Kendon (1988), who sees gestures in general as falling on a continuum from gesticulation – the spontaneous movements that accompany speech, through pantomimes and emblems – culturally regulated gestures, to signing proper. It is also reflected in Ekman's (1999) own distinctions among non-verbal signals.

The communicative content of facial expressions, like the communicative content of interjections, is also vague and context-dependent. This is captured in my analysis by claiming that what is activated (non-translationally) by the coded element of the facial expression is a cognitive state created by the (non-translational) triggering of a variety of emotion or attitudinal concepts, which then further constrain inferential processes.

Finally, the non-translational quality of the information conveyed by natural codes provides the key to capturing their analogicity. Natural codes do not encode digital conceptual structures, but rather point the audience in a certain direction. The resulting mental state is calibrated by the breadth of the smile, or the gravity of the frown. Of course, unlike the engineer assessing the pressure in the system, we do not read the quivering needle consciously. As discussed earlier, the interpretation is carried out by an automatic decoding process, rather like the honeybee calculating the distance between the hive and the nectar according to the intensity of the communicating honeybee's dance.

So what do natural behaviours indicate? An ostensive stimulus is typically a composite of natural (and semi-natural) as well as linguistic signals. When a natural behaviour is used as part of an utterance, it provides information about the speaker's intended meaning, and contributes to the construction of higher-level conceptual representations – in relevance-theoretic terms higher-level explicatures. Typically, the information conveyed is attitudinal or emotional.

This question is harder to answer when a natural behaviour is used alone as an ostensive stimulus. In Chapter 4, I suggested that when an interjection is used on its own, the ostensive stimulus has no explicit content and contributes only to implicatures – as is the case with non-verbal communication generally. I also mentioned that I thought there was something inherently problematic in this, and am reluctant to carry it over to my analysis of natural codes. Not only does it seem wrong to see naturally coded information as contributing only to implicatures, but within relevance theory, implicit content is, by definition, derived wholly via inference.

One solution would be to see naturally coded signals as contributing to explicit communication in their own right, whether or not they are accompanied by a linguistic signal. Another might be to introduce an explicit/implicit distinction for natural behaviours; thus, we might speak of both the explicit natural content and the implicit natural content of a communicative act. However, this proposal requires further thought and development, not least because in the current relevance-theoretic picture, ostensively used paralinguistic behaviours encourage the formation of higher-level explicatures whether or not they are coded signals (because of the coded linguistic material elsewhere in the utterance). One suggestion might be to appeal to the notion of degrees of explicitness and argue that natural signals, when used alongside linguistic utterances, make the higher-level explicatures more explicit than they would otherwise have been (because of the extra element of non-linguistic coding involved).

With regard to how natural behaviours are interpreted, I have argued that those natural behaviours that have the function of indicating are best analysed as governed by natural codes. On one level, they work in a similar way to animal communication systems. However, they can also be used by humans in overt intentional communication. This is not surprising, given that humans are aware of their involuntary responses in a way that animals are not (see Allen and Bekoff 1997 for discussion). As we saw in Chapter 2, natural behaviours are routinely deliberately shown to provide evidence about the communicator's informative intention. If some natural behaviours are coded signals, we would predict that they are interpreted by specialised, perhaps dedicated, neural machinery, and this prediction appears to be borne out. Both non-human primates and humans have neural mechanisms dedicated both to recognising faces and to processing facial expressions (Gazzaniga and Smiley 1991).

The term 'natural' covers a wide range of behaviours, and the distinctions presented here allow us to be more precise about what they have in common and where they differ. An utterance may sometimes be accompanied by ostensively used non-coded behaviours – a spontaneous shiver, for example. This may well be picked out by the relevance-based comprehension heuristic and used in constructing a hypothesis about the speaker's meaning. The same utterance may also be accompanied by other (non-ostensive) natural behaviours, which are inherently non-communicative (they are signs, as opposed to signals). These signs may still be picked up and processed by the audience's cognitive system, but, crucially, they will not be used in forming a hypothesis about the communicator's intended meaning. For if a natural behaviour is not used ostensively, or recognised as ostensive, it will not be picked up by the relevance-based comprehension heuristic.[25]

The information carried by these natural codes is non-translational in the sense described above. I have argued that it activates particular internal states which are analogous to the intensity of the signal. The decoding process is automatic, and leads to the non-translational activation of a range of attitudinal and emotion concepts, which constrain the inferential search for relevance. For the fact that a communicator has made it mutually manifest that there is an informative intention behind the deliberately shown behaviour means that the automatic decoding processes will be supplemented by other – perhaps equally specialised – processes that govern the search for the communicator's meaning.

There is a whole range of behaviours that encode non-translational information, from linguistic devices such as discourse connectives, pronouns and mood indicators on the one side, to interjections and coded facial expressions on the other; the approach might also be carried over to some of the prosodic aspects of speech. Following a suggestion from Dan Sperber (personal communication), the linguistic expressions might be described as encoding *meta-procedures*, which manage the accessibility or activation levels of the regular relevance-oriented procedures for perception, memory retrieval or inference.

Human speech, of course, exhibits a wide range of such features; speakers use stress, rhythm and pitch change in varying degrees to help convey their intended meaning. In many respects these too seem to fall at various points along the showing–meaning$_{NN}$ continuum. In languages such as Thai and Burmese, for example, pitch change is phonologically contrastive, and can be used to distinguish one lexical item from another. Even in languages with no lexical tone, intonation can be used to indicate interrogative mood. At the other extreme of the continuum – the showing end – we find affective tone of voice, which is universally accepted as non-linguistic; so Jack might infer that Lily is happy or sad, relaxed or tense, engaged or bored solely on the basis of the voice quality she uses. Other suprasegmental features of English, such as sentence stress and intonation, might be seen as falling at various points between the two extremes.

Carlos Gussenhoven (2002) presents evidence that some aspects of intonation are arbitrary and properly linguistic. However, he claims that other, universal, aspects of intonation are governed by 'biological codes' which correlate various aspects of prosody (e.g. high and low pitch, the presence or absence of articulatory effort) with what he describes as 'universal paralinguistic meanings' (2002, p. 47). Gussenhoven also notes that the linguistic aspects of intonation are digital, while the 'paralinguistic' aspects are analogue. This suggests that the study of prosody might yield exciting evidence concerning the existence of natural prosodic codes. In the next chapter I turn in more detail to Gussenhoven's proposals, and will also explore the possibility that in addition to natural codes, there may also be non-natural, non-linguistic ones.[26]

NOTES

1. I have put the word 'sign' in inverted commas here because according to the sign–signal distinction discussed in the introduction, and elaborated further upon in this chapter, what the semioticians refer to as a 'sign' I will refer to as a 'signal'.

2. See Sperber 1996 for an alternative, naturalistic approach to culture, within which the socio-cultural domain is partly analysed in terms of an inferential model of cognition and communication.

3. The factivity test does not work entirely smoothly in the case of bee-dancing. If the bee makes a mistake – as I'm sure bees occasionally do – then there is at least a sense in which the dance *still* meant 'nectar-at-location *x*'. The law-like link between, for example, black clouds and rain (from which it follows that if it doesn't rain then those black clouds can't be said to have meant rain any more) appears not to hold in the case of bee-dancing. However, if we are trying to fit bee-dancing into Grice's natural/non-natural dichotomy, I don't see that we have any choice but to view it as an example of *natural* meaning, since, as I go on to say, it seems fairly clear that bees do not possess the kind of higher-order intentional ability that would enable them to *mean* *non*-naturally (in the sense described by Grice). Such abilities are a prerequisite for the existence of non-natural meaning.

4. In the paper on which this chapter is based (Wharton 2003b) I applied the tests to the example of crying for the sake of completeness:

?His tears mean 'I am distressed or unhappy'.
?What was meant by his tears was that he is distressed or unhappy.

There are two reasons why discussion of crying is relegated to a footnote here: firstly, as I indicated in Wharton 2003b, I'm not as convinced by the results of the tests as applied to crying as I am by the results as applied to shivering and smiling; secondly, the dissociation between crying and tears makes it hard to say with any authority exactly what the adaptive value of crying is (as distinct from shedding tears). See Darwin 1872/1998, pp. 164–75, also Hauser 1996, p. 469 for discussion.

5. Hauser draws a further distinction between 'signs' and '*cues*'. The latter are communicative phenomena such as sexual ornaments and warning colours, which are permanently 'on'. The distinction has no bearing on the discussion in hand, but it is worth noting that these too are natural indicators.

6. The use of the notion of 'function' in evolutionary theory is not without its complications. For a neat summary of these see Brandon 2005. For a critical view of the 'functional' approach see Davies 1996.

7. This kind of exploitation of natural signs may well turn out to be highly adaptive. Indeed, it may be selected for and lead to the development of a kind of evolved cognitive reflex which correlates a particular feature of the environment with a certain reaction in a given organism. An example is the 'fear-reflex' most people feel when confronted by a large snake. Though I'm anticipating the discussion below to a certain extent, we would not want to call the relationship between the sign (the snake) and the reflex (fear) a 'code', since it is not the function of the *snake* to indicate that there is a snake in the vicinity; rather, it is the function of the *reflex* to keep the person safe.

8. Herb Clark (1994) makes a similar distinction, between the 'meaning' conveyed by natural signs – which he calls *symptoms* – and 'the meaning of certain deliberate human acts . . . *signals*'. There are interesting parallels between some of the issues discussed in this chapter and those covered in Clark's book. However, the 'sign–signal' distinction introduced above and Clark's 'symptom–signal' distinction are not co-extensive. Firstly, the sign–signal distinction *I* make is a distinction *within* the category of phenomena that Clark calls symptoms (see Fig. 2.1 on page 34 – the top node might be labelled *symptoms*). Secondly, as I have tried to show, many spontaneous, involuntary 'symptoms' that do not have an indicating function – that are *signs* in my terms – can still be deliberately *shown* in an

act of intentional communication. Although we might describe these as 'deliberate human acts', I don't think Clark would want to call them signals (in his terms).

9. Von Frisch (1967) proposes that the honeybee's dance has its evolutionary origins in primitive bees' pre-flight *intention* movements ('intention' in the ethological sense of reliably correlated with a certain course of action or behaviour – see note 2, chapter 1) which became refined, stylised and stereotyped over time. Signals, then, may well have their evolutionary origins in signs, and this seems to be a fairly standard ethological account of one of the ways in which coded behaviours (signals) might evolve from what started out as Gricean natural meaning. In Chapter 8, I present an account of how intentions might have played a role in the evolution from meaning$_N$ to meaning$_{NN}$ (as distinct from purely coded 'meaning').

10. Sperber (2001) notes that the fact that humans can reflect on the content of signals leads to differences in not only *how* humans communicate, but *why*. (I return to this in my final chapter.)

11. Robert Provine, in his book *Laughter: A Scientific Investigation* remarks that there is 'a strong association between smiling and social motivation and an erratic association with emotional experience' (2000, p. 45).

12. Hauser (1996, p. 54) credits the cognitive ethologist Peter Marler with being the first to apply the distinction to communicative systems.

13. The technical term is *magnetic flux density*.

14. To paraphrase Chomsky's (1988, p. 169) famous terminology.

15. In an insightful review of the paper which forms the foundation for this chapter (Wharton 2003b) Seth Sharpless pointed out I had misunderstood Peirce's notion of 'convention'. He was absolutely right: Peirce's description of a convention as 'depending upon habit (acquired or inborn)' [1895](CP 2.297) goes well beyond the idea of a convention as mere 'tacit agreement', the term I had originally used to describe Peirce's view.

16. Are there, for example, arbitrary *analogue* codes?

17. An anonymous reviewer of the paper from which this chapter is adapted (Wharton 2001) objected to my claim that there is a close correlation between analogue encoding and indexicality. S/he argued that there need be no proportional relationship between the sign and the object in cases of indexicality, whereas in cases of analogue encoding there must. It may well be that the two notions do not match up exactly, but I hope that my comparison is at least germane, given that the causal and temporal links between sign and object in cases of indexicality do parallel those at the heart of analogue codes.

18. I am reluctant to call iconic representations coded signals. However, this is not to suggest that they might not somehow become coded.

19. I have chosen not to list all ten assumptions here, since I intend to focus on Wierzbicka's Natural Semantic Metalanguage (NSM). However, I would briefly like to comment on two: (a) 'a semantic analysis of the human face . . . requires the identification of minimal meaningful units of facial behaviour'; (b) 'we need to distinguish the "semantics of human faces" from the "psychology of human faces"' (2000, p. 150). Regarding (a), rather than analysing 'eyebrow flashes', 'smiles' or 'frowns' Wierzbicka proposes that we should be analysing *'moving one's eyebrows upwards, doing something with one's mouth in such a way as the corners of one's mouth move upwards, moving one's eyebrows so that they will be (relatively) close together' (ibid.)*. She claims that these units can shed more light on the meaning of facial expression than, for example, Ekman's own sophisticated 'Facial Action Coding System' (FACS) (Ekman and Rosenberg 1997): 'if we are interested in *meaning* we must adopt the perspective of "the ordinary people" who want to communicate with one another, and not that of a physicist working in a laboratory' (Wierzbicka 2000, p. 159). I think Hauser's point about two different levels of analysis (see p. 116 above) is relevant here. FACS is a highly sophisticated, rigorous system for measuring facial movements in great detail: it is concerned neither with the recognition of facial expressions, nor directly with their communicative content. That being said, one alternative to Wierzbicka's proposal that the FACS should be replaced with her 'minimally meaningful units' (and one which I think I favour) would be to try and *integrate* Ekman's exhaustive work on facial expression into an account of their 'meaning'. It may, after all, prove more fruitful in the long term to build bridges between the two disciplines. This point carries over to assumption (b). Surely a plausible theoretical account of the semantics of facial expressions should *mesh* with theories of the psychology of facial expressions, not replace them.

20. And to my mind a prime candidate for a natural code.

21. Though she does not endorse the use of the expression. Wierzbicka is actually referring to a paragraph from Smith and Scott (1997, p. 239), and takes issue with their terminology: 'The problem with this approach is that it is not quite clear what precisely is meant by "attentional activity", and since this expression does not belong to ordinary language we can't use our ordinary linguistic intuitions to interpret what exactly the writers really have in mind' (2000, p. 164).

22. Allowing for my previous reservations over iconic representations being coded.

23. Wierzbicka's response to this quote from Ekman is to quote him again, this time from his rebuttal of Russell's critique (1994, p. 276): 'Russell complained that we and others had pre-selected our expressions [i.e. emotion labels, A.W.].' However, the word 'expressions' in this quote does *not* refer to 'emotion labels', as Wierzbicka indicates, but instead to photographs of the facial expressions themselves. (This is not to deny that Russell does in fact take issue with the 'forced-choice format' of Ekman's experiments – see Ekman (1994, pp. 273–5) for his response.)

24. Nods and headshakes made in response to linguistic utterances may be an exception. If I ask you if you *really* don't want another glass of wine, and in response you nod, I think I may well be justified in saying 'That's not true; you *do* want one.' On a different note, see Darwin (1872) for a proposal that behaviours such as head shakes have their roots in entirely natural behaviours, perhaps along the lines of ethological intention movements (Darwin's proposals are also discussed in Eibl-Eibesfeldt (1972, p. 305)).

25. Assuming it can make such subtle distinctions. There might, for example, be a situation where the procedure is triggered 'accidentally', as it were.

26. For reasons discussed in the introduction, I prefer 'natural code' to 'biological code' (language is a biological code too).

CHAPTER 6

Prosody and gesture

'How do I stop people getting angry?' I asked. In effect, this meant how could I stop them from having any vocal variation whatsoever? I also wanted to know why they made faces and insisted on making their voices dance even though they could see it upset me. 'How do other people learn these things?' I wanted to know. 'They learn them naturally,' Dr Marek said.

(Williams 1994, p. 103)

PROSODY

Commentators on the effects of prosody on comprehension are broadly agreed that prosodic inputs to the comprehension process range from the 'natural' (e.g. an angry, friendly or agitated tone of voice) to the properly linguistic (e.g. lexical stress or lexical tone). Some propose that prosodic effects range along a continuum from 'more to less linguistic', or from 'natural' to language-specific (Gussenhoven 2002, Pell 2002), but typically, accounts of prosody tend to favour either a predominantly natural view or a predominantly linguistic one.

Dwight Bolinger (1983) takes the view that we would be better to focus more on the natural side of intonation, for example. Indeed his analysis might be seen as an attempt to characterise intonation as one kind of natural code, focusing as he does on the interaction between intonation and other 'natural' components of the complex communicative stimulus:

If intonation is part of a gestural complex whose primitive and still surviving function is – however elaborated and refined – the signalling of emotions and their degrees of intensity, then there should be many obvious ways in which visible and audible gesture are coupled to produce similar and reinforcing effects. This kind of working parallel is easiest to demonstrate with exclamations. An ah! of surprise, with a high fall in pitch, is paralleled by a high fall on the part of the eyebrows . . . A similar coupling of pitch and head movement can be seen in the normal production of a conciliatory and acquiescent utterance such as 'I will' with the accent at the lowest pitch – we call this a bow when it involves the head, but the intonation bows at the same time. (1983, p. 98)

However, he is keen to stress that behaviours may be more or less natural and that even though we may feel some aspects of intonation to be properly linguistic, there still a sense in which they have their roots in natural behaviours:

Intonation . . . assists grammar – in some instances may be indispensable to it – but it is not ultimately grammatical . . . If here and there it has entered the realm of the arbitrary, it has taken the precaution of blazing a trail back to where it came from. (1983, pp. 106–8)

If, as Bolinger appears to suggest, there is a diachronic dimension to the continuum between display and language, then this continuum may turn out to be a useful tool with which to follow the trail back from arbitrary expressions to their natural origins.

Halliday's (1967) approach to intonation was based on his proposal that a theory of grammar should be rich enough to accommodate intonation patterns. In other words, the idea was to broaden the notion of 'language' to incorporate all prosody. Other linguistically oriented accounts of prosody can be found in Gussenhoven (2004), Ladd (1978, 1996), Tench (1996) and Steedman (2000). Indeed, even the 'pragmatic' account proposed by Hirschberg and Ward (1995) seems to depend on the Gricean notion of conventional implicature, itself – as was shown in Chapter 3 – a *semantic* notion (see Clark 2007).

Nonetheless, it is widely accepted that prosodic inputs to the comprehension process range from the 'natural' to the properly linguistic. It is also widely accepted that the effects of prosody are highly context-dependent: prosodic information interacts with information from many other sources during the comprehension process, and the same prosodic input may have different effects on different occasions. A further point of general agreement is that prosody typically creates impressions, conveys information about emotions or attitudes, or alters the salience of linguistically possible interpretations rather than expressing full propositions or concepts in its own right. An adequate account of prosody should accommodate these points.

Intuitively, one of the main functions of prosody is to guide the utterance interpretation process by altering the salience of possible interpretations of utterances (including possible disambiguations, reference resolutions, contextual assumptions, implicatures, speech-act descriptions, etc.). What relevance theory adds to this intuitive description is the idea that the salience of interpretations can be affected not only by altering processing effort but also by manipulating expected cognitive effects.

As I suggested in Chapter 3, many words encode quite general concepts, which must be fine-tuned by the hearer in inferring the occasion-specific sense intended by the speaker. Prosody is one of the many tools that can be used to guide the direction that this fine-tuning takes. Consider example (33) from Chapter 3, but this time uttered in a neutral tone, and repeated below as (139):

(139) Lily: I'm disappointed.

There are many degrees and shades of disappointment that Lily might have intended to convey, each of which would be relevant in a different way. While the neutral (or 'expected') prosody in this example would cause the hearer least phonological processing effort, it would give him little guidance on the type of cognitive effects he was expected to derive. By contrast, any departure from neutral (or 'expected') prosody would increase the hearer's phonological processing effort, but would thereby encourage him to look for extra (or different) effects. Which effects should he derive? According to the relevance-theoretic comprehension heuristic, he should follow a path of least effort, deriving whatever effects are made most accessible in the circumstances by the type of prosodic input used, and stopping when he has enough effects to justify the extra effort caused by the departure from neutral (or 'expected') prosody. Thus, the utterance of (139) in an angry tone of voice (as in (33)), with a wide pitch range and increased stress on 'disappointed', would indicate a degree and type of disappointment that would warrant the derivation of a particular range of positive cognitive effects via the automatic working of the relevance-theoretic comprehension heuristic.

Another idea often found in the literature on prosody (see, for example, Grice 1989, pp. 50–51) is that contrastive stress, like pointing or ostensive gazing, is a natural highlighting device, used to draw attention to a particular constituent in an utterance. This idea is explored from a relevance-theoretic perspective in Sperber and Wilson (1986/95: Chapter 4, Section 5). Here is a brief illustration of how this approach might work.

It follows from the Communicative Principle of Relevance that if two stress patterns differ in the amounts of processing effort required, the costlier pattern should be used more sparingly, and only in order to create extra, or different, effects. Thus, compare the effects on reference assignment of the neutral stress pattern in (140) and the costlier contrastive pattern in (141):

> (140) Federer played Nadal and he **béat** him
> (141) Federer played Nadal and **hé** beat **hím**.

A hearer using the relevance-theoretic comprehension heuristic in interpreting the second conjunct in (140) should follow a path of least effort in assigning reference, and interpret 'he' as referring to the Federer and 'him' to Nadal (an assignment made easily accessible by syntactic parallelism, on the one hand, and encyclopaedic knowledge, on the other). Use of the costlier contrastive pattern in (141) should divert him from this otherwise preferred interpretation towards the alternative, less accessible interpretation on which 'he' refers to Nadal and 'him' to Federer. On this account, contrastive stress is a 'natural' highlighting device which achieves its effects via the automatic working of the relevance-theoretic comprehension heuristic.[1]

A possible objection to this 'natural highlighting' account is that the acceptability of contrastive stress patterns seems to vary across languages (for an excellent survey of cross-linguistic variations and objections to 'highlighting' accounts of both contrastive and focal stress, see Ladd (1996, chapter 5). However, as noted in Sperber and Wilson (1986/95, pp. 213–4), this objection is not particularly compelling unless it can be shown that variations in contrastive stress are not explainable in terms of processing effort. For instance, French has a relatively flat intonation contour and a strongly preferred final placement of focal stress. English, on the other hand, has a relatively variable intonation contour and freer placement of focal stress. We might therefore expect the use of non-final contrastive stress in French to be more disruptive, hence costlier in terms of processing effort, and the use of alternative syntactic means (e.g. clefting) to be preferred.

Carlos Gussenhoven and his colleagues (e.g. Gussenhoven, 2002; Chen and Gussenhoven, 2003) have recently argued that the interpretation of prosody is governed by both biological and properly linguistic codes. An example of such a biological code is the Effort Code, which is seen as linking the amount of energy expended in speech production to a range of interpretive effects. Thus, an increase in effort may lead to increased articulatory precision, creating an impression of 'helpfulness', or 'obligingness'; or it may result in a wider pitch range, creating an impression of 'forcefulness' or 'certainty' or conveying affective meanings such as 'agitation' or 'surprise'. This account covers some of the same ground as my suggestion above that variations in the pitch range of (139) ('I'm disappointed') might achieve their effects by 'natural' pragmatic means. The relation between Gussenhoven's biological codes and the notions of natural sign and natural signal discussed above is an interesting one which I explore below.

The most obvious difference between the two approaches is that the type of effort appealed to in Gussenhoven's Effort code is speaker's effort, whereas the type of effort appealed to in the relevance-theoretic account is hearer's effort. Although both speaker's effort and hearer's effort affect the comprehension process, and both will ultimately need to be taken into account, they do not always vary in the same direction.[2] For instance, articulating clearly may cost the speaker some extra effort in production but is likely to diminish the hearer's overall effort in understanding (as the extra effort a writer puts into redrafting a text may save the reader some effort in comprehension). Is clear articulation a natural signal, interpreted (as Gussenhoven suggests) by an innately determined code? I would suggest that it might be better treated as a natural sign of the speaker's desire to help the speaker understand, which is interpreted via inference rather than decoding. Like other natural prosodic signs, it may be exploited in ostensive–inferential communication, as long as the fact that the speaker is making a special effort is salient enough, and relevant enough, to attract attention and be picked up by the relevance-theoretic comprehension heuristic.[3]

Notice, now, that the hearer's overall processing effort is analysable into several different components which may vary in opposite directions. For instance, the addition of an extra word or phrase may increase the hearer's linguistic processing effort but diminish the effort of memory and inference required to access a context and derive the intended cognitive effects, so that the utterance is less costly overall. By the same token, a departure from normal (or 'expected') pitch range may increase the hearer's phonological processing effort but reduce the effort of memory and inference required to arrive at the intended interpretation. Thus, the effort factor appealed to in the account of how pitch range affects the interpretation of (139) above is a special case of a more general factor that affects the pragmatic interpretation of every utterance. If this general account in terms of hearer's processing effort turned out to be descriptively adequate, it might be preferable on theoretical simplicity grounds to Gussenhoven's special-purpose account.

Gussenhoven and Chen (2003) show that the same pitch is interpreted as indicating different degrees of surprise by hearers from different languages. I do not think it follows (although of course it may be true) that such variations in pitch range have become grammaticalised, or properly linguistic. As suggested above, the same prosodic input may be more or less costly for hearers to process depending on what prosodic contours they are normally exposed to, and this may affect the comprehension process by 'natural' rather than coded means, via the automatic working of the comprehension heuristic. Variations in phonological processing effort may therefore need to be taken into account in deciding between a 'natural' and a properly linguistic treatment.

WHAT DOES PROSODY ENCODE?

At first sight, the claim that prosodic signals are naturally or linguistically coded might be seen as incompatible with the observation that they often create a diffuse impression or communicate a wide array of weak implicatures rather than conveying a determinate message. The same problem arose in Chapter 4 in dealing with the coded side of interjections. A code is standardly seen as a set of rules or principles pairing signals with determinate messages. How is it possible to maintain both that prosodic signals are coded and that what they convey may be no more than a wide array of weak non-propositional effects?

In this section, I would like to pursue the idea introduced in earlier chapters that the coded aspects of prosodic signals can be analysed in terms of a distinction between translational and non-translational or conceptual and procedural encoding. This idea has already been applied to different aspects of prosody by Vandepitte (1989), Clark and Lindsey (1990), House (1990, 2006), Escandell-Vidal (1998, 2002), Imai (1998) and Fretheim (2002) (see also König, 1991). To recap: if linguistic communication typically involves a combination of decoding and inference, then linguistic signals might be expected to encode information of two distinct types. First, there is regular conceptual encoding, where a word (e.g. 'cat') encodes a concept (e.g. CAT) which figures as a constituent of the logical form of sentences in which that word occurs. Second, we might expect to find a form of procedural encoding, where a word (or other linguistic expression) encodes information specifically geared to guiding the hearer during the inferential phase of comprehension. The function of such 'procedural' expressions would be to facilitate the identification of the speaker's meaning by narrowing the search space for inferential comprehension, increasing the salience of some hypotheses and eliminating others, thus reducing the overall effort required. I argue that both 'natural' and properly linguistic prosodic signals are procedural in this sense. Properly linguistic prosodic signals (e.g. lexical stress, lexical tone and fully grammaticalised aspects of sentence stress and intonation) might be analysed on similar lines, as facilitating the retrieval of certain types of syntactic, semantic or conceptual representation. Thus, the notion of procedural encoding applies straightforwardly to properly linguistic prosodic elements.

As we saw in Chapter 4, the function of an interjection such as *wow* might be to facilitate the retrieval of a range of speech-act or propositional-attitude descriptions associated with expressions of surprise or delight, which might be narrowed in context by information derived from prosody, facial expressions, background assumptions, discourse context, etc., and contribute to the speaker's meaning in the regular way, by falling under the relevance-theoretic comprehension heuristic.

In Chapter 5 I suggested that natural signals such as smiles and other spontaneous facial expressions should also be analysed as encoding procedural rather than conceptual information. On this approach, the function of facial expressions of surprise or delight would be to facilitate the retrieval of similar propositional-attitude descriptions to those activated by the interjection *wow*. This approach makes it possible, on the one hand, to capture the fact that natural signals, interjections and properly linguistic signals such as mood indicators or discourse particles all have a coded element, and on the other, to explain why what they communicate can sometimes be so nebulous, contextually shaded and hard to pin down in conceptual terms. It also makes it relatively easy to see how a given expression (e.g. an interjection) might move along the continuum from 'non-linguistic' to 'partly linguistic' to 'linguistic' without radically altering the type of information it conveys.

A spoken utterance is typically a composite of linguistic signals, natural signals and natural signs which interact in complex ways to yield a hypothesis about the speaker's meaning. As we saw from the quote above, Bolinger (who treats both facial expressions and intonation as signalling systems) endorses the view that prosody is a largely natural phenomenon.

Dolan *et al.* (2001) provide experimental evidence of cross-modal priming between facial expression and emotional tone of voice: for instance, a facial expression of fear was more quickly identified by experimental participants when accompanied by a frightened tone of voice. I look at the implications of some of these experiments in more detail in the next chapter. Meanwhile, I note that affective tones of voice, like affective facial expressions, appear to be better analysed as natural signals rather than natural signs, and hence, on the approach developed in this section, as conveying information by procedural encoding rather than inference alone.

Ladd (1996), Gussenhoven (2002, 2004) and Wichmann (2002) suggest that there is considerable cross-linguistic variation in the way these 'universal paralinguistic meanings' are realised, to a point where they may become heavily stereotyped or even fully grammaticalised and part of language proper. All of this might be seen as militating against the more natural view of prosody suggested by the Bolinger quote above.

My aim is not to come down on one side or other of this debate, but merely to draw attention to two possibilities that have not been so widely considered in the literature: first, it is possible not all prosodic inputs are coded at all; and second, the fact that prosodic patterns and their interpretations become stereotyped or vary from language to language does not provide conclusive evidence that they are linguistically coded.

Commenting on an earlier version of the paper on which this chapter is based, Dan Sperber pointed out to Deirdre Wilson and myself that some prosodic variation may be neither natural nor properly linguistic but *cultural* (Sperber, 1996; Origgi and Sperber, 2000; Sperber 2007). Examples of cultural prosodic inputs might include the stylised intonation patterns or 'calling contours' discussed by Ladd (1978). To the extent that such inputs have a signalling function, they might be seen as falling into the category of what – as we shall see in the next section – David McNeill calls 'emblems'. The framework proposed here also allows us to explore the parallels between various non-verbal behaviours. Using evidence from Danish, Scheuer (1995, p. 446) suggests that 'culture-specific mechanisms' might also be at work in the stabilisation of a range of prosodic phenomena. Just as emblems stabilise in a culture, so might certain prosodic patterns. Scheuer goes on to suggest that 'in order to provide hypotheses about prosody in spoken Danish . . . it seems to be necessary to go . . . beyond the scope of universal pragmatics, i.e. pragmatics based on universal principles' (1994, p. 46). Whilst it is true that relevance theorists have so far been more concerned with psychological rather than sociological factors in communication, this has been more a matter of expedience than of principle. Sperber and Wilson (1997) discuss a variety of possible interactions between cognitive and sociological factors in communication; the theoretical notion of a non-natural, non-linguistic code may be useful in exploring these areas of interaction in more detail. In the next section, I apply it to the analysis of gesture.

Of course, in the case of prosody the task of teasing out the various factors involved in these different distinctions is far from easy. At the end of a careful attempt to motivate a distinction between linguistic and paralinguistic intonation, Ladd (1996:283) concludes: 'But I concede that we must stop short of drawing a clear boundary between language and paralanguage. For now that question remains open.' Whilst leaving the question open, Ladd's fine-grained autosegmental analyses of intonational phonology shed considerable light on which parts of prosody are universal, and which are language-specific. I hope the distinctions drawn in this book will make some contribution to this debate.

The suggestion, then, is that natural and properly linguistic prosodic signals might encode procedural information of a type shared by borderline linguistic expressions such as interjections and properly linguistic expressions such as mood indicators, discourse connectives and discourse particles. This makes it possible to see how there could be a continuum of cases between purely natural prosodic signals and non-natural ones, whether cultural or properly linguistic. Studies of animal communication (e.g. Hauser, 1996) suggest, moreover, that natural signals often evolve from natural signs, perhaps via an intermediate stage of stylisation, providing a continuum of cases along the way. While many empirical questions remain about where the borderlines between these different categories should be drawn, and how items move from one category to another, the theoretical position is fairly clear. Prosodic inputs come in several broad types, which convey information in different ways, all of which may be exploited in ostensive–inferential communication.

GESTURE

Whilst the notion of a cultural, as opposed to linguistic, code has played little role in analyses of prosody, it is widely used in the study of gesture. As we saw in Chapter 1, communicators have a whole range of gestures at their disposal. At one extreme, there are the entirely natural, non-linguistic gesticulations that are spontaneously used to accompany speech. At the other, there is sign language proper, which is fully linguistic and non-natural in Grice's sense. Between these two extremes lie a range of gestures which, whilst clearly *non-linguistic*, are equally clearly non-natural in Grice's sense. This is the category of culture-specific 'emblems', exemplified in Fig. 1.1 from Chapter 1, repeated over as Fig. 6.1.

At the beginning of his 1992 book on gesture, David McNeill describes the various types of gesture in terms of a framework that is becoming something of a theme in this book. Gesture, he argues, is best seen as ranging along a *continuum* between natural display and language proper. The continuum McNeill presents is based on one originally shown in Adam Kendon (1988). 'Kendon's continuum' is reproduced (from McNeill 1992, p. 37) in Fig. 6.2. There are clear parallels with both the verbal and prosodic continua discussed earlier in the book.

The idea is that as we move from left to right on the continuum, the gestures become less natural, take on more 'language-like' properties and depend less and less on the co-presence of language itself. Those movements classified as 'gesticulation' in the continuum are the spontaneous movements of the arms and hands that accompany speech: what McNeill describes as 'the unwitting accompaniments of speech' (1992, p. 72); McNeill (1992) is devoted entirely to these movements, of which communicators are either unaware or, at best, only marginally aware.

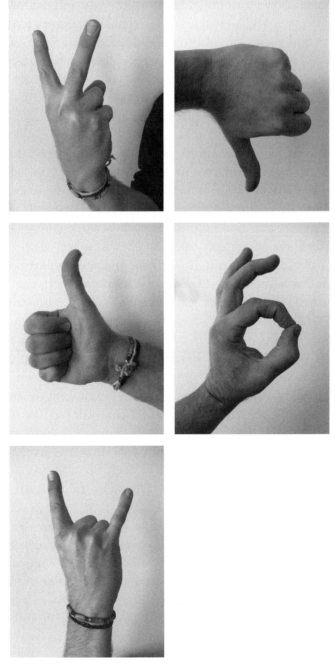

Fig. 6.1

Kendon's Continuum

Gesticulation → Language-like gestures → Pantomimes → Emblems → Sign Languages

Fig. 6.2 Kendon's Continuum

'Language-like' gestures are similar to gesticulations but are 'integrated' into a linguistic string in the sense that they must occur at a certain point and contribute to the interpretation of the string as a whole; so Jack might utter 'the dental examination was OK, but when he started [*gesture to represent drilling*] it was agony'. 'Pantomimes' are those movements that depict objects or actions; accompanying speech is no longer obligatory – 'there may be either silence or just inarticulate onomatopoetic [*sic*] sound effects ("whoops!", "click!" etc.)'. 'Emblems'[4] are those cultural-dependent symbolic gestures used to convey a wide range of both positive and negative meanings: the British 'thumbs up' signal and the two-fingered insult are two examples (see McNeill 1992, pp. 57–9 for an overview). Finally, Sign Languages are, of course, languages proper, with their own syntactic, semantic and phonological rules.

The study of gesture has a long history. Kendon (2004) devotes four chapters to an exhaustive and insightful survey, in which he traces the study of gesture from early Classical Antiquity through to the modern day. The work of Kendon and his colleagues has led to huge advances in the cataloguing and description of gestures, and our understanding of how gesture and language interact from a behavioural point of view has been greatly increased.

However, the pragmatics of gestural communication takes very much a second place to the description of the gestures themselves, and as in the case in work on prosody, distinctions that are important from a cognitive pragmatics point of view are not explored in as much detail as they might be. In some respects, there is even an element of inconsistency when pragmatic notions are introduced. For instance, Kendon (2004, p. 15) writes that the term gesture 'is a label for actions that have *manifest deliberate expressiveness*' (my italics). Yet the work of David McNeill is concerned almost entirely with 'gestures' that are largely not under a communicator's conscious control, and therefore – presumably – do not have manifest deliberate expressiveness. A better understanding of the role of gestures in non-verbal communication may be gained by making use of the idea that some 'natural' gestures (in particular, 'gesticulations') are deliberately shown, even if they have not been intentionally produced.

In general, the ostensive use of gestures in overt intentional communication is not really acknowledged. Kendon (1992, p. 328) writes:

If I clear my throat in the midst of an utterance this is not treated as part of what I am 'saying'. If I uncross my legs, take a drag on my cigarette or sip my coffee while another is speaking, such actions are not attended to by other participants as if they are contributions to the conversation. Overt acts of attention to activities of this sort are generally not made at all. Whereas spoken utterances and bodily movements, if perceived as gestures, are regarded as vehicles of explicitly intended messages, directly relevant to the business of the conversation, other aspects of behaviour are not regarded in this light.

But clearing the throat and uncrossing the legs can certainly contribute to the overtly intended speaker's meaning, just as bodily movement (and indeed, aspects of the spoken utterance) might convey information accidentally, or even be intended by the 'speaker' to convey information covertly. The distinctions drawn in Chapter 2, and applied to prosody earlier in this chapter, carry across to the study of gesture.

Kendon's comments reflect the fact that in accounts of human non-verbal communication generally, discussion of the role of intentions takes a very secondary role. In his account of facial expression Alan Fridlund (1994) abstracts away from it entirely: 'I have circumvented these "levels of intentionality" issues in the interests of space, and use intentionality in a purely functionalist sense' (p. 146). Kendon himself writes:

[T]he judgement of an action's intentionality is a matter of how it appears to others and not a matter of some *mysterious process by which the intention or intentions themselves that may guide the action may be known.* (2003, p. 15 – my emphasis)

The aim of a cognitive pragmatic framework such as relevance theory is very much to engage with these 'mysterious' processes and examine the role they play. Indeed, one of the main achievements of Grice's work was to begin the demystification of such processes.

Building on other distinctions drawn by McNeill, Marianne Gullberg (1998) articulates further dimensions that can be used in the analysis of gesture, which she presents in a framework she describes as 'Kendon's expanded continuum'. Kendon himself sees these further dimensions as motivating not so much the expansion of a single continuum as the introduction of a number of separate, albeit related, continua, and McNeill appears to concur. In more recent work (2000), he suggests that Kendon's continuum might be sub-divided into four distinct continua along which 'gesticulation', 'pantomime', 'emblems' and 'sign language' might be contrasted in four different ways: firstly, how the meaning of the gesture in question depends on the accompaniment of speech; secondly, the extent to which the gesture can be said to possess linguistic properties; thirdly, the extent to which these properties are conventionalised; and fourthly and finally, what McNeill describes as the 'character of the semiosis': McNeill contrasts the 'global-synthetic' properties of how gesticulation encodes meaning, with the 'segmented-analytic' properties of linguistic encoding.

However, as with Gussenhoven's notion of a biological code, even gestures at the natural end of the continuum (or continua) are analysed as at least partly coded. I suggest that gesticulations are better treated as natural *signs* of the speaker's desire to help the speaker understand, and are interpreted via inference rather than decoding. Like prosodic inputs, gestures come in several broad types. They convey information in different ways, all of which may be exploited in ostensive–inferential communication as long as the fact that the speaker is making a special effort is salient enough, and relevant enough, to attract attention and be picked up by the relevance-theoretic comprehension heuristic. I return to this issue in the Chapter 8, when I look more closely at the relationship between the showing–meaning continuum presented in Chapter 3, and the other continua discussed in this and previous chapters.

NOTES

1. In example (140), both syntactic parallelism and encyclopaedic knowledge facilitate the interpretation of 'he' as referring to Federer. In comments on a version of the paper upon which this chapter is based, Neil Smith reminded Deirdre Wilson and myself that syntactic parallelism and encyclopaedic knowledge do not always point in the same direction. Thus, in 'John telephoned Bill and he refused to **spéak** to him', it may be manifest to both speaker and hearer on the basis of encyclopaedic knowledge that, despite the syntactic parallelism, the most obvious candidate referent for 'he' is the direct object 'Bill' rather than the subject 'John'. We claim that in this case, use of a contrastive stress pattern should divert the hearer towards the otherwise less obvious interpretation on which John refused to speak to Bill. More generally, what counts as the 'path of least effort' is determined by a variety of linguistic and non-linguistic factors.

2. Speaker's effort is factored into the presumption of optimal relevance through a reference to the speaker's *abilities and preferences* (for discussion, see Sperber and Wilson, 1995: Section 3.3).

3. As Dan Sperber has pointed out, there is also a third possibility: some forms of clear articulation (e.g. in certain traditions of theatrical speech, or stylised emphasis of final consonants in utterances such as the comedy catchphrase 'I don't believe iT') may be neither purely natural nor properly linguistic but cultural. See below for discussion.

4. McNeill (p. 56) credits Ekman and Friesen (1969) with an earlier use of the term 'emblem'; Ekman and Friesen (1969) credit Efron (1941) with the original. McNeill also refers to them as 'Italianate' gestures: the term 'recognizes the richness of this type of gesture in Italy' (p. 56, fn. 3).

CHAPTER 7

Mindreaders

The words 'know' and 'feel' were like 'it' and 'of' and 'by' – you couldn't see them or touch them, so the meaning wasn't significant. People cannot show you a 'know' and you cannot see what a 'feel' looks like.

(Williams 1994, p. 95)

OTHER MINDS

According to the broadly Gricean account of communication adopted throughout this book, linguistic communication is an intelligent, intentional, inferential activity. Utterances do not encode the messages they convey; rather, they are used to provide evidence of the speaker's intentions, which hearers must infer. Although there is room for debate about precisely how important a role inference plays in communication (and indeed about the precise nature of 'inference' itself) most pragmatists now agree that verbal communication amounts to more than a simple coding–decoding process.

It's worth remembering, however, that the attribution of mental states to others plays an important role in cognition as well as communication. The human disposition to attribute mental states is so much a part of our individual (and collective, species-specific) psychological make-up that it is not something we can choose to do or not to do: it's something we just can't help, any more than we can help pulling our hand back from a source of extreme heat.

Plainly, other people's intentions and mental states generally are not objects to be perceived in the world in the same way as are their faces or bodies; they are 'out there', but they are invisible.[1] However, it is hard even to imagine what it would be like not to be able to sense the mental states of others in some way. The world would be such a different, potentially terrifying place. The human thumb accounts for over 50% of the function of the human hand; we can touch it, we can see it and we can feel it. Yet it is still very difficult to imagine how we might cope without one. In the case of our thumb, we are given a salutary reminder each time we injure it – just try tying your shoelace, or riding a bike with a sprained thumb. In order to know what it would be like to be unable to attribute mental states, we are left with thought experiments of the kind suggested by Baron-Cohen (1995, pp. 1–5) and the few first-hand accounts from people in whom this ability is impaired. Indeed, the central role the recognition of intentions plays in human interaction generally is no more clearly illustrated than by the accounts of those individuals for whom the mental states of others, rather than being merely out of sight, are locked away – permanently out of reach (Williams 1992, 1994, 1999; Holliday Willey 1999; see also Happé 1992 on the autobiographical writings of three Asperger syndrome adults, and Sacks 1994).

The author of the epigraph to this chapter – Donna Williams – is autistic. Her autobiographical works *Nobody Nowhere*, *Somebody Somewhere* and *Like Colour to the Blind* are vivid accounts of what it is like to be *mindblind* – to use the term adopted by Simon Baron-Cohen (1995). Donna's world is a strange, unfamiliar, frightening one: a world of 'inner isolation', of 'persistent aloneness' (1994, p. 95); a world it took enormous strength and courage to escape.

Our understanding of autism is still limited; while it is not in its infancy, research is certainly at an early stage of development. But great strides have been made, and there is a growing literature on both the precise nature of the deficits and impairments that give rise to the condition, and the effects autism has on the capacity of autistic people to communicate and interact with others (Leslie 1987, Happé 1994, Scholl and Leslie 1999).

Baron-Cohen (1995) suggests that autism is characterised by a (partial) breakdown in the mechanisms underlying the human mind-reading ability. The mind-reading system can be analysed into four sub-components – an Intentionality Detector, an Eye-Direction

Detector, a Shared-Attention Mechanism and a Theory of Mind Mechanism[2] – which play different roles at various stages in the cognitive development of normal children, and lead to more or less predictable consequences in instances of pathological breakdown (as, for example, in the case of autism).

Baron-Cohen's hypothesis is that autistic individuals show a deficit in their Shared Attention Mechanism.[3] This has two knock-on effects: firstly, it follows that people with autism cannot construct complex three-place relations, such as 'He sees (that) [I see her]', and as a result cannot grasp that they and another person are attending to the same object; secondly, and more crucially, there is no output from the Shared Attention Mechanism to trigger the development of the Theory of Mind Mechanism, which is seen as underlying the human ability to attribute complex epistemic mental states (or propositional attitudes) such as *believing that p* or *thinking that p*.

Imagine two people (A and B) running past you quickly down a road, one behind the other. Rather than viewing their movements as you might view the random movements of two billiard balls on a billiard table, you are likely to interpret their behaviour in terms of underlying mental states. At a basic, volitional level, you would perceive their actions as motivated by goals and desires; for instance, you might understand that A – the person behind – wanted to catch B – the person in front – or that B wanted to escape from A.[4] Volitional states, according to Baron-Cohen (1995), are 'primitive mental states in that they are the basic ones that are needed to be able to make sense of the universal movements of all animals: approach and avoidance' (pp. 32–3).[5]

However, as well as goals and desires, you would also be likely to attribute to A and B more complex, epistemic, states. So, for example, you might attribute to A the belief that B has done something wrong (which would help to explain why A has the goal of catching B), and to B the belief that A intends to catch him (which would help to explain B's desire to get away). Notice that the kind of beliefs you attribute may well be incompatible with the beliefs you yourself hold: you would have no problem attributing to

A the belief that B has stolen his wallet, even though you happen to know that this belief is false (because, for example, you have A's wallet in your pocket). Autistic people typically fail tests based on this kind of 'first order' ability to attribute false beliefs to others, and this is generally taken to be evidence that they lack a 'theory of mind', and are therefore unable to attribute more complex, epistemic mental states to others (Dennett 1978).

Since it is possible to attribute not only beliefs about the world but also beliefs about other people's beliefs, the mind-reading ability is recursive: we are capable of metarepresenting our own and others' mental states in a multi-layered way, to a number of different levels. Watching the chase, you have no problem entertaining the thought that B believes that A knows that he has done something wrong, or that A believes that B believes that A knows that he has done something wrong (or even, for that matter, that B knows that A believes that B believes that A knows that he has done something wrong).[6]

Overt intentional communication, as described in the Gricean literature, requires a recursive, metapsychological ability of this type. Here, Grice's philosophical concerns link up with those of modern cognitive science, psychology and (even) cognitive ethology. There is thus a point of contact between the Gricean philosophical literature discussed in Chapters 2 and 3, intentional accounts of pragmatics based on Grice's work, and recent psychological research on the capacity for mental-state attribution among humans and non-human animals. It is this point of contact between disciplines that this book aims to explore.

It seems clear that the kind of meta-communicative abilities necessary for overt intentional communication are related to the wider meta-psychological mind-reading ability discussed above. If A, pursuing B, shouts 'Stop! Thief!' with an accompanying glance at you, you might attribute to him the intention that you believe B is a thief (or at least the intention to get you to think that he believes B is a thief), and a desire to get you to help. By your hurried glance back, you might communicate to him that you do indeed intend to help.

However, there are good reasons to believe that there is more to the interpretive processes that underlie verbal comprehension (or, more generally, ostensive–inferential communication) than the general mind-reading abilities responsible for our interpretation of A's and B's actions in my example above. Firstly, the content of a speaker's intention – the 'meaning' she intends to convey – is invariably more complex than the kind of intention you might attribute to someone on the basis of observable evidence such as the chase between A and B in the example above. Secondly, what makes it possible for you to attribute to A the intention to catch B is that you can observe not only his efforts but also their consequences: from the fact that A's efforts are bringing him ever closer to B, you may conclude that this is just what they were intended to do. By contrast, the only real clue an audience has as to the content of the complex intention which constitutes the communicator's meaning is the fact that she has produced a certain utterance with a linguistic meaning which falls far short of determining what she intends to convey; until you have understood her meaning, her efforts will have no observable consequences from which her intentions can be inferred.[7] Observing someone climb a tree and picking a fig, we may infer that his intention in climbing the tree was to pick a fig. However, a speaker will achieve very few effects by producing an utterance unless she is first understood, so the normal procedures for recognising the intentions behind ordinary non-communicative actions won't work: the hearer can't *first* observe the effect of an utterance and *then* infer what it meant.

Thirdly, and perhaps most crucially, overt intentional communication always involves several layers of metarepresentations (she *intends* me to *believe* that she *intends* me to *believe* . . .); yet young children below the age of four – who regularly fail basic 'first order' theory of mind tests – master both verbal and non-verbal communication quickly and effortlessly well before this age.

For these and other reasons (see Sperber and Wilson 2002, Wilson and Sperber 2002) it has been proposed that verbal comprehension might be carried out by a specialised, domain-specific 'comprehension' mechanism or module[8] (Sperber 1996, 2000, Wilson 2005).

The task of this mechanism would be to interpret ostensive stimuli using the relevance-based comprehension heuristic outlined in Chapter 3. Such a comprehension sub-module may be seen as forming part of the wider mind-reading ability (in the same way as Baron-Cohen's 'Shared Attention Mechanism').

Indeed, although young children below the age of four regularly fail basic first order 'theory of mind' tests, there is some experimental evidence that they may be able to track false beliefs in performing word-learning tasks before they can pass standard false belief tests (Happé and Loth 2002). This confirms the view that the mind-reading abilities which are a prerequisite for verbal communication dissociate to some degree from the wider mind-reading ability, and supports the hypothesis that there is a separate, comprehension module.

There is a growing literature on how children can be adept interpreters of utterances, before they have a 'theory of mind' (in the sense of being able to pass regular false-belief tasks). Two camps appear to be emerging. On the one side, there are those (like Happé and Loth – see also Tomasello and Barton 1994, Akhtar, Carpenter and Tomasello 1996, Bloom and German 2000) who warn against underestimating the cognitive abilities of young children; on the other, there are those who claim that we overestimate the degree to which the inferential attribution of intentions is a prerequisite to verbal communication. Two recent papers from defenders of the latter view are Breheny (2006) and Recanati (2002).

Breheny proposes an account of 'basic' communication,[9] the central claim being that it does not require the attribution of propositional-attitude mental states (or presuppose a 'theory of mind'). His aim is to offer an account 'which does not involve propositional attitudes essentially nor presuppose folk-psychological abilities' (2006, p. 75). The account exploits aspects of relevance theory, in particular the relevance-theoretic notion of mutual manifestness, together with the notion of joint attention to a shared situation, as originally proposed in Barwise 1989. Breheny agrees with Sperber and Wilson that an act of basic communication 'involves one agent drawing another agent's attention to something' (2006, p. 96), but, in his view, the objects of such acts are not mental states but situations. No relevance-theorist would argue against Breheny's claim that communicators point to objects or situations, and in that sense his view is perfectly compatible with relevance theory.[10] Where the two approaches diverge is that Breheny goes on to deny that the attribution of proposition-attitude plays a role in basic communication. This is in contrast to the relevance-theoretic view discussed in Chapter 3, which is that the mental states of the shower or pointer invariably play a crucial role in determining: (a) *what* it is that has been shown or pointed out; (b) *why* it has been shown or pointed out in the first place.

There are, however, a number of issues which suggest the account may be unnecessarily minimalistic. In the first place, children are clearly attributing mental states to others well before they pass standard 'false-belief' tasks, perhaps as early as one year old (see Bretherton 1991). Indeed, Onishi and Baillargeon (2005) and Surian, Caldi and Sperber (in press) claim that children are able to pass *non-verbal* versions of the false-belief tasks at the age of thirteen or fourteen months.

Alan Leslie (1987, 1992) has argued extensively that the one-to two-year-old child's ability to engage in shared pretence depends on an ability to share 'imagined circumstances' and to identify with and respond to the mental states of others (see also Onishi, Baillargeon and Leslie 2007). More generally, very young children respond effortlessly and appropriately to non-verbal cues that indicate the mental state of a parent, carer or friend. If we put this together with the fact that children develop the shared attention ability between nine and eighteen months of age, it suggests that the requirement that acts of basic communication do not involve the attribution of the communicator's mental states is more minimalistic than it needs to be.

Secondly, as we saw in Chapters 2 and 3, even in the most basic acts of ostensive–inferential communication,[11] cases in which a communicator provides direct evidence of an intention to inform (e.g. my mad photograph-shower example) the mental states of the shower still play a role in recognising what it is that has been shown, and why. Evidence suggests that children begin to understand pointing gestures at around fourteen months (Blake *et al.* 1992); according to Leslie (1994): 'informative showing typically makes its appearance early in the second year along with verbal communication'. More recent work has explored this issue in more detail (see Lizskowski, *et al.* 2006 and Southgate, van Maanen and Csibra 2007). It is not clear how such behaviour is possible or can be done without providing some evidence of the mental states of the shower.

Finally (albeit anecdotally) as the father of two young children myself, I am constantly amazed by their communicative (and cognitive) precocity, rather than frustrated with their lack of such abilities.[12] It just seems unwise to underestimate them; the jury, however, is still out.

While Recanati (2002) does not specifically discuss theory of mind, his assertion that relevance theorists overestimate the role played by inference in verbal communication might also be said to put him in the second of the two camps described above. According to Recanati, communication is not constitutively inferential; instead, it is – at the explicit level at least[13] – 'as direct as perception' (2002, p. 105). Mature communicators may indeed use indirect means in order to convey their meanings – implicate them, for example – but the ability to infer speaker meaning is not a necessary condition of being able to communicate verbally. While relevance theorists stress the role of pragmatic inference in the derivation of the explicit content of an utterance, Recanati proposes that although these processes are indeed pragmatic, they are not inferential. As he puts it:

[T]hose pragmatic processes that are involved in the determination of truth-conditional content – primary pragmatic processes, in my terminology – need not involve an inference from premises concerning what the speaker can possibly intend by his utterance. Indeed, they need not involve any inference at all. (2002, pp. 113–14)

Ultimately, a great deal will depend on how we define inference. Indeed, Recanati's arguments rest on his appeal to a notion of inference that is distinct from the one adopted in relevance theory, a full discussion of which would take us too far afield here.[14]

Still, Recanati's approach does seem to make some counter-intuitive predictions (see Carston 2002b). To maintain his distinction between primary and secondary pragmatic processes (i.e. those processes responsible for the interpretation of cases in which a speaker means something over and above what they say) Recanati utilises a notion originally due to Millikan (1984). According to Millikan, in those cases where there is some divergence between what a speaker says and what a speaker means, communicators are effectively 'tinkering' with the 'mechanisms of normal language flow' (1984, p. 69). The mechanisms of 'normal' language flow are seen as determining what a speaker says, in the sense of the truth-conditional content of the utterance, or the proposition expressed. But at what point (and by what criteria) do we decide that language flow is not normal? As Carston shows, communicative exchanges involving the recovery of implicatures often appear more 'normal' than those in which the implicature is fully spelt out in linguistic terms; the latter often appear clumsily put, or inappropriately over-explicit.

More importantly, given the concerns of this book, we saw in Chapter 3 that the interpretation of patently non-linguistic, clearly non-coded natural behaviours – shivers, for example – plays a crucial role in an audience's recognition of what a speaker has said. On any conception of 'normal', we surely want to say that the mechanisms underlying the interpretation of natural signs which contribute to the truth-conditional content of an utterance are part of the mechanisms of normal language flow; but if they are not coded, then it is hard to see how (on any conception of 'inference') these interpretive mechanisms are not inferential. And in that case, inferential mechanisms must be capable of playing a role in the recognition of what is said.

Conspicuously absent from my discussion of the chase between A and B above is the question of how the facial expressions (and other coded natural behaviours) of each individual would provide the other with evidence about their respective emotional states. It is clear that these expressions would also play a large part in your interpretation of the situation, providing a window not only into A and B's thoughts, but also into their feelings; that B is (more or less) frightened, and A is angry (or furious).

Although the wider mind-reading ability is plainly involved to some extent in the attribution of such emotional states, the degree to which it is implicated is unclear. If, as I am proposing, some of the behaviours that indicate emotional states are coded, then we might predict that they are interpreted via their own dedicated cognitive mechanisms. Whatever the mechanisms involved, though, reading the faces of others is sure to be problematic to those for whom the mind behind the face is out of reach.

Here too, research into autism is suggestive. There is a growing literature charting the difficulties experienced by people with autism in attributing emotional states to others (Hobson, Ouston and Lee 1988; Muris *et al.* 1995). In an attempt to shed more light on the issue, Baron-Cohen, Spitz and Cross (1993) examined the recognition of emotion in autistic children. Given that people with autism have problems in recognizing beliefs, Baron-Cohen *et al.* theorised about the extent to which this would affect the recognition of the so-called 'cognitive' emotions. These are emotions such as surprise which are caused by epistemic states such as belief (one cannot just be surprised, one must be surprised *that such and such has happened*), and whose recognition therefore seems to presuppose an ability to attribute beliefs. Baron-Cohen *et al.* regard these 'cognitive' emotions as distinct from 'simple' emotions such as happiness and sadness, which can be recognised without the attribution of any belief. As predicted, the autistic children had more difficulty recognising surprise.[15]

To the extent that these findings (and the suppositions on which they are based) are correct, they might be taken to suggest that while the meta-communicative and meta-psychological abilities of people with autism are impaired, some of the natural coding–decoding mechanisms remain intact. This may pave the way to a fuller understanding of the precise nature of the relationship between the wider meta-psychological mindreading ability and those abilities responsible for the coding–decoding of natural signals. As we saw in Chapter 5, humans do have neural mechanisms dedicated to processing facial expressions (Gazzaniga and Smiley 1991). These specialised mechanisms, like the dedicated meta-communicative abilities that govern the search for relevance in verbal comprehension, may also be sub-modules of the wider mind-reading ability.

One striking feature of the literature on facial expressions is that the notion of intentionality is largely absent from it. As we saw in the last chapter, Fridlund (1994) abstracts away from it entirely: 'I have circumvented these "levels of intentionality" issues in the interests of space, and use intentionality in a purely functionalist sense' (p. 146). Of course, we underestimate the power of human facial expression at our peril too. It is certainly true that 'whereas the prosimian face is relatively unexpressive, the monkeys and apes tend to exhibit a quite significant range of expressions, culminating in the Marcel Marceau of expressiveness, modern humans' (Hauser 1996, p. 265). But if there is one moral to draw from my research, it is that what distinguishes human from non-human animal communication (and interaction generally) is not that we live in a world populated by other faces, but that we live in a world populated by other minds.

EXPERIMENTAL EVIDENCE AND FUTURE DIRECTIONS

Sabbagh (1999) surveys a wide variety of prosodic impairments in autism and right hemisphere damage. These include problems with the interpretation of: emotional and attitudinal prosody; 'inarticulate' prosody (e.g. grunts or sighs); contrastive stress; 'intrinsic' prosody (e.g. declarative/interrogative intonation). As noted above, he concludes that these difficulties are linked to a specifically communicative impairment rather than a more general impairment in the general mind-reading ability. In a careful review of studies on prosody in autism, McCann and Peppé (2003) cite additional evidence, showing that there are difficulties with the interpretation of types of affective prosody, while the ability to distinguish, say, a 'calm' from an 'agitated' attitude on the basis of prosodic clues remains intact. The framework outlined here and in previous chapters suggests two possible explanations for these differences: there may be selective impairment of the ability to interpret natural prosodic signals as opposed to natural prosodic signs; or there may be selective impairment of the ability to interpret natural prosodic indicators of mental rather than physical state. Both possibilities are worth investigating, and I will suggest some possible test cases below.

More generally, the right hemisphere appears to be relatively dominant in the interpretation of emotional prosody, and the left hemisphere in the interpretation of properly linguistic prosody (Ross *et al.* 1988, Baum and Pell 1999, Pell 2002a,b; though see Seddoh, 2002 for scepticism about the distinction between affective and linguistic prosody). For instance, right hemisphere damage in Parkinsonism seems to affect the interpretation of emotional and sentential prosody but not lexical prosody (perhaps suggesting a universal non-linguistic basis for sentential prosody). However, while right hemisphere damage may cause difficulties with emotional prosody, it does not necessarily lead to problems with the identification of emotional facial expressions; in general, recognition of emotion from faces is reliably better than from voices (Sabbagh 1999; Pell 2002a,b).

Lieberman (2000) provides a fascinating account of the type of sub-attentive processes involved in the production and interpretation of unintentional prosodic signs and signals, which may be seen as contributing more to accidental (or covert) information transmission than to ostensive communication:

> At all times, we are communicating information about our emotional state, attitudes, and evaluations of whatever we are currently confronting . . . Several of the nonverbal cues that reflect our internal state can be controlled consciously to some degree, but this will only occur if one directs one's conscious attention to the process of non-verbal encoding . . . Additionally, there are other cues to one's internal state (e.g. tone of voice, blinking, posture) that the vast majority of us have little or no control over. We produce most of our nonverbal cues intuitively, without phenomenological awareness. (Lieberman, 2000, p. 111)

This is 'the dance of non-verbal communication' referred to in Chapter 1. Lieberman comments further,

> The dance of nonverbal communication between two individuals often goes unnoticed by either participant . . . It is, however, noticeable when it is absent or out of sync. The dance occurs intuitively, and when we get a sense of the other's state of mind as a result of the nonverbal cues the other has emitted, we often have nothing other than our intuition to justify our inferences. (Lieberman, 2000, p. 123)

According to Lieberman, sub-attentive impressions of this type are dealt with in the basal ganglia. This may be seen as providing some evidence of a neurophysiological basis for the distinction between accidental, covert and overt information transmission discussed above. Further neurophysiological evidence may well shed light on the relations between prosody and linguistic, communicative and general mind-reading abilities.

In previous chapters, I have argued on theoretical grounds for two sets of distinctions: between natural signs, natural signals and non-natural signals (whether cultural or linguistic), on the one hand; and between accidental, covert and overt information transmission, on the other. Neither set of distinctions has been systematically applied to the literature on prosodic effects, or on gesture and facial expression, and it is perhaps not even obvious that they could be. However, if we could find a way of applying them, it might yield useful insights into the nature of the impairments in autism and right hemisphere damage (for instance, on whether they affect general mind-reading abilities or specific communicative abilities), and more generally, into the relation between non-verbal communication, mind-reading and comprehension.

I would therefore like to suggest a range of possible test cases which might be used in investigating the prosodic difficulties that arise in autism, Asperger's syndrome and right hemisphere damage, and – if these could be carried across to the study of facial expression and gesture – might provide a first step towards a more systematic application of these distinctions.

The first type of test case would consist of natural prosodic *signals* which are not overtly shown, and which would not normally be understood as contributing to a communicator's meaning. Examples might be someone trying to hide her anger while speaking, sighing while working alone in her room, or exclaiming with surprise when she drops something while no-one else is present. Comprehension of these non-ostensive signals in people with prosodic impairments might be compared with comprehension of cases where the same natural prosodic signal is ostensively used in addressing someone, and would normally be understood as contributing to the communicator's meaning.

The second type of test case would consist of natural prosodic *signs* which are not overtly shown, and which would not normally be understood as contributing to a communicator's meaning. Examples might be saying 'The bus is coming' while sounding bored, tired, shaky or ill. Interpretation of these natural prosodic clues might be compared with comprehension of cases where the same natural prosodic sign is ostensively used, and would normally be understood as contributing to the communicator's meaning.

NOTES

1. Though see Gibbs (1999) for a fascinating challenge to the claim that intentions exist solely in the minds of individuals.
2. The *Intentionality Detector* is responsible for the interpretation of the movement of 'agent-like' objects in terms of basic volitional concepts such as *goal* and *desire*; the *Eye-Direction Detector* (fairly transparently) detects 'eyes' and, more importantly, monitors them in order to decide whether they are directed towards *it*, or towards some other object or organism; given input from the Intentionality Detector and the Eye-Direction Detector, the *Shared-Attention Mechanism* allows individuals to monitor which objects, events and states they and another individual are jointly attending to (in relevance-theoretic terms, it keeps track of what is mutually manifest); the *Theory of Mind Mechanism* allows the individual to infer not only primitive volitional states (such as 'goal' and 'desire'), and perceptual mental states (such as 'see') but also what Baron-Cohen calls 'epistemic mental states' (1995, p. 51), such as 'believing' and 'thinking'. Baron-Cohen's Theory of Mind Mechanism is based on the one presented in Leslie (1994).

3. There is at least some evidence from Donna Williams' accounts that she may have some deficit with her *Intentionality Detector* too. Consider the following: 'Everything had its own, if limited, volition. Whether a thing was stationary or movable depended more on the thing's readiness to move than on the person's decision to move it. Statements like "It won't budge" only confirmed this assumed reality' (1994, p. 65).

4. You would almost certainly interpret a dog chasing a cat in terms of their respective goals and desires too, but like me you may find yourself less willing to attribute to either the cat or the dog more complex, epistemic mental states of the kind discussed below. (For discussion see Allen and Bekoff 1997, Chapters 2 and 6.) The behaviour of household pets is a commonly cited source of counter-evidence to claims concerning the uniqueness of the human mind-reading ability – 'But my dog knows *precisely* what I'm thinking', the argument goes. Interestingly, recent research by Mike Tomasello and his colleagues (Call *et al.* 2003, Hare and Tomasello 2005) suggests that dogs do have some ability to attribute mental states.

5. Given his hypothesis, many people with autism would indeed be able to interpret the situation described above in terms of the goals and the desires of the individuals concerned; Baron-Cohen notes, however, that 'this does not mean that they are able to understand all aspects of desire, or the more complex mental state of intention' (1995, p. 63).

6. Dennett (1988, pp. 185–6) wonders about the upper limits of the human recursive, meta-psychological ability: 'How high can human beings go? "In principle", forever, no doubt, but in fact I suspect that you wonder whether I realise how hard it is for you to be sure that you understand whether I mean to be saying that you can recognise that I can believe you to want me to explain that most of us can keep track of only about five or six orders.'

7. The solution might be the Communicative Principle of Relevance (and the relevance-theoretic comprehension heuristic it motivates).

8. I use the term 'module' in the sense of Sperber 1996 and, indeed, much of the literature on evolutionary psychology: that is, in a somewhat 'looser' sense than the one proposed by Fodor 1983.

9. A communicative act typified by the assertive utterance of a declarative sentence.

10. And, incidentally, no relevance theorist I know would claim that the 'objects' of communicative acts are mental states.

11. Breheny does not provide a definition of 'ostensive-inferential communication' since, as an everyday concept, 'communication' cannot be defined (in this he is following the methodological strategies of Fodor 1998 and Chomsky 2000): 'a communicative situation is that kind of communication

which our concept of communication locks onto as a result of exposure to stereotypical instances of communication' (Breheny 2006, p. 51). Surely, though, as theorists, we should specify what domain our intended generalisations are intended to apply to.

12. Of course, it may be that I am simply guilty of projecting onto my children abilities they do not have in a manner analogous to the individual in note 4 above, who projects abilities onto his/her household pet.

13. Recanati does not use the notion of explicit content, preferring his own (pragmatically enriched) notion of *what is said*.

14. Sperber 1995, p. 195 writes 'when most of us talk of reasoning, we think of an occasional, conscious, difficult and rather slow activity. What modern psychology has shown is that something like reasoning goes on all the time – unconsciously, painlessly and fast.' It is in this latter, broader sense that relevance theorists regard linguistic communication as *inferential*. As I understand it, Recanati's claim is that the relevance theory notion of *broad* inference actually falls somewhere *between* what he takes to be more satisfactory definitions of inference in the broad and the narrow sense. He goes on to argue that primary pragmatic processes may only be regarded as inferential in a *very* broad sense – the same sense in which we might regard the processes underlying perception (e.g. vision) as inferential.

15. The difference between 'simple' and 'cognitive' emotions is complicated by the fact that just as I can be 'happy', I can also be 'happy that P'. However, as noted above, you can only be 'surprised that P': you can't just feel 'surprised'. It might also be argued, in fact, that 'emotion' is not the correct word to use for simply 'feeling' happy (see my earlier discussion of Rey's distinction between 'feelings' and 'emotions' in Chapter 4).

CHAPTER 8

The showing–meaning$_{NN}$ continuum and beyond

The three of them stood and looked at each other. Then, as so often happened with the people, there were feelings between them. Fa and Nil shared a picture of Ha thinking.

(William Golding – *The Inheritors*)

TWO 'SHOWING–MEANING' CONTINUA

An ongoing concern in this book has been to draw parallels between the 'showing–meaning$_{NN}$' continuum presented in Chapter 3 and the other continua introduced at various points: Goffman's continuum between response cries and words, Gussenhoven's continuum between natural and linguistic prosody and Kendon's continuum between gesticulation and sign-language. However, as I have also pointed out, there are differences. The aim of the following discussion is to focus on these. For while the continua reflect similar underlying intuitions, in key regards they are actually quite distinct. To be more precise, we are dealing with two different types of continua. My conclusion will be that while continua of the kind proposed by Goffman, Gussenhoven and Kendon are useful descriptive tools, and capture the intuition that there is a continuity of some sort between display and language proper, they lack real explanatory power. By contrast, I will argue that the showing–meaning$_{NN}$ continuum developed in this book is useful in both descriptive and explanatory terms.

Continua of the kind proposed by Goffman and Kendon are based entirely on the role played in communication by coding: in semiotic terms, the nature of the 'sign' and the type of relationship that links signals to messages. The principal observation on which the continua are based is that as we move across the full spectrum of behaviours from display to language, there is an increase in 'language-like' codification. Among the features typical of such 'language-like' coding, McNeill lists 'segmentation', 'compositionality', a 'lexicon', a 'syntax', 'distinctiveness' and 'arbitrariness'; these features are highly reminiscent of Hockett's list of the distinguishing features of language discussed briefly in Chapter 5.

It should be noted, however, that although the point of such a continuum is to show a change in the type of coding involved as we move from left to right, the ultimate aim appears to be to analyse all the behaviours along the continuum as codes of one sort or another:

> The first point to establish is that, in performing gestures,[1] the speaker's hands are no longer just hands, but symbols. Gestures are not just movements and can never be fully explained in purely kinesic terms. They are not just the arms waving in the air, but symbols that exhibit meanings in their own right. (McNeill 1992, p. 105)

> Our purpose is thus to bring out semiotic values, and this has led us to build semiotic distinctions directly into the gesture classification; that is, to classify the gesture by means of asking (a) is the movement a symbol? and (b) what type of symbol is it? The categories of iconic, metaphoric and deictic . . . correspond to the fundamental types of semiotic sign. (*ibid.* p. 77)

For obvious reasons, I call a continuum of this type – which clearly has its roots in the code model of communication – a Code-continuum, or a C-continuum. Essentially, a C-continuum is a continuum between non-linguistic coding and linguistic coding. As was pointed out in Chapter 6, Gussenhoven's continuum is also one between natural signals (as opposed to natural signs) and linguistic signals.

By contrast, the continuum proposed in Chapter 3 is based on the role played in ostensive communication by the inferential attribution of intentions; it has its roots in Gricean notions such as those discussed in Chapters 2 and 3. Positions on the continuum reflect the extent to which hearers are required to attribute intentions to speakers[2] in order to get from the evidence provided to the information being communicated (the first, basic layer which constitutes the content of the communicator's informative intention). I call this continuum an Ostensive behaviour-continuum, or an O-continuum.

My claim is that the O-continuum can be extended so as to incorporate all the elements on the C-continuum; after all, if there is a high degree of coding in the communicative stimuli, it follows that the evidence provided will be of the less direct variety. The C-continuum, however, cannot be extended to incorporate all the elements on the O-continuum.

One thing that the C-continuum and the O-continuum have in common is that they provide a 'snapshot' of the types of evidence used in communicative acts. So at one extreme of both continua lie clear cases of spontaneous, natural display (though in the case of the C-continuum, these are also treated as coded signals); while at the other extreme lie clear cases of linguistic coding. However, while both continua illustrate the increase in 'language-like' codification as we move toward language proper, there are several points about which the C-continuum has little or nothing to say. This, I argue, is because it takes no account of the inferential nature of human communication.

Because the C-continuum is based on the code model and concerned mainly with classifying 'signs', it says little about how communicative behaviours are used, apart from noting that they are coded signals and that different types of coding relationship exist. The positions of various behaviours on the C-continuum are fixed or static: facial expressions 'display'; words 'mean'; interjections belong at some half-way point. On the face of it, this seems fair enough, but a moment's reflection reveals that it captures neither the way people communicate, nor the variety of ways in which a given piece of behaviour can be used to convey information.

For example, it misses the crucial point that just as communicators use language to say things, we can also use language to display or show. Equally, communicators can use what are essentially 'displays' in order to mean$_{NN}$. In the O-continuum the same stimulus can occupy different points depending on how it is used.

Suppose I intend to communicate to you that I have a sore throat. I might choose to communicate this by saying (142) in an extremely hoarse voice:

(142) The moon looks beautiful tonight.

Or suppose Lily approaches Jack at a party and asks him if he speaks any French; Jack replies as in (143):

(143) Pouvez-vous parler moins vite s'il vous plaît?

Both these utterances qualify as clear cases of showing or display, since they provide direct evidence of the first, based layer of information – in (142) that I have a sore throat, in (143) that Jack can indeed speak French (see Sperber and Wilson 1986/1995, pp. 177–8).

Now consider ostensive uses of natural signs, such as those discussed in Chapter 3: for example, the case in which Lily uses a shiver to mean$_{NN}$ that she does not want to stay outside. Here, as I argue above, a behaviour that is essentially a display is used (in virtue of the intentions behind the display) to mean$_{NN}$. Though the O-continuum also provides a snapshot of the positions occupied by different items at a given point in time, that is not all it tells us; it suggests not only how the items on the continuum are interpreted (via a mixture of direct and indirect evidence – or, if you prefer – natural and coded behaviour), but how it is that they might occupy different points at different times.

In discussing interjections in Chapter 4 I suggested that since we have a continuum in which a given item can occupy different points depending on how it is used, we would expect some expressions to move along it as a result of being frequently used in one way or another. In historical terms, when an interjection, for example, moves far enough along the continuum, it may become linguistically productive ('to wow', 'yucky'), and some of its uses may be properly linguistic (verbs, adjectives etc.). This suggests a historic, diachronic dimension to the continuum. A C-continuum, however, can shed little light on this dimension. Since behaviours occupy fixed positions on the continuum, it can only, at best, represent diachrony in a series of still pictures.

By contrast, the O-continuum, which can also been seen as a series of still pictures, has the added advantage that it can represent the fluidity and constant change that results in expressions coming to form part of language. In many historical linguistic accounts

(Aitchison 1991, Lightfoot 1991), children are seen as converging on the simplest grammar that reflects the practice of the speech community to which they are exposed. The O-continuum could allow us to explore the idea that pragmatic factors may affect this convergence, and to see language change in terms of the micro-processes involved in the emergence of new encoded meanings. Language change might then be characterised in terms of population-scale macro-processes resulting from an accumulation of those micro-processes, leading to the stabilization of new senses.

It is also plausible that interactions between cognitive and social factors might influence the direction of linguistic change. Dan Sperber (1996) uses the notion of 'attractor' in what he terms 'epidemiological' models of ephemeral and longer-lasting cultural change.

> To say that something is an attractor is just to say that, in a given space of possibilities, transformation probabilities form a certain pattern: they tend to be biased so as to favour the transformations in the direction of some certain point, and therefore cluster at or around that point. An attractor is not a material thing; it does not physically 'attract' anything. To say that there is an attractor is not to give a causal explanation; it is to put in a certain light what is to be causally explained. (Sperber 1996, p. 112)

Various factors can be responsible for attractors – cognitive, social, environmental – each operating on different timescales. Whilst this notion has been discussed in the context of historical linguistics (Lass 1997), there has been little application of epidemiological models to historical linguistics (one notable exception is Enfield 2003). More work on Linguistic Epidemiology may shed light on the distinction between short-term linguistic fashions and longer-lasting trends, and the causal processes that influence them.

It might also be worth exploring whether the O-continuum has an evolutionary-diachronic as well as a historical-diachronic dimension. In fact, when it comes to evolutionary concerns, the O-continuum is doubly suggestive. Firstly, as we have seen, the flexibility inherent in the continuum allows for the fact that behaviours might move along it; secondly, and perhaps more importantly, by using the O-continuum to shed light on the evolution of language and communication, we are setting our account within the wider context of the evolution of human cognitive abilities. I turn to this in the next section.

A PRINCE AMONG PRIMATES

Over the past twenty years, there has been a tremendous resurgence of interest in the evolution of communication, cognition and language. In a proliferation of recent publications, researchers have proposed different aspects of human language as the evolutionary cornerstone around which the edifice of the language capacity might have been built. For Terrence Deacon (1997), it is the fact that language uses 'symbols'; for Jean Aitchison (1996), it is what she refers to as 'the naming insight' deployed in the early stages of the acquisition of language by children; for Andrew Carstairs-McCarthy (1999) it is subject–predicate structure, which he argues has its origins in syllable structure. Michael Corballis (2002) proposes that language evolved from manual gestures; Steve Mithen (2005) suggests that it was the propensity of early hominids to make music that led eventually to the evolution of language.

What is interesting to note is that all these authors base their accounts on a view of ancestral hominid linguistic communication as a simple coding–decoding affair. The same stance is adopted in one of the seminal papers on the topic: Steven Pinker and Paul Bloom's 'Natural language and natural selection' (1990). However, this view is problematic (see Sperber 2000): it is hard to see why, if human linguistic communication began as a pure coding–decoding process, it should have changed in character so drastically at a certain evolutionary stage, and come to rely so heavily on inferential intention recognition.

Another tacit assumption in the works cited above is that the evolution of the human linguistic ability preceded the development of a human metarepresentational capacity.[3] This view is also problematic: firstly, without a capacity for metarepresentation, it is hard to see how humans could ever have become aware of the representational character of their signals; secondly, and perhaps more importantly, it is hard to see how a language faculty could have been adaptive.

For one of the key problems in formulating a plausible evolutionary account of the language faculty based on natural selection is that an individual who acquired some novel linguistic coding and decoding ability as a result of mutation would have had no advantage in 'fitness' in a community with no capacity for inferential communication, which would have been unable to understand what she meant. Her abilities would have been entirely useless: she would have had no one to talk to, and no one to listen to. However, the problem is more tractable if we hypothesise that metarepresentational abilities developed before linguistic abilities. Humans with a capacity for metarepresentation would have been involved in inferential communication before a language faculty evolved, and a plausible evolutionary scenario might go as follows: the biological evolution of the language faculty resulted from the emergence of ever more precise coded signals, which increased the efficiency of inferential communication by saving effort and making its effects more precise. If humans were communicating inferentially before language developed, then showing – in the sense described in Chapter 3 – clearly came before saying, and evolutionary considerations might provide useful insights into why there is a continuum between the two, and why modern humans are so adept at doing both. As Patrick Suppes (1986, p. 113) puts it:

language must have begun from attempts at communication between a few individuals. At first these efforts at communication did not have very much stability of literal meaning. Only slowly and after much time did a stable community of users lead to the abstract concept of literal meaning . . . There is no hard and fast platonic literal meaning that utterers' meanings attach themselves to . . . The story surely is exactly the other way round.

A striking feature of much work on the evolution of the human metarepresentational capacity is that while there is disagreement about the factors that may have led to its development, there is broad agreement at least that it could have evolved – or begun to evolve – independently of communication. Leda Cosmides and John

Tooby (2000) suggest that the ability to mentally 'detach' ourselves from the here-and-now, to entertain a representation of a situation as something other than a true belief about the world, would have improved our adeptness in reacting and responding to local aspects of the environment. This would have enabled humans to adapt to the environment spontaneously – for example by making plans – rather than having to adapt (as does the rest of the animal kingdom) on an evolutionary timescale. Such improvisational skills would have proved highly adaptive.

Another view – The Machiavellian Intelligence Hypothesis (Byrne and Whiten 1988) – suggests that the metarepresentational capacity might have developed in response to a particular challenge for humans (and, indeed, primates generally): the task of dealing with the complexity of social interaction. In the human case, it is argued, this challenge led to a kind of 'Cognitive Arms Race' in which human cognitive abilities spiralled – mainly in order to help individuals compete with their conspecifics and perhaps out-manoeuvre them. The ability to interpret behaviour in terms of underlying mental states would have given our ancestors strong predictive powers, and it would therefore have been adaptive to become increasingly adept at working out the thoughts and feelings of others (Humphrey 1984).

Tomasello *et al.* (2005) point out that as well as evolving the ability to compete and deceive, humans also evolved the ability to collaborate and cooperate. This unique human disposition to share intentions – which also involves a metarepresentational ability – may form the foundation upon which much human interaction (and possibly human culture) is built.

Of course, sensing how someone else is feeling does not necessarily require complex metarepresentational abilities. Well before they are capable of passing false-belief tests and acquiring a full-blown human 'Theory of Mind', young infants can sense the emotional state of their carers. Indeed, intention recognition plays a rather limited role in recognising the emotional states of others. Consider the automatic way in which we interpret facial expressions, or the way panic spreads through a crowd. The cries that alert others to danger in this situation may not be uttered with intentions, and are on the whole not understood by attributing intentions. Presumably at some early stage in our evolution, this was how we were able to sense whether or not people were friendly or a threat, or whether a situation was safe or dangerous.

Before the evolution of a metarepresentational capacity, our ancestors would have been 'ignorant of an inner explanation for their own behavior' (Humphrey 1984, p. 49). But once rudimentary metarepresentational abilities appeared, they could have spiralled and spiralled until they eventually led to the evolution of the kind of complex mechanisms that underlie full-blown 'theory of mind' (including a capacity for overt intentional communication). In their foreword to Baron-Cohen 1995, Cosmides and Tooby put it like this:

Unobservable entities . . . are 'visible' to natural selection . . . Over innumerable generations, the evolutionary process selected for modules . . . that could successfully isolate, out of the welter of observable phenomena, exactly those outward and visible signs in behavior that reliably signaled inward and invisible mental states.

The metarepresentation-before-language hypothesis, then, is independently endorsed by evolutionary psychologists, primatologists and ethologists working on the evolution of human social intelligence, who argue that the social pressures of ancestral hominid life would have led to the evolution of metarepresentational abilities either to outmanoeuvre opponents or to detect cheats in the community (Cosmides 1989). In the words of Nicholas Humphrey:

Once a society has reached a certain level of complexity, then new internal pressures must arise which act to increase its complexity still further . . . If intellectual prowess is correlated with social success, and if social success means high biological fitness, then a heritable trait which increases the ability of an individual to outwit his fellows will soon spread through the gene pool. In these circumstances there can be no going back; an evolutionary 'ratchet' has been set up, acting like a self-winding watch to increase the general intellectual standing of the species. (Humphrey 1988, p. 21)

Interestingly, this kind of view does not fit with the traditional philosophical view of the function of communication. Recall from

Chapter 2 Stephen Neale's concern over Grice's modification of his 1957 characterisation of meaning$_{NN}$, which led him to distinguish between *exhibitive* and *protreptic* utterances. In an exhibitive utterance, U's intention is not to induce a belief in A, but rather to get A to think that U holds a particular belief: thus, the utterance exhibits U's belief. In a protreptic utterance, U exhibits a belief with the *further* intention of inducing the same belief in A (on the strength of A's recognising that U holds it too). Neale's concern was that the modification 'does not comport well with the commonly held view that the primary purpose of communication is the transfer of information about the world' (1992, p. 549); on Grice's revised account, Neale goes on, 'the primary purpose seems to be the transfer of information about one's mental states' (*ibid.*).

Some arguments from a recent paper by Dan Sperber (2001) might be seen as militating against this view. In the case of honeybees, the 'primary purpose' of communication does indeed appear to be to transfer information about the world. Having perceived a source of nectar, the forager bee returns to the hive and performs its dance. By decoding the dance, the receiver bees end up in precisely the same cognitive (mental) state as the forager bee was in when it discovered the source. Communication is beneficial to the bees insofar as they benefit from the perceptions of other bees; it results in what Sperber calls 'cognition by proxy'.

As we saw in Chapter 3, human inferential communication does not result in the straightforward replication of cognitive states that is achieved by coded communication. As Hauser (1996, p. 497) puts it: 'whereas bees are informational laser beams, humans are informational floodlights'. Sperber points out that even when human communicators seem to be offering information, they are not always benevolent. If it is in their interests, they are capable of lying and deception. While there is some evidence to suggest that some non-human primates are capable of rudimentary forms of deception, humans are capable of highly elaborate, novel deceptions. Equally, of course, audiences are not always trusting: a communicator's motives may be entirely benevolent, but she may still not be believed.[4]

A plausible account of the function of communication must accommodate these observations; furthermore, a plausible account of the evolution of communication must accommodate the fact that despite this possibility of deception, and despite the possibility that a communicator and her audience may have conflicting goals, communication must have been advantageous to both in order to stabilise (or be selected for).

Sperber argues that the human ability to present arguments for a conclusion the audience is intended to draw, or to evaluate the arguments of others, may have been one of the factors involved in this stabilisation: for communicators, argumentation is a means of persuasion; for an audience, it is a means of assessing the content of a message, regardless of how much they trust the communicator. Indeed, Sperber suggests that the human capacity for reasoning may well have evolved in a communicative context rather than in the course of individual knowledge acquisition. Understanding the first, basic layer of communicated information already involves embedding it under a higher-level mental state (or propositional attitude) representation: a human communicator indicates that she believes, desires or regrets that *p*. Checking the coherence of argumentation would have required an even more sophisticated metarepresentational ability. It is not Sperber's aim in his 2001 paper to present an account of the evolution of language, but he does suggest that as argumentation evolves, so a logical vocabulary – words such as 'if', 'however', 'so' – would be beneficial; and some of these expressions may have been the evolutionary forerunners of the *non-translational* vocabulary.

Whatever the implications for the evolution of the human reasoning ability, notice that construed in this way, human communication has at least as much to do with the transfer of information about the communicator's mental states as it does with the transfer of information about states of affairs per se. This extra dimension of human communication may have been part of Humphrey's evolutionary 'ratchet' that helped spark the cognitive arms race from which natural language finally emerged. Language would have been a perfect adaptation to increase the efficiency of inferential communication: the vehicle by which thoughts and ideas are carried, and through which they proliferate.[5]

In many ways, the most surprising contribution to the debate on the evolution of language is that of Hauser, Chomsky and Fitch (2002). Hauser *et al.* seek to sever the link between the evolution of language and the evolution of communication. They argue that language – in the sense of a 'narrow syntax' (2002, p. 2) which generates linguistic representations and maps them on to the conceptual-intentional and sensory-motor interfaces – could have evolved as a by-product of other human computational abilities: in evolutionary terms, it may be a 'spandrel'.

The *spandrels* of San Marco Cathedral are, in Gould and Lewontin's words, 'the tapering triangular spaces formed by the intersection of two rounded angles at right angles' and 'are necessary architectural by-products of mounting a dome on rounded arches'. Each spandrel 'contains a design . . . so elaborate, harmonious and purposeful that we are tempted to view it as the starting point of any analysis'. However, 'this would invert the proper path of analysis', since 'the system begins with an architectural constraint: the necessary four spandrels and their tapering triangular form'. Gould and Lewontin go on to comment, 'anyone who tried to argue that structure [spandrels] exists because of [the designs] would be inviting the same ridicule that Voltaire heaped on Dr. Pangloss . . . Yet evolutionary biologists, in their tendency to focus on immediate adaptation to local conditions, do tend to ignore architectural constraints and perform just such an inversion of explanation' (Gould and Lewontin 1979, pp. 147–9).

One of the reasons for severing the link between the evolution of language and the evolution of communication, and the main motivation behind Hauser, Chomsky and Fitch's belief that 'investigations of this capacity should include domains other than communication (e.g. number, social relationships, navigation)' (2002, p. 2) is that 'the core recursive aspect of FLN [faculty of language in a narrow sense] appears to lack any significant analog in animal communication' (*ibid.*). By contrast, features of what Hauser *et al.* call 'FLB' (faculty of language in the broad sense – including the conceptual-intentional and sensory-motor systems) do appear to have homologues in non-human animals.

However, these arguments do not militate against the metarepresentation-before-language view presented above. Firstly, the proposal that humans were capable of entertaining representations of the form 'She meant that p' or 'She intended me to believe that p' before the evolution of FLN is not inconsistent with FLN having emerged entirely as a spandrel. Secondly, and more importantly, the claim that FLN evolved partially as a by-product of other abilities is not necessarily inconsistent with its having evolved to meet largely communicative ends. For while it is certainly true that 'the core recursive aspect of FLN appears to lack any significant analog in animal communication' it is not true that it is the only human recursive ability. The human metarepresentational ability is a recursive, syntactic ability par excellence: a plausible candidate, it might be argued, for exaptation into syntax in Hauser *et al.*'s narrow linguistic sense. The degree of metarepresentation required for overt inferential communication presupposes a considerable recursive ability, and the syntax of FLN could quite plausibly have been inherited from the syntax of the language of thought. As Tooby and Cosmides point out in their commentary to Pinker and Bloom's 1990 article, just as we should not ignore architectural constraints, we should be wary of 'naïve spandrelism'.[6]

Precisely what kind of existing behaviours might have been co-opted into the service of inferential communication, and hence laid the foundations for the emergence of public language, is unclear. There are a number of possibilities. An existing repertoire of coded vocal signals, such as the warning calls of modern day vervet monkeys is one possibility; another is that in tandem with vocal calls, ancestral communication may well have involved the use of gesture, facial-signalling or mime (Donald 1998). Yet another possibility is that the source is instinctive emotional calls. This last option is one endorsed by Ray Jackendoff, who suggests that interjections – those semiwords discussed in Chapter 4 – might represent 'fossils of the one word stage of language evolution' (1999, p. 273). Indeed, there is some evidence that interjections do represent some kind of more primitive communicative system: in neurological terms, use of interjections is associated with the phylo-genetically ancient limbic sub-cortical circuitry linked with emotion, as opposed to the more recent cortical structures implicated in the production of language proper.

Proposals of this kind have not met with universal appeal: '[T]he universals of language are so different from anything else in nature . . . that origin as a side consequence of the brain's enhanced capacity, rather than as a simple advance in continuity from ances-tral grunts . . . seems indicated' (Stephen Jay Gould 1989, p. 14). In this view Gould had an unlikely early ally in Chomsky himself: 'in the case of such systems as language or wings it is not easy even to imagine a course of selection that might have given rise to them' (1988, p. 167).

Dennett (1996) discusses Gould's and Chomsky's scepticism over the role natural selection may have played in the evolution of language:

> Gould and Chomsky . . . float the suggestion that nothing we know yet rules out the possibility that . . . change in brain size . . . could have as an adventitious consequence radical discontinuities in behavioural repertoire (hint: such as the sudden blossoming of a Language Acquisition Device). Right. And nothing we know yet rules out the hypothesis that given a few lucky mutations and a slight change in their diet, pigs may suddenly sprout wings or start spinning magnificent pigwebs for the first time in their biological history. (Dennett 1996, p. 264)

Accounts of the evolution of language are fraught with problems, the main one being that there is, of course, none of the evidence that is usually used to confirm (or disconfirm) evolutionary hypotheses: e.g. a fossil record. It may be that, for the moment at least, we will have to content ourselves with a myth.

MYTHS

Grice (1982) presents us with just such a 'myth' about how human cognitive capacities might have spiralled in such a way that mean-ing$_{NN}$ might have emerged from meaning$_N$. He goes on:

But can such a link be explained by a myth? The question is perhaps paralleled, as was recently suggested to me, by the question how the nature and validity of political obligation (or perhaps even of moral obligation) can possibly be explained by a mythical social contract. (1989, p. 297)

Would that Grice's scrupulousness were observed by all researchers looking into evolutionary issues. Some work on the evolution of communication and language seems to start from the assumption that since there presumably is an evolutionary explanation, any evolutionary explanation is probably worth pursuing. Moreover, as I mentioned above, there is a strong case for concluding that in the case of brains (which do not fossilise), and languages (which, unlike linguists, do not fossilise either) a myth is the best we have to offer at the present time.

Grice asks us to imagine a creature[7] which, when in pain, involuntarily emits a noise – for the sake of argument, a groan (of course, the groan could just as easily be a spontaneous gesture, or a naturally coded behaviour, such as an alarm call). At this stage, we might say – just as we did in discussing such examples in Chapter 2 – that the groan means$_N$ that the creature is in pain. Grice then moves through a succession of four further stages designed to show what needs to be added to this scenario in order to arrive at a full-fledged case of meaning$_{NN}$.

In the second stage, Grice adds two further conditions: firstly, that creature X is able to produce the behaviour in question voluntarily, and secondly, that another creature – creature Y – recognises the voluntary nature of the sound X has produced. At this stage, Y's recognition that X is voluntarily producing a noise that is normally involuntary will most likely lead Y to conclude that X is not in pain.

At the next stage, Grice adds a further condition: not only does Y recognise that X has produced the noise voluntarily, but X intended Y to recognise his behaviour as such. The possibility that X was intending to deceive Y is now no longer the only one:

we have now undermined the idea that this is a straightforward piece of deception. Deception consists in trying to get a creature to accept certain things as signs of something or other without knowing that this is a faked case. Here, however, we would have a sort of perverse faked case, in which something is faked but at the same time a clear indication is put in that the faking has been done. (1989, p. 293)

At this stage, Y is likely to be in something of a quandary. Creature X is not only simulating the behaviour of someone in pain, but overtly simulating the behaviour of someone in pain. It does not seem unreasonable to suggest that one way Y might proceed is to presume that X is 'engaging in some form of play or make-believe' (*ibid.*).[8] If Y indeed draws this conclusion, we have reached stage four.

At the fifth stage, Y comes to suppose not that X is playing a game, but rather that X is trying to get Y to believe (or at least accept) that X is in pain: that is, that X's intention in voluntarily producing the normally involuntary behaviour was to convey the very same information of which the involuntary behaviour is a natural sign. The idea may seem far-fetched, but it is not. As just one example, consider how often fake yawns are used to convey the information that one is tired. By this stage, of course, Y may wonder precisely why X should choose to communicate that he is in pain by using a faked expression of pain as opposed to an involuntary sound. Grice suggests various reasons: it might be 'uncreaturely' to act so spontaneously, or (more likely) X's voluntary production might be intended to convey only some, as opposed to all, of the features associated with spontaneous yawns. To this we might add the possibility that, following the discussion in Chapter 2, X may have good reason to 'show' an involuntary behaviour. In this regard, consider the earlier examples in which Lily shows Jack her spontaneous smile, or her spontaneous shiver. Grice does not discuss this possibility, since he was interested in characterising meaning$_{NN}$, which for him could not involve the deliberate showing of spontaneous natural behaviours or, indeed, anything that provided direct evidence of its own for the existence of a certain state of affairs.[9]

By the time we have reached the fifth stage, it is the intention behind the behaviour, rather than the behaviour itself, that plays a central role in Y's successful understanding of X. In Grice's terms, we have now reached:

a stage in which the communication vehicles do not have to be, initially, natural signs of that which they are used to communicate; provided a bit of behaviour could be expected to be seen by the receiving creature as having a discernible connection with a particular piece of information, then that bit of behaviour will be usable by the transmitting creature, provided that the creature can place a fair bet on the connection being made by the receiving creature. (1989, p. 296)

It is not hard to translate Grice's 'myth' about creatures into a myth about humans. Consider the following scenarios, which are to be seen as taking place over many, many generations. Imagine a tribe of our hominid ancestors. When these ancestors are tired, they involuntarily yawn. To other hominids a yawn reliably correlates with tiredness in the same way that, say, black clouds correlate with rain, or spots correlate with measles. Crucially, though, a meta-representational ability is already evolving along the hominid line (perhaps, as we saw earlier, to help better exploit the environment; perhaps to facilitate more complex social interaction). Our ancestors already have rudimentary metarepresentational abilities, and the evolution of the capacity for overt intentional communication should be seen against the backdrop of this independently evolving metarepresentational prowess.

In the first scenario, one member of the tribe – call him Jack – is able to fake a yawn. Another member – call her Lily – recognises the voluntary, **un**spontaneous nature of Jack's yawn. At this stage, the fact that Lily recognises that Jack has faked the yawn may lead her to come to the conclusion that he is not tired. Jack is voluntarily producing a normally involuntary behaviour and could, after all, be trying to deceive her.

In the second scenario, we imagine not only that Lily recognises Jack's yawn as faked, but also that Jack **intends** Lily to recognise his behaviour as such. Jack and Lily can already metarepresent in a rudimentary way: he is thus 'aware' of his intention and capable of metarepresenting it as in (144), while she is capable of recognizing his intention and representing it as in (145):

(144) I intend *that Lily recognises my intention to fake this yawn.*
(145) Jack intends *that I recognise that he intends to fake a yawn.*

The possibility of deception – a plausible interpretation in the previous stage – is now no longer the only possibility. Of course, Lily is still likely to be in something of a quandary, since Jack is not only apparently faking a yawn, but is also doing so *overtly*. It does not seem unreasonable to suggest that one way Lily might proceed is to presume that Jack is engaging in make-believe or being playful. If Lily indeed arrives at this conclusion, we have reached a third scenario.

Consider now a fourth scenario. Lily has come to suppose not that Jack is playing a game, but rather that he is trying to get her to believe that he **is**, in fact, tired. That is, she presumes that Jack's intention in voluntarily producing the normally **in**voluntary yawn was to convey the very same information the involuntary yawn normally conveys. By this stage, of course, Lily may wonder precisely why Jack should choose to communicate that he is tired by using a faked yawn as opposed to an involuntary one. There may be various reasons for this: for instance, Jack's voluntary production might be intended to convey only some, as opposed to all, of the features associated with an involuntary yawn. Perhaps Jack is tired, but not so tired as to yawn involuntarily; perhaps he is feeling drowsy because he feels unwell. (Recall the example described in Chapter 2, where a faked yawn is used to communicate boredom.) Whatever he intends to inform Lily of, he is at this stage entertaining the metarepresentation in (146):

(146) I intend *Lily to realise that I intend to inform her that* . . .

And Lily, if she recognises his intention, is entertaining the metarepresentation in (147):

(147) Jack intends me to *realise that he intends to inform me that* . . .

At this stage, according to Grice's myth, the vehicles of communication (and communication itself) can be characterised in terms of the O-continuum. We have arrived at full-fledged ostensive communication as characterised in earlier chapters. Were we tempted, we might extend Grice's myth and imagine further scenarios in which the evidence provided by a communicator becomes less and less and direct, with successful communication depending to an ever greater extent on attributing intentions to X. The stimulus itself may begin to consist of ever more stylised imitations of spontaneous emissions, and might thus be seen as occupying various points along the continuum. We thus have a framework within which to analyse the evolution of coded behaviours, verbal and non-verbal.

At a given point, the success of communication need no longer depend on any prior natural connection between the ostensive stimulus and the intended meaning, but perhaps instead on some prior stylised version of that connection. What I have in mind is something analogous to the development of writing systems, in which representations that were originally iconic become increasingly stylised. Over the course of time, the final figure (or letter) that emerges as a result of historical processes bears no resemblance at all to the object that was originally represented by the stylised representation, but continues to bear some relation to the original representation itself. In such a way the increase in codification discussed in Chapter 3, and illustrated by the C-continuum, is accounted for in terms of increased reliance by the audience on the intentions behind a stimulus. The C-continuum is thus accommodated within the O-continuum.

Of course, this is only a myth. In 1922, Otto Jesperson wrote '[One] theory [of the evolution of language] is the interjectional, nicknamed the "pooh-pooh", theory: language is derived from instinctive ejaculations called forth by pain or other intense feelings or sensations' (1922, p. 414). I am no pooh-pooh theory revivalist. It is difficult to imagine how full-blown language might have emerged from an accumulation of basic communicative exchanges, how something so complex and sophisticated could ever have crystallised from such beginnings. Here, Hauser *et al.*'s 'spandrel' account may be the best we have, and we may well have to accept that we will never know the true nature of the forces which shaped the emergence of all the components of language proper.

As Sperber and Wilson put it:

[Grice's myth] is reminiscent of the story of how Rockefeller became a millionaire. One day, when he was very young and poor, Rockefeller found a one-cent coin in the street. He bought an apple, polished it, sold it for two cents, bought two apples, polished them, sold them for four cents . . . After one month he bought a cart, after two years he was about to buy a grocery store, when he inherited the fortune of his millionaire uncle. (1986/ 1995, p. 53)

Nonetheless, if communication did play a role in the evolution of language, the myth is still illuminating. Firstly, as I mentioned earlier, those metarepresentational – in a sense, syntactic – abilities that underlie inferential communication are just the kind of abilities that may have been exapted for the syntax of natural language. Secondly and more generally, it doesn't matter what kind of behaviours were used in early inferential communication – existing coded warning calls, instinctive emotional calls, mimes, gestures, facial expressions; what we have is a plausible, naturalistic frame-work on which to build.

It is hard to see how comparable insights are achievable within semiotic, code-based accounts. The semiotic view does not sit comfortably with the Chomskyan view of the human ability to acquire, speak and comprehend language as a natural, biologically inherited one. Semiotic accounts of language and communication characteristically stress its unnatural aspects, focusing on the socially regulated, arbitrary, conventional nature of meanings.

Seen in the light of Grice's myth, however, the unnatural '[arbitrary/conventional] symbol-using mind' (Vol. 2, p. 299) of Peirce and the semioticians can be re-interpreted. Once we have reached a stage where words no longer have to be 'natural signs of that they are used to communicate', we have reached a stage where individuals have the ability to reflect not only on the intentions behind instances of their use, but also on the content of the signals themselves. Indeed, it could be argued that the two abilities are fundamentally the same. Construed in this way, non-natural doesn't mean 'unnatural', and that, I think, means that we're probably on the right track.

BEYOND

In my introductory chapter, I asked four questions. The first – what is the relation between natural non-verbal behaviours and intentional communication? – raised issues about the domain of pragmatic principles. Intentional verbal communication, as we saw, involves a mixture of both natural and non-natural meaning, and an adequate pragmatic theory needs to take account of both. The consequences for the analysis of non-verbal behaviours are threefold: while some non-verbal behaviours betray our thoughts and feelings to others in a way that does not amount to intentionally communicating them, others may be deliberately produced in a way that clearly amounts to intentional communication. A third class – and one which has so far been largely ignored – involves behaviours that are involuntarily produced but deliberately (or overtly) shown.

In discussing the second question – how are non-verbal behaviours interpreted? – I drew a distinction between natural *signs* and natural *signals*. Natural signs (e.g. tree rings, footprints in the snow) carry information which provides evidence for a certain conclusion (e.g. about the age of the tree, the presence of an animal) and are interpreted via inference. Natural signals (e.g. the alarm calls of vervet monkeys, the waggle-dance of honey-bees, bird song) have the function of conveying information: they are governed by *natural codes* and interpreted by specialised decoding mechanisms. Signs and signals alike may convey information accidentally, covertly or overtly.

The third question – what do these behaviours convey? – requires a complex answer. In rare cases (such as, perhaps, affirmative nodding and negative shaking of the head in response to a yes–no question) non-verbal behaviours may contribute to explicit communication. However, since non-verbal behaviours usually communicate vaguer information about emotions, impressions or moods, I made use of the relevance-theoretic distinction between *strong* and *weak* communication, or *strong* and *weak implicatures*. As noted in previous chapters, utterances are rarely uttered in a behavioural vacuum: they typically involve a mixture of strong and weak communication, with non-verbal behaviour generally contributing to the weaker side. Relevance theory provides a framework in which this fact can be accommodated and explained. The final question – What is the relation between natural non-verbal behaviours and those non-verbal behaviours that are not natural? – was explored in Chapter 6. As we saw, the notion of a natural code needs to be augmented with the notion of a cultural code.

I would also argue that the distinctions drawn in answering these four questions have applications for a wide range of disciplines related to pragmatics, and not just for the study of non-verbal behaviours. As I also said in Chapter 1, pragmatics is necessarily a cross-disciplinary subject, with its roots in philosophy and linguistics, but reaching out into such diverse areas as cognitive science, psychology, sociology and even the study of non-human animal communication. The broader aim of this book has been to underline and explore the consequences of this fact. What excites me personally (and has always excited me) about pragmatics is the potential this cross-disciplinary dimension opens up. In the postface to the second edition of *Relevance*, Sperber and Wilson (1986/1995 pp. 258–60) outline some of the wider domains to which the relevance-theoretic approach to pragmatics has begun to be applied: these range from linguistic semantics (Blakemore 1987, 1992, 2002) to lexical acquisition (Akhtar and Tomasello 1996, Happé and Loth 2002, Wharton forthcoming); from translation studies (Gutt 1992) to work in the literary domain on stylistic and poetic effects (Pilkington 2000 Simonin 2006, Vega Moreno 2007); from the analysis of autism (Happé 1993) to evolutionary psychology (Origgi and Sperber 2000, Sperber and Girotto 2003). In recent years, work in *experimental pragmatics* has seen considerable advances (see Noveck and Sperber 2004), and there is great potential for other applications. There is potential to extend pragmatic analyses further, into other aesthetic and even musical domains.

One discipline to which the cognitive pragmatic framework outlined in this book might be fruitfully applied is sociolinguistics. In many ways, it is surprising that rather few attempts have been made in this direction. The anthropologist and sociolinguist John

Gumperz has gone on record as saying: '[i]t is the philosopher Paul Grice who lays the foundation of a truly social perspective on speaking' (2001, p. 216). However, with the notable exception of Penelope Brown, Steven Levinson and their colleagues (see Brown and Levinson 1979, 1987, Enfield 2003, Enfield and Levinson 2006a,b), researchers who adopt a sociolinguistic/anthropological perspective have not so far been very interested in building on the foundations of a 'truly social perspective' that Grice laid.

How might this be done? Earlier in this chapter, when discussing possible implications of the showing–meaning$_{NN}$ continuum for the analysis of historical language change, I noted that the stabilisation of new lexical senses might be characterised in terms of population-scale macro-processes resulting from the accumulation of individual micro-processes. Just as much work in historical linguistics is largely concerned with the patterns of linguistic change themselves (though see Hopper and Traugott 1993/2003), so work in discourse analysis and sociolinguistics often centres on social notions such as power relations and inequality, and examines how they are mani-fested, reinforced and even *constructed* by discourse. Approaching the sociolinguistic domain from a different perspective – that is, starting with the minds of the individuals who create the discourse, and treating macro-level sociolinguistic phenomena as resulting from an accumulation of individual micro-level acts – may yield interesting and worthwhile results.

NOTES

1. By which McNeill means 'gesticulations' on Kendon's continuum; 'I use the term "gesture" in this book specifically to refer to the leftmost, "gesticulation" end of the spectrum' (1992, p. 37).
2. Or producers of ostensive acts generally.
3. Deacon is quite specific on this matter: he proposes that the human capacity for symbolic thought could have led to the development of a Theory of Mind.
4. Actually, there is some evidence that honeybees are able – to some degree at least – to maintain a level of scepticism about the dance of a returning forager. In an ingenious experiment, Gould (1990) removed some forager

bees from a hive and introduced them to a source of pollen on a land-bound boat. He then prevented the bees returning to the hive. Over time, he moved the boat further and further towards the middle of a nearby lake (forcing the bees to fly further and further), and only allowed them to return to the hive and perform their dance when the boat – and therefore the pollen source – was situated right in the middle of the lake. When the foragers finally returned to their hive and danced, *none* of the bees in the hive visited the boat. Gould's interpretation of this was that the bees were comparing the supposed location of the pollen with their knowledge of their environment, and (in a manner of speaking) not *believing* the dancers.

5. If human communication is causal in this way, then it raises another question. In the case of human natural signals such as smiles, do we produce them to let others know that we are happy (i.e. are they, in Grice's terms, *exhibitive*), or do we produce them to encourage others to be happy too (i.e. are they *protreptic*)?

6. Origgi and Sperber 2000 devote the last few pages of their paper to an account of how a rudimentary syntax might have evolved.

7. Much of Grice's work in philosophical psychology involves what he calls 'creature construction'. That is, we imagine ourselves as benevolent *genitors*, designing and constructing organisms (or *operants*) so that their chances of survival might be maximised (Grice is not solely concerned with survival *per se*, but for present purposes that will do). I concentrate on the small section from Grice (1982) rather than the longer, considerably more developed work from 1975 (published in 2000) for reasons of space (my own psychic-conceptual space, that is).

8. The myth is only designed to shed light on phylogeny; nonetheless, in the light of Leslie's proposal that pretence is the first epistemic mental state that children come to recognise and use (if pretence can be regarded as an epistemic mental state), it may have ontogenetic implications too.

9. As we saw earlier, and in contrast to Grice, Schiffer (1972) was happy to describe some of those cases of 'deliberately and openly showing' as meaning$_{NN}$ (the case of the bandaged leg, for example). It's unclear whether he would have come to the same conclusion about intentionally shown spontaneous behaviours.

References

Aitchison, J. (1991) *Language Change: Progress or Decay?* Cambridge: Cambridge University Press.

(1996) *The Seeds of Speech.* Cambridge: Cambridge University Press.

Akhtar, N., M. Carpenter and M. Tomasello (1996) The role of discourse novelty in children's early word learning. *Child Development* 67; 635–45.

Allen, C. and M. Bekoff (1997) *Species of Mind.* Cambridge, MA: MIT Press.

Ameka, F. (1992) Interjections: the universal yet neglected part of speech. *Journal of Pragmatics* 18; 101–18.

Avramides, A. (1989) *Meaning and Mind: An Examination of a Gricean Account of Language.* Cambridge, MA: MIT Press.

Austin, J. (1962) *How to Do Things with Words.* Oxford: Clarendon Press.

Bach, K. (1994) Conversational impliciture. *Mind and Language* 9; 124–62.

(1999) The myth of conventional implicature. *Linguistics and Philosophy* 22; 327–66.

(2001) You don't say? *Synthese* 127; 11–31.

Bach, K. and R. Harnish (1979) *Linguistic Communication and Speech Acts.* Cambridge, MA: MIT Press.

Banfield, A. (1982) *Unspeakable Sentences: Narration and Representation in the Language of Fiction.* Boston, MA: Routledge and Kegan Paul.

Baron-Cohen, S. (1995) *Mindblindness: An Essay on Autism and Theory of Mind.* Cambridge, MA: MIT Press.

Baron-Cohen, S., A. Spitz and P. Cross (1993) Do children with autism recognise surprise? A research note. *Cognition and Emotion* 7(6); 507–16.

Barwise, J. (1989) *The Situation in Logic.* Centre for the Study of Language and Information – distributed by University of Chicago Press.

Bateson, M-C. (1996) On the naturalness of things. In Brockman, J. and K. Matson (eds.) *How Things Are: A Science Tool-kit for the Mind.* Phoenix: London.

Baum, S. and M. Pell (1999) The neural basis of prosody: insights from lesion studies and neuroimaging. *Aphasiology* 13; 581–608.

Benfey, T. (1869) *Geschichte der Sprachwissenschaft.* Munich.

Besemeres, M. and A. Wierzbicka (2003) The meaning of the particle *lah* in Singapore English. *Pragmatics and Cognition* 11; 13–38.

Bickerton, D. (2000) Calls aren't words, syllables aren't syntax. *Psycoloquy* 11(14).

Blake, J., S. McConnell, G. Horton and N. Benson (1992) The gestural repertoire and its evolution over the second year. *Early Development and Parenting* 1; 127–36.

Blakemore, D. (1987) *Semantic Constraints on Relevance.* Oxford: Blackwell.

(1992) *Understanding Utterances: An Introduction to Pragmatics.* Oxford: Blackwell.

(2002) *Relevance and Linguistic Meaning: The Semantics and Pragmatics of Discourse Markers.* Cambridge: Cambridge University Press.

Blass, R. (1990) *Relevance Relations in Discourse: A Study with Special Reference to Sissala.* Cambridge: Cambridge University Press.

Bloom, P. and T. German (2000) Two reasons to abandon the false belief task as a test of theory of mind. *Cognition* 77; B25–B31.

Bolinger, D. (1983) The inherent iconism of intonation. In Haiman, J. (ed.) (1983) *Iconicity in Syntax (Typological studies in language, Volume 6).* Amsterdam/Philadelphia: John Benjamins; 97–109.

Bradbury, J. and S. Vehrencamp (1998) *Principles of Animal Communication.* Sunderland, MA: Sinauer Associates.

Brandon, R. (2005) The theory of biological function and adaptation. Online conference on Adaptation and Representation at. Accessed on 5 August 2008 at www.interdisciplines.org/adaptation/papers/10

Breheny, R. (2006) Communication and Folk Psychology. *Mind and Language* 21(1); 74–107.

Bretherton, I. (1991) Intentional communication and the development of an understanding of mind. In Frye, D. and C. Moore (eds.) *Children's Theories of Mind: Mental States and Social Understanding.* Hillsdale, NJ: Lawrence Erlbaum; 49–75.

Brown, G. and G. Yule (1983) *Discourse Analysis.* Cambridge: Cambridge University Press.

Brown, P. and S. Levinson (1979) Social structure, groups and interaction. In Giles, H. and K. Scherer, (eds.) *Social Markers in Speech.* Cambridge: Cambridge University Press; 291–341.

(1987) *Politeness: Some universals in language usage.* Cambridge: Cambridge University Press.

Byrne, R. and A. Whiten (eds.) (1988) *Machiavellian Intelligence: Social Expertise and the Evolution of Intellect in Monkeys, Apes and Humans.* Oxford: Clarendon Press.

Call, J., J. Bräuer, J. Kaminski and M. Tomasello (2003) Domestic dogs (Canis familiaris) are sensitive to the attentional state of humans. *Journal of Comparative Psychology* 117; 257–63.

Carstairs-McCarthy, A. (1999) *Origins of Complex Language.* Oxford: Oxford University Press.

Carston, R. (1996) Enrichment and loosening: complementary processes in deriving the proposition expressed. *UCL Working Papers in Linguistics* 8; 61–88.

(2000) Explicature and semantics. *UCL Working Papers in Linguistics* 12; 1–44.

(2002a) *Thoughts and Utterances: The Pragmatics of Explicit Communication.* Oxford: Blackwell.

(2002b) Linguistic meaning, communicated meaning and pragmatics. *Mind and Language* 17(1/2) 127–48.

Chen, A. and C. Gussenhoven (2003) Language-dependence in signalling of attitude in speech. In Suzuki, N. and C. Bartneck (eds.) *Proceedings of Workshop on the Subtle Expressivity of Emotion, CHI 2003 Conference on Human and Computer Interaction.*

Cheney D. and R. Seyfarth (1990) *How Monkeys See the World: Inside the Mind of Another Species.* Chicago: Chicago University Press.

Chomsky, N. (1986) *Knowledge of Language.* London: Praeger.

(1988) *Language and Problems of Knowledge: The Managua Lectures.* Cambridge, MA: MIT Press.

(1995) *The Minimalist Program.* Cambridge, MA: MIT Press.

(1999) An Online Interview with Noam Chomsky: on pragmatics and related issues. *Brain and Language,* 68(3) 393–401.

(2000) *New Horizons in the Study of Language and Mind.* Cambridge: Cambridge University Press.

Clark, B. (2007) 'Blazing a trail': moving from natural to linguistic meaning in accounting for the tones of English. In Nilsen, R. A., Appiah Amfo, N. A. and K. Borthen (eds.) *Interpreting Utterances; Pragmatics and its Interfaces. Essays in Honour of Thorstein Fretheim.* Novus, Oslo; 69–81.

Clark, B. and R. Gerrig (1990) Quotations as demonstrations. *Language* 66; 764–805.

Clark, B. and G. Lindsey (1990) Intonation, grammar and utterance interpretation. *University College London Working Papers in Linguistics* 2; 32–51.

Clark, H. (1996) *Using Language.* Cambridge: Cambridge University Press.

Clark, H. and J. Fox Tree (2002) Using 'uh' and 'um' in spontaneous speaking. *Cognition* 84; 73–111.

Corballis, M. (2002) *From Hand to Mouth: The Origins of Language.* Oxford: Oxford University Press.

Cole, P. and J. Morgan (eds.) (1975) *Syntax and Semantics 3: Speech Acts.* New York, Academic Press.

Cosmides, L. (1989) The logic of social exchange: has natural selection shaped how humans reason? Studies with the Wason selection task. *Cognition* 31; 197–276.

Cosmides, L. and J. Tooby (2000) Consider the source: The evolution of adaptations for decoupling and metarepresentation. In Sperber, D. (ed.) *Metarepresentations: A Multidisciplinary Perspective. Vancouver Studies in Cognitive Science*. New York: Oxford University Press; 53–115.

Crystal, D. (1995) *The Cambridge Encyclopaedia of Linguistics*. Cambridge: Cambridge University Press.

Cuxac, C. (1999) The expression of spatial relations and the spatialization of semantics in French Sign Language. In Fuchs, C. and S. Roberts (eds.) *Language Diversity and Cognitive Representations*. Amsterdam: Benjamins; 123–42.

Dale, R. (1996) Theory of Meaning. PhD Thesis. City University of new York. Available online at http://russelldale.com/dissertation/parts.html.

Darwin, C. (1872) *The Expression of the Emotions in Man and Animals*. London: John Murray. Republished (1998). (Edited with foreword, commentary and afterword by P. Ekman.) London: Harper Collins.

Davidson, D. and G. Harman (eds.) (1975) *The Logic of Grammar*. Dordrecht: Reidel.

Davies, M. (1996) Philosophy of language. In Bunnin, N. and E. P Tsui-James (eds.) *The Blackwell Companion to Philosophy*. Oxford: Blackwell; 90–139.

Davies, P. (1994) Troubles for direct proper functions. *Noûs* 28(3); 363–81.

Davis, S. (1991) *Pragmatics: A Reader*. Oxford: Oxford University Press.

Deacon, T. (1997) *The Symbolic Species*. London: Penguin.

Demko, T. (1995) Which came first: bees or flowers? *Science Times; The New York Times*. Tuesday 23 May 1995; B7–B8.

Dennett, D. (1978) Beliefs about beliefs. *Behavior and Brain Sciences* 4; 568–70.

(1987) *The Intentional Stance*. Cambridge, MA: MIT Press.

(1988) The Intentional Stance in Theory and in Practice. In Byrne, R. and A. Whiten (eds.) (1988) *Machiavellian Intelligence: Social Expertise and The Evolution of Intellect in Monkeys, Apes and Humans*. Oxford: Clarendon Press; 180–202.

(1995) *Darwin's Dangerous Idea – Evolution and the Meanings of Life*. London: Penguin.

(1996) Granny versus Mother Nature – No Contest. *Mind and Language* 11; 263–9.

Dolan, R., J. Morris, and B. de Gelder (2001) Crossmodal binding of fear in voice and face. *Proceedings of the National Academy of Sciences USA* 9; 10006–10.

Donald, M. (1998) Mimesis and the executive suite. In Hurford, J., M. Studdert-Kennedy and C. Knight (eds.) *Approaches to the Evolution of Language*. Cambridge: Cambridge University Press; 44–68.

Dreller, C. and W. Kirchner (1993) How honeybees perceive the information of the dance language. *Naturwissenshaften* 80; 319–21.

(1994) Hearing in the Asian honeybees Apis dorsata and Apis florae. *Insectes Socieaux* 42; 115–25.

Duchenne, G. (1862) Mécanisme de la Physionomie Humaine, republished as (1990) *The Mechanism of Human Facial Expression* (edited and translated by R. A. Cuthbertson) Cambridge: Cambridge University Press.

Dummett, M. (1981) *The Interpretation of Frege's Philosophy.* London: Duckworth.

Dunbar, R. (1998) Theory of mind and the evolution of language. In Hurford, J., M. Studdert-Kennedy and C. Knight (eds.) *Approaches to the Evolution of Language.* Cambridge: Cambridge University Press; 92–111.

Eco, U. (1976) *A Theory of Semiotics.* London: Macmillan.

Eibl-Eibesfeldt, I. (1972) Similarities and differences between cultures in expressive movements. In Hinde, R. (ed.) *Non-Verbal Communication.* Cambridge: Cambridge University Press; 297–312.

Efron, D. (1941) *Gesture and Environment.* Morningside Heights, NY: King's Crown Press.

Ekman, P. (1989) The argument and evidence about universals in facial expressions of emotion. In Wagner, H. and A. Manstead (eds.) *Handbook of Social Psychophysiology.* New York: Wiley; 143–64.

(1992) An argument for basic emotion. *Cognition and Emotion* 6(3/4); 169–200.

(1994) Strong evidence for universals in facial expressions: A Reply to Russell's Mistaken Critique. *Psychological Bulletin* 115(2); 268–87.

(1999) Emotional and conversational nonverbal signals. In Messing, L. and R. Campbell (eds.) *Gesture, Speech and Sign.* Oxford: Oxford University Press; 45–57.

Ekman, P. and W. Friesen (1969) The repertoire of non-verbal behaviour categories: Origins, usage and coding. *Semiotica* 1; 49–98.

Ekman, P. and E. L. Rosenberg (1997) *What the Face Reveals.* New York: Oxford University Press.

Enfield, N. (2003) *Linguistic Epidemiology: Semantics and Grammar of Language Contact in Mainland South East Asia.* London: Routledge.

Enfield, N. and S. Levinson (eds.) (2006a) *Roots of Human Sociality. Culture, Cognition and Interaction.* New York: Berg Publishers.

Enfield, N. and S. Levinson (2006b) Introduction: human sociality as a new interdisciplinary field. In Enfield, N. and S. Levinson (eds.) *Roots of Human Sociality,* 1–35. New York: Berg Publishers: 1–35.

Escandell-Vidal, V. (1998) Intonation and procedural encoding: The case of Spanish interrogatives. In Rouchota, V. and A. Jucker (eds.) *Current Issues in Relevance Theory.* Amsterdam: John Benjamins; 169–203.

Escandell-Vidal, V. (2002) Echo-syntax and metarepresentations. *Lingua* 112; 871–900.

Feibelman, J. (1960) *An Introduction to Peirce's Philosophy*. London: Allen and Unwin.

Fernandez-Dols, J. and M.-A Ruiz Belda (1995) Are smiles a sign of happiness? Gold medal winners at the Olympic Games. *Journal of Personality and Social Psychology* 69; 1113–19.

Fretheim, T. (2002) Intonation as a constraint on inferential processing. In Bel, B. and I. Marlien (eds.) *Proceedings of the Speech Prosody 2002 Conference*: 59–64.

Fodor, J. (1975) *The Language of Thought*. New York: Crowell.

(1981) *Representations*. Hassocks: Harvester Press.

(1983) *The Modularity of Mind*. Cambridge, MA: MIT Press.

(1998) *Concepts: Where Cognitive Science Went Wrong*. Oxford: Clarendon Press.

Fodor, J., J. Fodor and M. Garrett (1975) The psychological unreality of semantic representations. *Linguistic Enquiry, Fall* 1975; 515–31.

Fridlund, A. (1994) *Human Facial Expression: An Evolutionary View*. San Diego: Academic Press.

von Frisch, K. (1967) *The Dance Language and Orientation of Bees*. Cambridge, MA: Belknap Press of Harvard University Press.

Gardiner, A. (1951) *The Theory of Speech and Language*. 2nd edition. Oxford: Clarendon Press. (First published: Oxford, 1932.)

Garfinkel, H. (1967) *Studies in Ethnomethodology*. Englewood Cliffs, NJ: Prentice Hall.

Gazzaniga, M. and C. Smiley (1991) Hemispheric mechanisms controlling voluntary and spontaneous facial expressions. *Journal of Cognitive Neuroscience* 2; 239–45.

Gibbs, R. (1999) *Intentions in the Experience of Meaning*. Cambridge: Cambridge University Press.

Gigerenzer, G. and P. Todd (1999) Fast and frugal heuristics: the adaptive toolbox. In Gigerenzer, G., P. Todd and the ABC Research Group. *Simple Heuristics That Make Us Smart*. Oxford: Oxford University Press.

Gigerenzer, G., P. Todd and the ABC Research Group. *Simple Heuristics That Make Us Smart*. Oxford: Oxford University Press.

Goffman, E. (1964) The neglected situation. *American Anthropologist* 66(6), part 2; 133–6.

(1981) *Forms of talk*. Oxford: Blackwell.

Goodglass, H. (1993) *Understanding Aphasia*. New York: Academic Press.

Goodwin, C. (1981) *Conversational Organisation: Interaction between Speakers and Hearers*. New York: Academic Press.

Gould, J. (1990) Honeybee cognition. *Cognition* 37; 83–103.

Gould, S. J. (1989) Tires to Sandals. *Natural History*, April 1989, 8–15.

Gould, S. J. and R. Lewontin (1979) The spandrels of San Marco and the Panglossian paradigm: A critique of the adaptationist program. In Selzer, J. (1993) *Understanding Scientific Prose*. Wisconsin: University of Wisconsin Press.

Grandy, R. and R. Warner (1986) Paul Grice: a view of his work. In Grandy, R. and R. Warner (eds.) *Philosophical Grounds of Rationality: Intentions, Categories, Ends*. Oxford: Clarendon Press; 1–44.

Green, M. (2007) *Self-expression*. Oxford: Oxford University Press.

Grice, H. P. (1957) Meaning. *Philosophical Review* 66; 377–88.

(1967) *William James Lectures* I-VII. Unpublished typescripts.

(1968) Utterer's meaning sentence meaning and word-meaning. *Foundations of Language* 4; 225–42.

(1969) Utterer's meaning and intentions. *Philosophical Review* 78; 147–77.

(1975) Logic and conversation. In Cole, P. and J. Morgan (eds.) *Syntax and Semantics 3: Speech Acts*. New York: Academic Press; 41–58.

(1982) Meaning revisited. In Smith, N. (ed.) *Mutual Knowledge*. London: Academic Press.

(1989) *Studies In The Way of Words*. Cambridge, MA: Harvard University Press.

(2001) *Aspects of Reason*. (Edited by Warner, R.) Oxford: Clarendon Press.

Gullberg, M. (1998) *Gesture as a Communication Strategy in Second Language Discourse: A Study of Learners of French and Swedish*. Lund: Lund University Press.

Gumperz, J. (1964) Linguistic and social interaction in two communities. In Gumperz, J. and D. Hymes (eds.) The ethnography of communication. *American Anthropologist* 66(6), part 2; 137–54.

(1982) *Discourse Strategies*. Cambridge: Cambridge University Press.

Gumperz, J. (2001) Interactional linguistics: a personal perspective. In Schiffrin, D., D. Tannen and H. Hamilton (eds.) *The Handbook of Discourse Analysis*. Oxford: Blackwell.

Gumperz, J. and D. Hymes (1972) (eds.) *Directions in Sociolinguistics*. New York: Holt, Reinhart and Winston.

Gussenhoven, C. (2002) *Intonation and interpretation: Phonetics and Phonology. Speech Prosody 2002: Proceedings of the First International Conference on Speech Prosody*. Aix-en-Provence, ProSig and Université de Provence Laboratoire Parole et Langage. 47–57.

(2004) *The Phonology of Tone and Intonation*. Cambridge: Cambridge University Press.

Gutt, E. (1992) *Relevance Theory: A Guide to Successful Communication in Translation*. Dallas, Summer Institute of Linguistics, and New York, United Bible Societies.

Halliday, M. (1963) *Explorations in the Function of Language*. London: Arnold.

(1967) *Intonation and Grammar in British English*. The Hague: Mouton.

Hamilton, E. and H. Cairns (1989) *The Collected Dialogues of Plato*. Princeton, NJ: Princeton University Press.

Happé, F. (1993) Communicative competence and theory of mind in autism: A test of relevance theory. *Cognition* 48; 101–19.

(1994) *Autism: An Introduction to Psychological Theory*. Cambridge, MA: Harvard University Press.

(1992) The autobiographical writings of three Asperger syndrome adults: Problems of interpretation and implications for theory. In Frith, U. (ed.) *Autism and Asperger Syndrome*. Cambridge: Cambridge University Press; 207–42.

Happé, F. and E. Loth (2002) *Theory of mind and tracking speakers' intentions. in Mind and Language* 17 (1/2); 24–36.

Hare, B. and M. Tomasello (2005) Human-like social skills in dogs? *Trends in Cognitive Sciences* 9; 439–44.

Hart, H. L. A. (1952) Signs and words. *Philosophical Quarterly Vol. 2*. The University of St. Andrews for The Scots Philosophy Club.

Hauser, M. (1996) *The Evolution of Communication*. Cambridge, MA: MIT Press.

Hauser, M., N. Chomsky, and T. Fitch (2002) The faculty of language: what is it? Who has it, and how did it evolve? *Science* 298; 1569–79.

Hirschberg, J and G. Ward (1995) The interpretation of the high-rise question contour in English. *Journal of Pragmatics* 24; 407–12.

Hobson, P., J. Ouston and A. Lee (1988) What's in a face? The case of autism. *British Journal of Psychology*. 79(4); 441–53.

Hockett, C. (1959) Animal 'languages' and human language. In Spuhler, J. N. (ed.) *The Evolution of Man's Capacity for Culture*. Detroit: Wayne State University Press; 32–9.

Holliday Willey, L. (1999) *Pretending to be Normal*. London: Jessica Kingsley.

Holloway, J. (1951) *Language and Intelligence*. London: Macmillan.

van Hooff, J. (1972) A comparative approach to the phylogeny of laughter and smiling. In Hinde, R. (ed.) *Non-verbal Communication*. Cambridge: Cambridge University Press; 209–38.

Hopper, P. and E. Traugott (1993) *Grammaticalization*. Cambridge: Cambridge University Press. (Revised edition published 2003.)

House, J. (1990) Intonation structures and pragmatic interpretation. In Ramsaran, S. (ed.) *Studies in the Pronunciation of English*. London: Routledge; 38–57.

(2006) Constructing a context with intonation. *Journal of Pragmatics* 38(10); 1542–58.

Humphrey, N. (1984) *Consciousness Regained.* Oxford: Oxford University Press.

(1988) The social function of intellect. In Byrne, R. and A. Whiten (eds.) (1988) *Machiavellian Intelligence: Social Expertise and The Evolution of Intellect in Monkeys, Apes and Humans.* Oxford: Clarendon Press; 271–86.

Hymes, D. (1972) On communicative competence. In Pride, J. and J. Holmes (eds.) *Sociolinguistics.* Harmondsworth: Penguin.

Ifantidou-Trouki, E. (1993) Sentential adverbs and relevance. *Lingua* 90 (1); 65–90.

Ifantidou, E. (2001) *Evidentials and Relevance.* Amsterdam: John Benjamins.

Imai, K. (1998) Intonation and relevance. In Carston, R. and S. Uchida (eds.) *Relevance Theory: Applications and Implications.* Amsterdam: John Benjamins; 69–86.

Itani, R. (1995) Semantics and Pragmatics of Hedges in English and Japanese. University of London. PhD Thesis.

Iten, C. (2000) 'Non-truth-Conditional' Meaning, Relevance and Concessives. University of London PhD Thesis.

Jackendoff, R. (1999) Possible stages in the evolution of the language capacity. *Trends in Cognitive Sciences* 3(7); 272–9.

Jakobson, R. and M. Halle (1956) *Fundamentals of Language.* The Hague: Mouton.

Jespersen, O. (1922) *Language: Its Nature, Development and Origin.* London: Allen and Unwin.

Kaplan, D. (1977) Demonstratives. In Almog, J., J. Perry and H. Wettstein (eds.) (1989) *Themes from Kaplan.* Oxford: Oxford University Press; 481–563.

(1997) What is meaning? Explorations in the theory of meaning as use. Unpublished manuscript.

Kazantzakis, N. (1965) *Travels in Greece (Journey to the Morea).* Translated by F. A. Reed. Oxford: Bruno Cassirer.

Kendon, A. (1988) How gestures can become like words? In Poyotas, F. (ed.) *Cross-cultural Perspectives in Nonverbal Communication.* Toronto: Hogrefe; 131–41.

(1992) The negotiation of context in face-to-face interaction. In Duranti, A. and C. Goodwin (eds.) *Rethinking Context: Language as an Interactive Phenomenon.* Cambridge: Cambridge University Press.

(2004) *Gesture: Visible Action as Utterance.* Cambridge: Cambridge University Press.

König E. (1991) *The Meaning of Focus Particles: A Comparative Perspective.* London: Routledge.

Kraut, R. and R. Johnston (1979) Social and emotional messages of smiling: An ethological approach. *Journal of Personality and Social Psychology* 42; 1529–53.

Ladd, R. (1978) *The Structure of Intonational Meaning*. London: Indiana University Press.

(1996) *Intonational Phonology*. Cambridge: Cambridge University Press.

Lass, R. (1997) *Historical Linguistics and Language Change*. Cambridge: Cambridge University Press.

Levinson, S. (2000) *Presumptive Meanings*. Cambridge, MA: MIT Press.

Leslie, A. (1987) Pretense and representation: The origins of 'theory of mind'. *Psychological Review* 94; 412–26.

(1992) Pretense, autism, and the 'theory-of-mind' module. *Current Directions in Psychological Science* 1; 18–21.

(1994) ToMM, ToBY and Agency: core architecture and domain-specificity. In Hirschfeld, L. and S. Gelman (eds.) *Mapping the Mind: Domain Specificity in Cognition and Culture*. Cambridge: Cambridge University Press; 119–48.

Leslie, A. and F. Happé (1989) Autism and ostensive communication: The relevance of metarepresentation. *Development and Psychopathology* 1; 205–12.

Levinson, S. (1989) *Pragmatics*. Cambridge: Cambridge University Press.

Lewis, D. (1969) *Convention*. Cambridge, MA: Harvard University Press.

Lieberman, M. (2000) Intuition: A social-cognitive neuroscience approach. *Psychological Bulletin* 126; 109–37.

Lightfoot, D. (1991) *How to Set Parameters: Arguments from Language Change*. Cambridge, MA: MIT Press.

Lizskowski, U., M. Carpenter, T. Striano and M. Tomasello (2006) 12- and 18-month-olds point to provide information for others. *Journal of Cognition and Development* 7; 173–187.

Lycan, W. (1991) Review of Avramides, A. (1989) *Meaning and Mind: An Examination of a Gricean Account of Language*. In *Mind and Language* 6; 83–6.

Lyons, J. (1972) Human Language. In Hinde, R. (ed.) *Non-Verbal Communication*. Cambridge: Cambridge University Press; 49–86.

McCann, J. and S. Peppé (2003) Prosody in autism spectrum disorders: A critical review. *International Journal of Language and Communication Disorders* 38; 325–50.

McDowell, J. (1980) Meaning, communication and knowledge. In Z. van Straaten (ed.) *Philosophical Subjects. Essays Presented to P. F. Strawson*. Oxford: Clarendon Press.

McNeill, D. (1992) *Hand and Mind: What Gestures Reveal about Thought*. Chicago: University of Chicago Press.

(ed.) (2000) *Language and Gesture*. Cambridge: Cambridge University Press.

Miller, G. (1978) Semantic relations among words. In Halle, M., J. Bresnan and G. Miller (eds.) *Linguistic Theory and Psychological Reality*. Cambridge, MA: MIT Press; 60–118.

Millikan, R. (1984) *Language, Thought and Other Biological Categories*. Cambridge, MA: MIT Press.

Mithen, S. (2005) *The Singing Neanderthals: The Origins of Music, Language, Mind and Body*. London: Weidenfeld and Nicholson.

Moles, A. (1963) Animal language and information theory [Originally published as 'Langage animal et théorie de l'information']. In Busnel, R. (ed.) *Acoustic Behaviour of Animals*. Amsterdam: Elsevier; 112–31.

Morris, C. H. (1938) Foundation of the theory of signs. Reprinted in Morris, C. (1971) *Writings on the General Theory of Signs*. The Hague: Mouton; 13–71.

Muller, M. (1862) *Lectures on the Science of Language*. New York: Charles Scribner.

Muris, P., C. Meesters, H. Merckelbach and M. Lomme (1995) Knowledge of basic emotions in adolescent and adult individuals with autism. *Psychological Reports* 76(1), Feb 1995; 52–4.

Neale, S. (1992) Paul Grice and the philosophy of language. *Linguistics and Philosophy* 15(5); 509–59.

Noveck, I. and D. Sperber (eds.) (2004) *Experimental Pragmatics*. Palgrave Macmillan.

Ogden, C. and I. Richards (1923) *The Meaning of Meaning: A Study of the Influence of Language upon Thought*. London: Routledge and Kegan Paul.

Okanoya, K. (2002) Sexual selection as a syntactical vehicle: The evolution of syntax in birdsong and human language through sexual selection. In Wray, A. (ed.) *The Transition to Language*. Oxford: Oxford University Press; 46–64.

Onishi, K. and R. Baillargeon (2005) Do 15-month-old infants understand false beliefs? *Science* 308: American Association for the Advancement of Science; 255–8.

Onishi, K., R. Baillargeon and A. Leslie (2007) 15-month-old infants detect violations in pretend sequences. *Acta Psychologica* 124; 106–28.

Origgi, G. and D. Sperber (2000) Evolution, communication and the proper function of language. In Carruthers, P. and A. Chamberlain (eds.) *Evolution and the Human Mind: Modularity, Language and Meta-cognition*. New York: Cambridge University Press; 140–69.

Ozonoff, S., B. Pennington and S. Rogers (1990) Are there emotion perception deficits in young autistic children? *Journal of Child Psychology and Psychiatry and Allied Disciplines* 31(3); 343–61.

Peirce, C. (1897, 1903) Logic as semiotic: the theory of signs. In Buchler, J. (ed.) (1955) *The Philosophical Writings of Peirce*. New York: Dover Press.

Pell, M. (2002a) Surveying emotional prosody in the brain. In Bel, B. and I. Marlien (eds.) *Proceedings of the Speech Prosody 2002 Conference*; 77–82.

(2002b) Evaluation of nonverbal emotion in face and voice: Some preliminary findings on a new battery of tests. *Brain and Cognition* 48; 499–514.

Pilkington, A. (2000) *Poetic Effects: A Relevance Theory Perspective*. Amsterdam: John Benjamins.

Pinker, S. and P. Bloom (1990) Natural Language and Natural Selection. *Behavioural and Brain Sciences* 13; 707–84.

Provine, R. (2000) *Laughter: A Scientific Investigation*. London: Faber and Faber.

Quirk, R., S. Greenbaum, J. Leech and J. Svartik (eds.) (1985) *A Comprehensive Grammar of the English Language*. London: Longman.

Recanati, F. (1987) *Meaning and Force: The Pragmatics of Performative Utterances*. Cambridge: Cambridge University Press.

(1993) *Direct Reference*. Oxford: Blackwell.

(1998) Pragmatics. In *Routledge Encyclopaedia of Philosophy*, Vol. 7. London: Routledge; 620–633.

(2002) Unarticulated Constituents. *Linguistics and Philosophy* 25; 299–345.

(2002) Does linguistic communication rest on inference? *Mind and Language* 17(1/2); 105–26.

(2004) *Literal Meaning*. Cambridge: Cambridge University Press.

Rey, G. (1980) Functionalism and the emotions. In Rorty, A. (ed.) *Explaining Emotions*. Los Angeles: University of California Press; 163–98.

Rinn, W. (1984) The neuropsychology of facial expression: a review of the neurological and psychological mechanisms for producing facial expressions. *Psychological Bulletin* 95; 52–77.

Ross, E., J. Edmonson, G. Seibert and R. Homan (1988) Acoustic analysis of affective prosody during right-sided Wada test: a within-subjects verification of the right hemisphere's role in language. *Brain and Language* 33; 128–45.

Russell, J. (1994) Is there universal recognition of emotion from facial expression? A review of cross-cultural studies. *Psychological Bulletin* 115; 102–41.

Sabbagh, M. (1999) Communicative intentions and language: Evidence from right-hemisphere damage and autism. *Brain and Language* 68; 29–69.

Sacks, O. (1994) A neurologist's notebook: An Anthropologist on Mars. *New Yorker*, 27 December 1993–3 January 1994.

Sadock, J. and A. Zwicky (1985) Speech act distinctions in syntax. In Shopen, T. (ed.) *Language Typology and Syntactic Description*. Volume 1. Cambridge: Cambridge University Press; 155–96.

Sapir, E. (1970) *Language: An Introduction to the Study of Speech*. London: Harvest.

Saussure, F. de (1974) *Course in General Linguistics*. (First published 1916.) London: Peter Owen.

Scheuer, J. (1995) Relevance and prosody in spoken Danish. *Journal of Pragmatics* 23; 421–47.

Schiffer, S. (1972) *Meaning*. Oxford: Clarendon Press.

Schiffrin, B. (1987) *Discourse Markers*. Cambridge: Cambridge University Press.
(1994) *Approaches to Discourse*. Oxford: Blackwell.

Scholl, B. and A. Leslie (1999) Modularity, development and 'theory of mind'. *Mind and Language* 14; 131–53.

Searle, J. (1965) What is a speech act? In Black, M. (ed.) *Philosophy in America*. Allen and Unwin; 221–39.
(1969) *Speech acts*. Cambridge: Cambridge University Press.
(1979) *Expression and Meaning*. Cambridge: Cambridge University Press.

Sebeok, T. (1972) *Perspectives in Zoosemiotics*. The Hague: Mouton.

Seddoh, S. (2002) How discrete or independent are 'affective' prosody and 'linguistic' prosody? *Aphasiology* 16; 683–92.

Seeley, T. (1989) The honey-bee colony as a superorganism. *American Scientist* 77; 546–53.

Seyfarth, R. and D. Cheney (1992) Meaning and mind in monkeys. *Scientific American* 267(6); 78–86.

Seyfarth, R., D. Cheney and P. Marler (1980) Vervet monkey alarm calls: semantic communication in a free-ranging primate. *Animal Behaviour* 28; 1070–94.

Shannon, C. and W. Weaver (1949) *The Mathematical Theory of Communication*. Urbana, IL: University of Illinois Press.

Simonin, O. (2006) Literary meaning and speaker's intention. Paper delivered at the 1st International Literature and Cognitive Science Conference (University of Connecticut, Storrs).

Smith, C. and H. Scott (1997) A componential approach to the meaning of facial expressions. In Russell, J. and J. Fernandez-Dols (eds.) *The Psychology of Facial Expression*. New York: Cambridge University Press;

Smith, N. and I. Tsimpli (1995) *The Mind of a Savant*. Oxford: Blackwell.

Southgate, V., C. van Maanen and G. Csibra (2007) Infant pointing: Communication to cooperate or communication to learn? *Child Development* 78; 735–40.

Sperber, D. (1990) The Evolution of the language faculty: A paradox and its solution. *Behavioural and Brain Sciences* 13; 756–8.
(1994) The modularity of thought and the epidemiology of representations. In Hirschfeld, L. and S. Gelman (eds.) *Mapping the Mind: Domain Specificity in Cognition and Culture*. Cambridge: Cambridge University Press; 39–67.

(1995) How do we communicate? In Brockman, J. and K. Matson (eds.) *How Things Are: A Science Tool-kit for the Mind*. Phoenix: London; 191–9.

(1996) *Explaining Culture: A Naturalistic Approach*. Blackwell: Oxford.

(2000) Metarepresentations in an evolutionary perspective. In Sperber, D. (ed.) *Metarepresentations : A Multidisciplinary Perspective*. Oxford: Oxford University Press; 117–37.

(2001) An evolutionary perspective on testimony and argumentation. *Philosophical Topics* 29; 401–13.

(2007) Seedless grapes: nature and culture. In Laurence, S. and E. Margolis (eds.) *Creations of the Mind: Theories of Artifacts and their Representation*. Oxford: Oxford University Press; 124–37.

Sperber, D. and V. Girotto (2003) Does the selection task detect cheater detection? In Fitness, J. and K. Sterelny (eds.) *From Mating to Mentality: Evaluating Evolutionary Psychology*. Monographs in Cognitive Science. Psychology Press.

Sperber, D. and D. Wilson (1986/1995) *Relevance: Communication and Cognition*. Oxford: Blackwell.

(1997) Remarks on relevance theory and the Social Sciences. *Multilingua* 16; 145–51.

(1998) The mapping between the mental and public lexicon. In Carruther, P. and J. Bouchers (eds.) *Language and Thought: Interdisciplinary Themes*. Cambridge: Cambridge University Press; 184–200.

(2002) Pragmatics, modularity and mindreading. *Mind and Language* 17; 3–23.

Stalnaker, R. (1978) Assertion. In Cole, P (ed.) *Pragmatics: Syntax and Semantics Volume 9*. New York: Academic Press.

(2002) Common Ground. *Linguistics and Philosophy* 25; 701–21.

Stanley, J. (2000) Context and logical form. *Linguistics and Philosophy* 23; 391–434.

Steedman, M. (2000) Information structure and the syntax-phonology interface. *Linguistic Inquiry* 31(4); 649–89.

Stevenson, C. (1944) *Ethics and Language*. New Haven and London: Yale University Press.

Strawson, P. (1964) Intention and convention in speech acts. *Philosophical Review* 73; 439–60.

Suppes, P. (1996) The primacy of utterer's meaning. In Grandy, R. and R. Warner (eds.) *Philosophical Grounds of Rationality: Intentions, Categories, Ends*. Oxford: Clarendon Press; 109–29.

Surian, L., L. Caldi and D. Sperber (in press) Attribution of beliefs by 13-month-old infants. To appear in *Psychological Science*.

Tench, P. (1996) *The Intonation Systems of English*. London: Cassell.

Tomasello, M. and M. Barton (1996) Learning words in non-ostensive contexts. *Cognitive Development* 10; 201–24.

Tomasello, M., M. Carpenter, J. Call, T. Behne and H. Moll (2005) Understanding and sharing intentions: The origins of cultural cognition. *Behavioral and Brain Sciences* 28; 675–91.

Trask, R. L. (1993) *A Dictionary of Grammatical Terms in Linguistics*. London: Routledge.

Traugott, E. and P. Hopper (1993/2003) *Grammaticalization*. Cambridge: Cambridge University Press.

Vega-Moreno, R. (2007) *Creativity and Convention: The Pragmatics of Everyday Figurative Speech*. Amsterdam: John Benjamins.

Vandepitte, S. (1989) A pragmatic function of intonation. *Lingua* 79; 265–97.

Vygotsky, L. (1962) *Thought and Language*. (Translated by E. Hanfmann and G. Vakar) Cambridge, MA: MIT Press.

Welby, Lady Victoria (1893) Meaning and metaphor. *Monist* 3(4); 510–25. Reprinted in Welby (1985).

(1896) Sense meaning and interpretation. *Mind* 5(17); 24–37 and *Mind* 5(18) (1896). Reprinted in Welby (1985).

(1911) Reprinted as Welby (1985) H. Walter Schmitz (ed.) *Signifcs and Language: The Articulate Form of Our Expressive and Interpretive Resources*. Amsterdam and Philadelphia: John Benjamins.

Wharton, T. (2000a) Interjections, evolution and the 'showing'/'saying' continuum. *Paper presented at* The Third International Conference on the Evolution of Language (Evolang). Paris, 3–6 April 2000.

(2000b) Interjections language and the 'showing'/'saying' continuum. *UCL Working Papers in Linguistics* 12; 173–213.

(2001) Natural pragmatics and natural codes. *UCL Working Papers in Linguistics* 13; 109–58.

(2002) Paul Grice saying and meaning. *UCL Working Papers in Linguistics* 14; 207–48.

(2003a) Interjections language and the 'showing'/'saying' continuum. *Pragmatics and Cognition.* 11(1); 39–91.

(2003b) Natural pragmatics and natural codes. *Mind and Language* 18; 447–77.

(2008) Meaning and showing: Gricean intentions and relevance theoretic intentions. *Intercultural Pragmatics* 5(2); 131–52.

Whiten, A. and R. Byrne (1988) Taking (Machiavellian) Intelligence Apart: editorial. In Byrne, R. and A. Whiten (eds.) (1988) *Machiavellian Intelligence: Social Expertise and The Evolution of Intellect in Monkeys, Apes and Humans*. Oxford: Clarendon Press; 50–66.

(1997) *Machiavellian Intelligence II: Extensions and Evaluations*. Cambridge: Cambridge University Press.

Wichmann, A. (2000) The attitudinal effects of prosody, and how they relate to emotion. In *Proceedings of Speech Emotion-2000*; 143–48.

(2002) Attitudinal intonation and the inferential process. In Bel, B. and I. Marlien (eds) *Proceedings of the Speech Prosody Conference*; 11–16.

Wierzbicka, A. (1992) The semantics of interjection. *Journal of Pragmatics* 18; 159–92.

(1994) Cognitive domains and the structure of the lexicon: The case of emotions. In Hirschfeld, L. and S. Gelman (eds.) *Mapping the Mind: Domain Specificity in Cognition and Culture*. Cambridge: Cambridge University Press; 431–53.

(1996) *Semantics: Primes and Universals*. Oxford: Oxford University Press.

(2000) The semantics of human facial expression. *Pragmatics and Cognition* 8(1); 147–83.

Wilkins, D. (1992) Interjections as deictics. *Journal of Pragmatics* 18; 119–58.

Willey, L. Holliday (1999) *Pretending to be Normal*. London: Jessica Kingsley.

Williams, D. (1992) *Nobody Nowhere: The Remarkable Autobiography of an Autistic Girl*. London: Jessica Kingsley.

(1994) *Somebody Somewhere*. London: Jessica Kingsley.

(1999) *Like Colour to the Blind*. London: Jessica Kingsley.

Wilson, D. (1998) Linguistic Structure and Inferential Communication. In Caron, B. (ed.) *Proceedings of the 16th International Congress of Linguists*. Oxford: Pergamon.

(2000) Metarepresentation in linguistic communication. In Sperber, D. (ed.) *Metarepresentations: A Multidisciplinary Perspective*. Oxford: Oxford University Press; 411–48.

(2003) Relevance theory and lexical pragmatics. *Italian Journal of Linguistics/Rivista di Linguistica* 15; 273–91.

(2005) New directions for research on pragmatics and modularity. *Lingua* 115; 1129–46.

Wilson, D. and R. Carston (2007) A unitary approach to lexical pragmatics: Relevance, inference and ad hoc concepts. In Burton-Roberts, N. (ed.) *Pragmatics*. London: Palgrave; 230–59.

Wilson, D. and D. Sperber (1981) On Grice's theory of conversation. In Werth, P. (ed.) *Conversation and discourse*. Croom Helm, London.

(1988) Mood and the analysis of non-declarative sentences. In Dancy, J., J. Moravcsik and C. Taylor (eds.) *Human Agency: Language, Duty and Value*. Stanford, CA: Stanford University Press; 77–101.

(1993) Linguistic form and relevance. *Lingua* 90(1); 1–25.

(2002) Truthfulness and Relevance. *Mind* 111 (443); 583–632.

(2004) Relevance theory. In Horn, L. and G. Ward (eds.) *The Handbook of Pragmatics*. Oxford: Blackwell; 607–32.

Wilson, D. and T. Wharton (2006) Relevance and prosody. *Journal of Pragmatics*.

Index

adverbials 63–4
after all 63
Aitchison, Jean 175, 176
Akhtar, Nameera 65, 160
Allen, Colin 109, 132, 169 n.4
Ameka, Felix 71, 73, 93, 97
analogue versus digital codes 56, 117–21,
    120–1
    advantages of digital over analogue
      codes 118
    analogue codes 117
    digital codes 117–18
animal communication systems 109–15
    see also grasshoppers, honey bees,
      vervet monkeys
attractors 175
Asperger's Syndrome 57
    see also autism
Austin, John 60
autism 15, 156–8, 163–5
    test cases for people with prosodic
      difficulties 167–8
Avramides, Anita 26, 35 n.4, 67 n.6

Bach, Kent 49, 50
Baillargeon, Renée 161
Banfield, Ann 106
    see also impliciture
Baron-Cohen, Simon 156, 164, 179
Barton, M. 160
Bateson, Mary Catherine 4
Baum, S. 166
Bekoff, Marc 109, 132, 169 n.4
Benfey, Theodor 70
Benson, Nancy 162
Besmeres, Mary 71
biological codes 138 n.26, 143–4, 153

see also natural codes, Gussenhoven,
    Carlos
Blake, Joanna 162
Blakemore, Diane 13, 59, 60, 62, 64, 128
    see also conceptual–procedural
      distinction
Blass, Regina 86
Bloom,Paul 160, 176, 183
Bolinger, Dwight 1, 121
    prosody as a natural phenomena 139–40
Bradbury, Jack 115
Brandon, Robert 113, 135
Breheny, Richard 160–2, 169 n.11
Bretherton, Inge 161
broadening 53
    see also loosening
Brown, Gillian 2
Brown, Penelope 193
but 59, 65
    see also discourse connectives
Byrne, Richard 178–9

'C'-continuum 171–2, 173–5, 187–9
    versus 'O'-continuum 171–6
    see also Kendon, Adam, Goffman,
     Erving
Caldi, Stefania 161
Carpenter, Malinda 160
Carstairs-McCarthy, Andrew 176
Carston, Robyn 9, 39, 49, 53, 68 n.14, 163
character and content 61–2
    see also Kaplan, David
Chen, Aoju 143, 144
Cheney, Dorothy 81, 110, 122
Chomsky, Noam 1, 4, 8, 9, 182, 184
Clark, Billy 140, 145
Clark, Herb 48, 49, 62, 67 n.6, 101–2

211